Your Confidence Compass

From Self-Doubt to Self-Leadership

LISA J ALLEN

Your Confidence Compass: From Self-Doubt to Self-Leadership

Copyright © 2025 Lisa J. Allen

Published by Market Refined Publishing
193 Cleo Circle Ringgold GA 30736
marketrefinedmedia.com

All rights reserved.

No part of this publication may be reproduced, distributed, or transmitted in any form or by any means, including photocopying, recording, or other electronic or mechanical methods, without the prior written permission of the publisher, except in the case of brief quotations embodied in critical reviews and certain other non-commercial uses permitted by copyright law.

Unless otherwise notes, all Scripture quotations are taken from The Holy Bible, New International Version® NIV® Copyright © 1973, 1978, 1984, 2011 by Biblica, Inc. Used with permission. All rights reserved worldwide.

Print ISBN: 979-8-9924512-3-8
Digital ISBN: 979-8-9924512-4-5
Audio ISBN: 979-8-9924512-5-2
LCCN: 2025902381

Cover and Interior Design by Nelly Murariu at PixBeeDesigns.com
Manuscript Edits by Market Refined Media & Publishing

Printed in the United States of America

First Edition: April 2025

Table of Contents

Endorsements — vii
Preface — ix

Introduction: What is True Confidence? — xi

Part 1: Self-Awareness Through Self-Discovery — 1

Chapter 1: Who Am I? — 5
Chapter 2: Who Am I Alongside Others? — 33
Chapter 3: Who Is with Me? — 59
Chapter 4: What Do I Value? — 79

Part 2: Self-Leadership Through Self-Reflection — 95

Chapter 5: What Is My Calling? — 99
Chapter 6: Where Do I Want to Go Next? — 133
Chapter 7: How Do I Let Go When Things End? — 153
Chapter 8: How Do I Get There? — 171

Part 3: Self-Acceptance Through Self-Control — 197

Chapter 9: How Can I Guard My Capacity? — 201
Chapter 10: How Can I Maintain My Mindset? — 223

Conclusion: Self-Acceptance That Grows Our Confidence — 237

Acknowledgments — 247
About the Author — 249
Appendix — 251
Endnotes — 255

To my Mom (and Dad in heaven),
Bill, Kelsey, Justin, Connor and Mckenzie . . .
and to Noah and the future generations of the Allen Family.

May this book be a legacy to help
guide you for years to come.

Endorsements

"In this book, Lisa Allen invites you into a journey of small, deliberate steps of obedience that take you from self-doubt and self-reliance to self-confidence and self-leadership. Drawing from her years of coaching, her carefully crafted exercises and tools will equip and enable you to discover and boldly step into your calling, to become the confident woman God created you to be. Please know, I write these words from personal experience. Lisa's words in this book helped transition me from my career as a trial attorney to my God-given calling as a Bible teacher, speaker and author."

Wendy Blight
Biblical Content Specialist for Proverbs 31 Ministries
Author of *Rest for Your Soul: A Bible Study on Solitude, Silence and Prayer*

"I am SO in love with this book. In fact, I feel like I want to get this for all the Christian Image Consultant's and Color Consultants that I train. From a business owner's perspective, this book is a game-changer. The concept of pairing self-awareness with self-leadership was eye-opening to me. After having read it, I can see a renewed importance on the self-leadership piece that is so often missing. An unexpected bonus was how relevant the message of this book would be to me personally. Lisa is a fantastic writer with spiritual insights combined with practical application."

Shari Braendel
CEO Style By Color

Preface

Is confidence something you are born with, or can it be cultivated?

While some personality styles are naturally more assertive, boldly journeying into the uncertain future, confidence can be cultivated and redefined. This book will serve as a compass for you starting with God as your true north. The chapters unfold to help you collect confidence from various areas of your life. The exercises within these pages have been administered to hundreds of clients who have grown in their ability to gain self-awareness leading to increased confidence. We will learn how self-awareness, while important, on its own is *only* a starting point. We then will create a pathway from self-awareness to self-leadership opening you up to the changes you desire, but have not yet achieved.

These pages will help you to:

- Determine where you are "now" in your life as a starting point which is crucial to know as you dream about where you want to land personally, professionally, spiritually or physically.

- Identify your creative design (at its best and worst) to infuse you with self-awareness, self-reflection and ultimately, self-acceptance.

- Take your new-found self-awareness full circle by identifying action steps of self-leadership for new mindsets, changed behaviors or strong habits that have been keeping you stuck.

- Take you from your life's dreams to decisions required to reach your preferred future.

- Create a life-changing statement of purpose to aim your time, energy and resources at the dream you've been pondering.

Are you ready to take this trip toward connecting with *Your Confidence Compass*? Let's Go!

Introduction

What is True Confidence?

> *". . . being confident of this, that he who began a good work in you will carry it on to completion."* Philippians 1:6

I was gazing at a spectacular beach from my balcony in a five-star hotel. This is not my typical travel accommodation. I'd been invited as a Confidence Coach to administer a strengths assessment I'd been certified in. My assignment was to do a workshop and then coach ten-to-twelve couples throughout the conference. Event number one was a dinner on the beach, which I could see being set up from my balcony.

It was then that the voices in my head that sounded coincidentally like mine started chipping away at my confidence. *"What in the world are you doing here? These are professional athletes. I mean, yeah, you love football, but these are professional baseball players. What do you have to offer them?"*

If it had been a women's conference, I would have had no problem. I would have owned the room. But these were men and women, and most of them were young enough to be my kids. Did they really want to hear about their strengths from this middle-aged woman?

I felt myself growing smaller.

It's easy to have confidence when you've been introduced from the stage as a speaker or an expert—I'd done that many times before. But this beach dinner would require confidence without any props like that. Suddenly, I was terrified. I could imagine how they would all see right through me, would roll their eyes when I wasn't looking and laugh at me together later.

My insecurity only added to my sense of imposter syndrome. I was a Confidence Coach, for goodness sake! I was supposed to be a pro at this. I felt like the Wizard of Oz about to have the curtain pulled back and be exposed as a fraud to all the world.

It was then that God Himself interrupted those thoughts and reminded me, "Lisa, you have been invited to have a seat at this table. You are a seasoned expert in this assessment that helps people gain self-awareness and increase confidence through these coaching conversations. You can do this."

I didn't feel *confident*. But I did feel *called*.

Remembering that was all I needed to flip the switch in my head and start coaching myself with all the skills I used to help others. I coached my own mindset by writing down the words "invited and experienced." This phrase was a reminder that I had years of experience in this topic and I could trust my experience as I walked out the invitation to attend, speak and coach at this couples' conference.

Before long, I was ready to boldly place my toes in that sand and enjoy all the new friends I would meet that night at dinner. They would never have known I'd been close to curling up in my bed and watching *Modern Family* reruns by the way I mixed and mingled on that beach.

My point in sharing this story is this: everyone battles insecurity. Even a seasoned Confidence Coach. Sometimes insecurity is predictable, and sometimes it interrupts (or tries to interrupt) important assignments like that one. The key is to know how to redirect your thoughts into a confident mindset.

There's no escaping those feelings of insecurity in this life, not entirely. But you have the ability to develop a way to walk forward despite those feelings. This book will help you do that.

INTRODUCTION: WHAT IS TRUE CONFIDENCE?

Ready for More

If you've picked up this book, chances are you're ready for a change.

Your life isn't *bad*. In many ways, it's actually pretty good. But you can't shake this gnawing sense of restlessness—the conviction that there's something *more* in store for you.

You might feel like you're on a hamster wheel, going from one task to the next, never able to stop or pause long enough to figure out if that's really the wheel you want to be on.

You've been living on auto-pilot for so long, helping everyone else reach their goals—your kids, your spouse, your boss maybe—that you don't remember what it's like to pursue your own dreams or have your own goals.

Maybe you've been staying home with your kids, and while you wouldn't trade that for the world, they don't need you as much anymore. And you're ready to step into the next season of your life—if only you can figure out what that next season is. Or perhaps you've been working outside the home for years, and you're tired of the grind of corporate life. You're ready to stop answering to everyone else and start forging your own path.

You've spent countless sleepless nights plagued by the question, "Why am I here? What is my purpose?"

Whatever your past, you've picked up this book because you're ready to focus on yourself and your calling.

Maybe you want to write a book. Maybe you're ready to switch careers. Maybe you're navigating changing relationships—with your kids, your husband, your family, or your friends. Maybe you're facing a new season of life due to a suddenly empty nest or retirement, and you need a plan.

CONFIDENCE IS A SKILL ANYONE CAN DEVELOP— INCLUDING *YOU!*

XIII

But you're also holding back because you're not sure you can do it. You've been resisting the call you feel on your life because you don't feel confident. You may be a high-achiever with many accomplishments under your belt, but now you feel like you are past your prime. You may have suffered with insecurity for most of your life and feel like you have little to show for your efforts, so how could you possibly do great things now? You may think that confidence is a personality trait you simply don't have. But part of you hopes you're wrong, and that's why you've picked up this book. Part of you—a bigger part—wants to push past the fear and find the confidence you need to follow your dreams.

You don't want to look back at this season of your life and feel regret. You don't want to feel like you wasted the limited time you were given. You want to feel content, maybe even proud of what you contributed to the world and to the Kingdom. You want to know that you used your time and your gifts well.

You don't want to miss out on what God has in store for you because you were too scared to step out in faith.

In short, you need the confidence and the capacity to pursue your calling in this new season of life.

I Can Help

The earliest use of the word "coach" dates back to the 1500s and was associated with the word "wagon," ultimately giving rise to the word "stage coach." It was a form of transportation to get you from where you are to where you need to be. While the word is now used to refer to people rather than vehicles, the meaning is the same: a coach is someone who helps you get where you want to go.

In the decade and a half, I've dedicated to being a Confidence Coach, I've worked with hundreds of clients to help them identify where they are in their lives—personally, professionally, and relationally—and then craft a pathway to get their lives where they want them to be.

My method has helped hundreds of women spring into confident action. Specifically, I've helped them to:

- Develop the consistency to pursue ministry or a side hustle, instead of a singular focus on a corporate job.

- Set necessary boundaries with family, friends, and coworkers by finding their voice and engaging in conversations that honor others while still getting their own needs met.

- Take control of their calendars to make space to write the book, pursue the ministry, or start the non-profit that God has put on their hearts.

- Learn to say "no" to good things in order to say "yes" to greater things.

- Reframe their mindset for growth instead of stagnation.

- Your goal may be similar to some of those I just listed, or it may be something a little different. Whatever it is, your destination will be defined by your sense of calling combined with your unique gifts and circumstances.

While this book will not replace the role of a professionally trained coach in your life, it does serve as a stepping stone that will help you create an action plan based on self-awareness, defined success, a realistic pace, and clarity on the season of life you're in.

In this book, I've collected the best exercises, frameworks, and resources that I use with my clients, so that you can apply them to your own circumstances and achieve the behaviors required to move forward and to reach your goals.

True Confidence

If you're like many of my clients, you probably think confidence is something you have to manufacture, that it's about appearing a certain way. Or you believe it's a quality that some people are just born with—and you're not one of them.

I'm here to tell you that confidence is a skill anyone can develop—including *you*! It just takes practice, like learning to play the piano or ride a bike.

You can think of confidence like a muscle that needs to be exercised to the point of discomfort in order to grow. In fact, I like to call it our "confidence muscle" because that helps remind us that the only way to build it is to keep pushing yourself to do a little more and a little more, allowing your confidence to slowly expand.

Confidence muscles are built especially when we face new circumstances. Get ready to build your confidence muscle if you are:

- Transitioning in your career
- Aging with a body that isn't cooperating with your typical health habits
- Finding your leadership style no longer fits your team or organization
- Experiencing compounded loss requiring a season of grief and adjustment
- Raising teens and caring for aging parents
- Empty nesting
- Divorced or widowed
- A new mom

You see, uncertainty in a new experience is actually the training ground for confidence. The opposite of confidence is denial, leading to a refusal to change, an unwillingness to accept your circumstances, or robotically trying to recapture something that is evaporating. Instead, we can build confidence during those hard seasons by accepting the discomfort that comes with change and moving forward in faith.

INTRODUCTION: WHAT IS TRUE CONFIDENCE?

And I'll let you in on a secret: some people *appear* more confident than others, but *everyone* has some insecurities. No one *feels* confident all the time.

You may have heard that courage is not the absence of fear, but the determination to do something despite that fear. Confidence is exactly the same.

We mistakenly believe that confidence feels like strength, victory, and familiarity. In fact, confidence feels like courage based in trust—trust in ourselves *and* in God.

The goal isn't to never feel afraid of what people will think or that you might fail. Rather, the goal is to pursue your purpose no matter how you feel in the moment and to move forward in the face of uncertainty because you know it's the direction you're called to go—even if you don't yet know how the details will work out.

***CONFIDENCE MUSCLES* ARE BUILT ESPECIALLY WHEN WE FACE NEW CIRCUMSTANCES.**

The truth is that you'll never feel confident until you face the fear that's keeping you small.

True confidence comes from identifying and living your values. True confidence requires that you appreciate the strengths you have, develop the things you can change, and accept the limitations you have as part of your humanity. True confidence comes from knowing you can trust yourself to do what you set out to do and that you will adapt when new challenges arise.

But it's more than that. It's also knowing that you have the support of the One for whom nothing is impossible. As a believer, you know that God is in control, directing your steps and sheltering you under His wings. And you can turn to scripture for support and comfort when times are tough. Plus, when you make mistakes or fail or run into your limitations, the Gospel reminds you that brokenness is beautiful. As 2 Corinthians 12:9 states, God's "power is made perfect in [our] weakness."

YOUR CONFIDENCE COMPASS

True confidence is harnessing the best of who you are with quiet acceptance. It's understanding who you are, recognizing your God-given strengths *and* weaknesses, and trusting that God will fill in the gaps to help you fulfill the purpose to which He is calling you.

The Journey to Confidence

Ok, so how do you get there? How do you journey from the valley of self-doubt in which you find yourself to the mountaintop of radical self-acceptance?

Over the last twelve years, I've developed a three-part process:

1. Engage in self-discovery in order to develop self-awareness.
2. Engage in self-reflection in order to develop self-leadership.
3. Engage in self-control in order to develop self-acceptance.

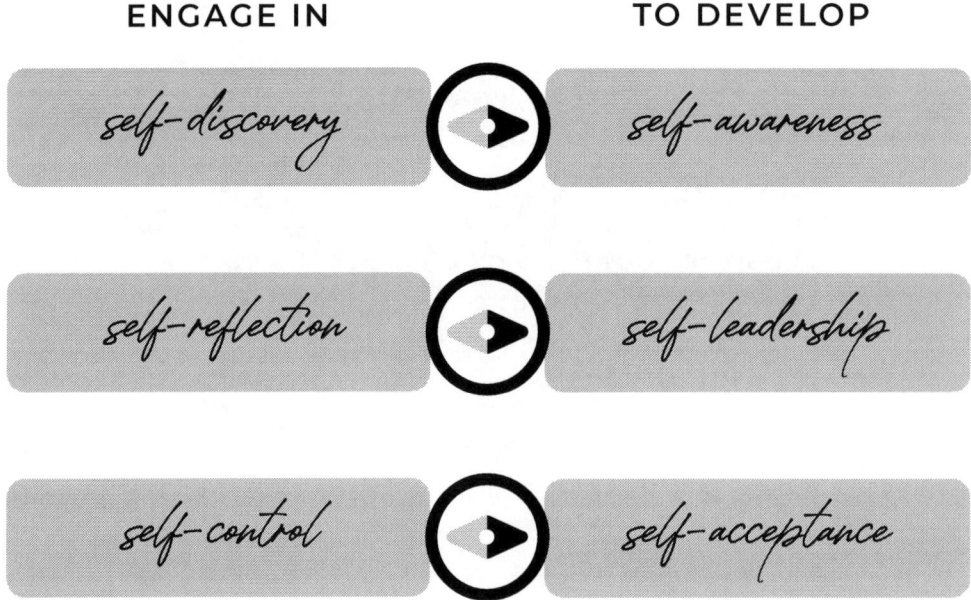

Self-discovery leads to self-awareness—a deep understanding of your personality, relational support system, and values. Self-awareness leads to self-reflection, which involves discerning what God is calling you to do with your life, deciding where you want to go next, and discovering who God is calling you to become. That enables you to practice self-leadership by setting goals and making a clear plan for how to achieve them. Then, you'll begin exercising self-control in your life by managing your reactions, habits, and time. You'll continue to develop your self-control by accepting your limitations, guarding your capacity, and really owning what you're responsible for. You'll be letting go of what you can't control and controlling what is in your sphere of influence. All of this leads to self-acceptance, which is the heart of true confidence.

As I write this, western North Carolina is in the aftermath of Hurricane Helene, which devastated the landscape, destroying entire towns and roadways. As I've spoken with friends who have family members making their way back to their Charlotte homes, they no longer have the advantage of cell service or navigation systems. Road signs and roads themselves are gone, and the journey requires patience, creativity, and careful attention to the changed landscape.

Of course, that's how we always navigated long journeys before GPS software and smartphones. When you wanted to take a trip, careful planning was required before the trip began. You made note of major roadways, alternate routes, on-ramps, off-ramps, rest stops, fueling stations, and restaurants. When we encountered road closures or construction, we had to find alternate routes to continue our journey. We also had to identify hotels and rest stops ahead of time. Without such planning, a simple trip could be a disaster. But by making a clear plan, thinking through the possible curveballs that might be thrown our way, and anticipating the support we'd need, we would make it to our destination safely.

So, it will be for you on your way to your dream destination in this season of your life. This is how we participate with God, our Guide, on our journey to our confident life. He is sovereign, providing on-ramps and off-ramps, rest stops, and alternate routes to make sure we arrive at His best place for our lives. It is a two-pronged approach. We do our part praying, planning, and preparing. Then God does His part by giving us the courage and creativity to adjust to roadblocks and unexpected travel interruptions.

Planning well requires that we understand where we want to go, the best way for us to get there, and what we'll need along the way. That's why it all starts with self-discovery. Only by knowing ourselves well can we be confident in our destination and in our ability to get there.

Self-Discovery Leads to Self-Awareness

Self-discovery is the key to open the door to deepened confidence. In this part of the process, we answer questions like, "Who am I, really? What are my values? What are my strengths? What are my areas of struggle?"

You might think you know yourself pretty well after spending a handful of decades with yourself, but my clients are often surprised about how much they actually don't know. Some find they have never known themselves very well, not in the deep, compassionate but honest way they do by the end of our time in this phase. Others find they have changed so much over the last few years (or decades) that their sense of who they are needs a major update.

You might be wondering why this matters, or you might be thinking this sounds awfully self-focused when what you want to do is impact the world around you for good. Especially for Christian women, it can feel foreign to take time to think about yourself and to look inward. We're so used to focusing on everyone else and meeting the needs of others that we forget about ourselves. After all, doesn't the Bible tell us to sacrifice ourselves in the service of others?

INTRODUCTION: WHAT IS TRUE CONFIDENCE?

Yes, sacrificial love is at the center of a life surrendered to Jesus, but here's what we forget: understanding ourselves will enable us to love others better.

When we really understand ourselves—our God-given gifts, limits, and weaknesses—we can better maximize our strengths, minimize our weaknesses, and see how we are meant to fit into the larger plan. Self-discovery allows us to recognize the lens we're seeing through when we look at the world, coloring and distorting everything we encounter, just like tinted sunglasses might turn the sky an odd shade of green.

Here's a hard truth: if you don't know yourself deeply, it can alter or limit your view of God. Why? Because without self-awareness, you have no idea how your personal lens is coloring your understanding of God. When we more fully know ourselves, we can begin to more fully know God and others, too. As we begin to know God better, we can then continue the journey of self-discovery as He reveals, guides, and convicts us.

That is why the journey to true confidence must begin with self-discovery. In Part I, I will walk you through several powerful exercises to help you unlock a deep understanding of who you are and how God made you.

But our journey of discovery doesn't stop there. We will also look at who you are in relation to those around you. Typical self-awareness that stops at "Who am I?" remains self-focused, but what we want is what I call *full-circle self-awareness*, which also asks, "Who am I alongside you, and what happens when we come together?"

Full-circle self-awareness considers how our gifts and tendencies interact with others' to create an outward-focused self-awareness. In this second part of the self-discovery step, we ask questions like:

- Who is on this journey with me?
- Who do I become when I'm around those people?
- How can I use my gifts in the best way to complement the gifts and needs of these other people?

My approach keeps the goal in mind. Rather than seeing self-discovery as the goal, which can lead to navel gazing and self-focus, we pursue self-discovery because it is the path to the full-circle self-awareness that will enable you to more effectively serve others with true confidence.

Self-Reflection Leads to Self-Leadership

Once you are more deeply self-aware, you can begin to engage in self-reflection. This stage focuses on asking yourself, "Why am I here? Where do I want to go next? What is the path from where I am to my destination? What is holding me back that I need to let go of?" Through the process of self-discovery, you'll have gained a fuller sense of *how* you were made. Now it's time to consider what you were made *for*.

Through self-reflection, you'll gain a clearer sense of your purpose and craft a picture of where you want to go, summarized in your Calling Statement. Next, you'll outline the steps it will take to get there and what is required to close that distance. You'll create your own map and chart your course to the person you want to become.

This is all part of self-leadership, putting your self-awareness into action.

> **THIS IS ALL PART OF SELF-LEADERSHIP, PUTTING YOUR SELF-AWARENESS INTO ACTION.**

I knew one woman I did life with for close to a decade. She is an assertive personality gifted with incredible strategic skill, vision, and the ability to tackle anything life and work throw her direction. She is a Workboot (which you will learn about in Chapter 1), which means she is driven and dominant. This personality likes to take action and keep things moving. Because of that, my friend often would grow impatient in discussions that seemed to hold her back from any given task at the moment. From time to time, she would cut someone off a little too directly and end up hurting their feelings. Over and over, I would hear her confess, "I know I was rude the way I shut them down in our committee today," or, "I know better than to cut people's heads off with my curt words." This clearly demonstrates self-awareness. But that self-awareness never led to self-leadership, so she didn't change her behavior.

It takes genuine humility to be self-aware and to admit it to someone else like she did. But though confession is good for the soul, without self-leadership, self-awareness is just information you know about yourself. This information needs to be processed through self-reflection and turned into action through self-leadership.

James 1:22 (AMP) says, "Do not merely listen to the word, and so deceive yourselves. Do what it says." God guides us in our hearts and through His Word about how He wants us to act. When our actions don't align with His best, He allows His Holy Spirit to convict us and show us a better way. Our obedience is evident when we change our behavior and walk out His direction. I've lost touch with my friend, but I trust that God has helped her to control her urges to shut someone down too quickly and instead engage in reciprocal dialogue, allowing her to achieve self-leadership in this area.

> **WITHOUT SELF-LEADERSHIP, SELF-AWARENESS IS JUST INFORMATION YOU KNOW ABOUT YOURSELF.**

Self-leadership means we are using our self-awareness to help us navigate the path God has called us to walk. We're putting what we've learned into action and asking ourselves, "Given my unique strengths and weaknesses, what is the best way for me to move forward in faith?" Knowing who you are gives you a better understanding of how you will walk out your calling. Someone with a different wiring than you can have a similar calling, but may need to approach it completely differently than you and have different motivations.

Central to self-leadership is having a clear vision of where you're headed—what you want to accomplish and why that matters to you. Knowing your "why" will help you re-center when the pressures of life threaten to push you off track into old, self-sabotaging behaviors. Having a clear sense of calling will give you the confidence to keep trying when you face obstacles, because you know that God will help you reach the land He has promised you.

Self-Control Leads to Self-Acceptance

After all of this, you'll be ready for the final stage of the journey: practicing self-control to develop self-acceptance. This stage is all about making sure that the goals you want to pursue and the priorities you've identified for your life actually show up in your daily actions and that you have the time and energy to pursue them. It's about staying on the path for the long haul and starting again when you get side-tracked.

This concept is represented in Romans 7:15, which says, "I do not understand what I do. For what I want to do I do not do, but what I hate I do." It's one thing to know what we want to do, and even to start doing it, but it's another to keep acting in accordance with our purpose day in and day out, even when it feels hard.

Your purpose is unique, but the struggles you face to pursue it are not. Consider this example: You have been given the luxury of a warning about your cholesterol by your doctor. There is time to make changes to your nutrition, exercise, and stress levels before your current behaviors lead to a heart attack, stroke, or worse. You are aware of the issue and agree with it (self-awareness). You decide you need to make a change (self-reflection), so you join a gym and eat a salad every day for lunch for a week (self-leadership). It feels good! But then stress picks up at work, and you're too busy to go to the gym for a few days.

INTRODUCTION: WHAT IS TRUE CONFIDENCE?

You skip the salad because you run out of lettuce, and it's easier to grab those chips and a sandwich. When you see a platter of cookies in the break room at work, you can't resist. Pretty soon, you're right back where you started.

Everyone I've coached has experienced something similar. So have I. The book you are holding is a clear reminder of that. My annual goal list for the last four years has included writing this book. I was quite aware of this goal. I reflected on it and knew why it mattered to me. I had a plan for how to do it, researching all of the steps to publication. I even had the beginnings of a few chapters and a rough table of contents saved. But my book remained a dream in my heart, not a book in your hands. Until 2024, my self-leadership lacked the self-control it took to pull the trigger and start the official writing process with an editor to provide the accountability I needed and put my money where my mouth was, so to speak.

What is it for you? Knowing the direction you want your finances to take, but lacking the discipline to implement changes? Or maybe it's your health as you take the gamble to miss annual checkups for several years, hoping you will be fine. Or maybe you want to get an important certification for your career pathway, but instead of studying for it, you waste your evenings scrolling social media and streaming Netflix.

Without self-control, our self-leadership will be ineffective and inconsistent, at best. That's why Part III focuses on helping you develop the self-control you'll need to move purposefully and effectively toward your goals, staying the course even when storms threaten to blow you off track.

> SELF-LEADERSHIP MEANS VIEWING YOURSELF BOTH COMPASSIONATELY AND REALISTICALLY.

The vision casting you'll do in Part II will prepare you to practice focused self-control. In any given situation, you'll ask yourself, "What is needed at this moment to keep me moving in the direction I've chosen to go?" You'll continue to rely on your self-awareness to consider how your unique wiring comes into play on your journey as you ask, "What does this situation require of me, and how can I best respond given what I know about myself?"

You'll also learn to distinguish between what is in your control and what is outside it. You'll be able to evaluate, "What has this season dealt me, and how can I respond to it well? Do I need to rush or rest? Hustle or hush? Speak or maintain silence?" We can't control a lot of what happens in life, but we *can* control our response to it. When we focus on our response and let go of the rest, we walk in accordance with God's plan for our lives. Galatians 5:22-23 reminds us that self-control is one of the fruits of the spirit, given to us by God when we walk in His will.

Now, self-control is about more than gritting your teeth and making yourself do something. It's about more than willpower. Instead, the key is to set ourselves up for success so that less willpower is required. By applying self-leadership to the little things in our lives, we'll be able to practice the self-control that will help us reach our goals.

In Part III, I'll teach you to manage yourself by reading your "gauges" and guarding your capacity as you develop the habits that will bring you to your goals. A good leader doesn't ask a team member to do something he or she is not capable of doing, either due to a lack of training or a lack of skill. Likewise, self-leadership means managing your resources—your time, energy, strengths, and weaknesses—in a way that maximizes your positive impact within the limitations of your circumstances. Self-leadership means viewing yourself both compassionately and realistically. When you know what you are capable of—and what you are *not* capable of—your confidence soars because you're no longer setting yourself up for failure by committing to things that are beyond your capacity.

You'll also learn to remove distractions and maintain the mindsets that keep you on track. You will add tools to your toolbox that help you take captive the thoughts that are keeping you from the abundant mindset required to move forward.

We'll also discuss the essential parts of ourselves that many clients struggle to accept: our pasts, our ages, our seasons, our scars, and our appearances. One of the challenges of self-awareness is when we are aware of something we wish we could change, but it is simply out of our control. (Welcome to aging!) Part of self-control in those situations is accepting that we can't change it and refusing to waste our time and energy trying to. In this chapter, I'll share practical tips for creating and maintaining a mindset of deep self-acceptance so you can feel comfortable with the "skin" you're in, both literally and metaphorically.

True confidence stems from unconditional self-acceptance, which results from understanding that everything about you—including the weaknesses you may have wished away at times—is perfectly designed to bring about God's plan and help you achieve your purpose. When sin entered the garden of Eden in Genesis 3, our bodies became susceptible to decay, illness, and aging. Violence and cruelty became common, causing us to hurt others and be hurt by others. We've all made mistakes we wish we could undo. But because of God's saving grace, we can stand victorious on this side of eternity as we look forward to the perfect conditions we will experience in Heaven.

True confidence uses what you have, including the hard parts of your past. Have you survived a divorce? The death of a loved one? Maybe you are sober and in recovery. Perhaps you experienced early childhood abuse and now mentor other abuse survivors. Self-acceptance means taking your life experiences and weaving them into the fabric of confidence.

When you accept your wiring, your past, and the limitations of the season you're in—seeing them all as strengths rather than frustrating or embarrassing faults—you will finally feel that confidence that has seemed so elusive for so long. You'll no longer have anything to hide or anything to prove, and you'll be ready to use your unique strengths to achieve the purpose God has prepared for you.

Self-Acceptance Is Not Selfish

Confidence develops by truly understanding who you are at your best *and* at your worst—by recognizing your blind spots, your biases, and your barriers—and then by practicing self-control to manage how your unique personality shows up in any given situation.

When we achieve this peaceful acceptance, we can shift our focus to serving and loving those around us without competition or comparison. I love the quote in Rick Warren's *The Purpose Driven Life*: "True humility is not thinking less of yourself, but thinking of yourself less." As we gain confidence, we can walk into any room, situation, or relationship and create space for others.

This is why self-discovery, self-reflection, and self-control are not selfish.

When you develop self-awareness and self-leadership, bolstered by the power of self-control, you'll begin to live in a state of unconditional self-acceptance, confident in your abilities and aware of your limitations. Only then will you be able to love and serve others in the fullness of God's power and design for your life.

Your Guide

My husband and I took the trip of a lifetime in 2019, journeying through Greece and Italy. We paused to spend extra time in the city of Rome, and it was there we connected with our guide, Luciano.

He was nothing short of amazing. He knew Rome like the back of his hand. He understood history, art, food, and shopping. As an ex-commander of the Swiss Guard, he knew how to maneuver the Vatican visit without long lines and provided strategic insights within the tour. At the Coliseum, we gained VIP access because of his contacts and learned about everything from architecture to gladiators to the unusual tidbits about bathroom habits during the fights. At Luciano's recommendation, we left our hotel at six in the morning to arrive at Trevi Fountain where we found ourselves being three of only a handful of guests as the sun rose, and we were able to throw our coins in without crowds or a wait. But, most importantly, Luciano understood

Bill and I and the kind of trip we wanted while visiting Rome.

The journey you're about to embark upon also requires a guide, at least if you want it to be successful. Sure, this book is a kind of guide, and I am a guide for my coaching clients. But a book or even a coach can only take you so far.

Luckily, we all have a Guide far greater than any book, One who knows everything there is to know about you and your destination. That guide is Jesus.

These chapters will serve you whether you have faith in Him or not. But my faith and experience have taught me that God is my Guide, whether I acknowledge it or not. He knows how to help me maneuver life, helps me wait until the right timing for the perfect "sunrise," and helps me know how I am wired for His perfect plans, the seasons my life will encounter, and who will journey along with me.

You can take this trip without a guide. But I wouldn't recommend it.

Instead, as Proverbs 3:5-6 states, I encourage you to "Trust in the LORD with all your heart and lean not on your own understanding; In all your ways, acknowledge him and he will make your paths straight."

We can't change the fact that life is full of uncertainty, risk, and hardship. But we can change the way we respond. The exercises in this book will help you to accept your assignments and face uncertainty with confidence grounded in the tools you've gained and the support of the One who never fails so that you're ready to move forward with anticipation of the future rather than fear or dread.

No matter your specific goals, this book will help you develop a quiet confidence that halts comparison and catapults you into the courage to accomplish the dream God has placed on your heart.

Reflect & Respond

1. What's your current view of confidence? What does the "confident you" look like? Take a few minutes to imagine this confident version of yourself. How are things different in your life because of your newfound confidence?

2. The most important question I ask my clients at our first session is, "How will we know my coaching worked?" I ask you that now. What does your life look like at the end of implementing the strategies in this book? Try to name something external in addition to any feelings you might name. This is important because feelings are subjective and hard to measure. What external, observable differences would you like to see in your life?

   Some clients will say to me, "I finally want to launch my own ministry." Others will say, "I am tired of not having a quiet time or not following through with my goals or taking care of my health." Ultimately, what is your goal in picking up this book?

3. Are you a person of faith? If so, how do you experience the guiding hand of God? Think back on a difficult season when you had to make big or difficult decisions. Did your faith offer you guidance during that time? How so?

4. What would it feel like to know that Jesus is guiding every step on your journey into this next phase of your life? How would you respond differently to challenges if you knew, really knew, that He was right there with you, leading you forward?

WHAT IS
NEEDED
AT THIS
MOMENT TO
KEEP ME
MOVING
IN THE
DIRECTION
I'VE CHOSEN
TO GO?

PART 1

Self-Awareness Through Self-Discovery

> *"Search me, God, and know my heart; test me and know my anxious thoughts. See if there is any offensive way in me, and lead me in the way everlasting."*
>
> Psalm 139:23-24

Let's try an experiment. On the inside cover of this book, write your name *(if you're reading digitally, find a Post-it Note)*. Now put your pen in your opposite hand and write your name again. That's right, I want you to write your name with your non-dominant hand. I can imagine you carefully switching hands, tilting your head to the right or left, and even positioning your mouth and tongue in such a way as to somehow assist writing in this unnatural posture.

One of the things that strikes me whenever I ask groups to do this in person is that no one ever looks at me like I'm nuts when I ask them to write their name. They simply find their pen and paper and get to it. Some people will question details like, "Do you want my first and last name? Do you want it in cursive or printed?" (If you had any of these questions, you probably have some Mary Jane in our SHOE Assessment because you need details, want to do things right, and don't want to mess up the inside cover of your book.) But no one struggled to write their name with their natural hand.

No, it wasn't until our pens switched hands that three things probably happened:

1. It took you longer.
2. It was uncomfortable.
3. It didn't look as good as the name you wrote with your natural hand.

This exercise is a powerful illustration of what it feels like to work within your natural strength zone (using your dominant hand) and what it feels like to have to work outside of your comfort zone (using your non-dominant hand).

Take a moment to recognize how much easier it is to do things that are in your natural strength zone. Let's say you have a task that should take about four hours. If it's in your natural strength zone, it will feel like two hours. You'll glance at your watch and think, "Where has the time gone? It's past lunchtime." It actually energizes you, rather than drains you. Now imagine that task is something that's well outside your natural strength zone. The four hours will feel like six because the task is uncomfortable for you. Plus, it may take you longer because it requires more effort and concentration to make sure you did it right.

God will call us to do things outside of our natural strength zones and wiring from time to time. For example, I am not wired for statistics, analytics, or strategy. Math isn't my thing. I never got geometry or algebra beyond eking by with a passing grade. I checked out of math the year my teacher started putting tiny little letters into math problems like "X" and "Y." Yet, throughout my professional roles, I have had to write annual budgets that were reviewed monthly. Whenever budget time rolls around, I know I will be less comfortable than others might be and will need to allow a lot of focused time to create or review the numbers and maybe even have someone double-check a few things for me.

While we want to try to utilize our natural strengths as much as possible, there will be times when we have to do things that don't come as naturally to us. Knowing our personalities doesn't give us a "pass" on everything that's not our preference. Rather, it helps us understand when certain things might be more difficult for us and to seek help when we need it.

Understanding and accepting the way you're wired is a crucial prerequisite for success of any kind. If you are naturally more reserved and you want to be belly-laugh, life-of-the-party extroverted, you will find yourself exhausted and competitive. There may be times when you need to be more social or outgoing than feels natural to you, and that's ok. Recognizing that it will be more challenging for you due to your wiring enables you to get the support you need for that challenge, and it empowers you to avoid positions where you have to do a lot of socializing. Instead, you can focus on opportunities that capitalize on your unique strengths.

Part I offers you a toolkit to help you look more closely at yourself and your life—your preferences, biases, and blind spots. You'll need a magnifying glass to help you zoom in on certain areas of your life. Next, you'll want a flashlight to illuminate things that may have been kept in the dark. Don't forget to grab a mirror to look intently at yourself and view an accurate reflection. You will also need a pair of lenses to help you see your perspective and to also consider others' perspectives on your journey. Finally, you'll need a compass to keep you oriented on what matters most.

With these tools at the ready, you'll understand yourself and how you interact with those around you better than ever before, entering into full-circle self-awareness, which is the first stop on the journey to true confidence.

Before you can decide where you want to go or how to get there, you have to first know where (and who) you are.

Let's begin.

Chapter 1
Who Am I?

> *"For we are God's handiwork, created in Christ Jesus to do good works, which God prepared in advance for us to do."*
>
> Ephesians 2:10 NLT

One client, whom I'll call Susie, came to me feeling ill-equipped and not enough, frustrated that she became exhausted from being all things to all people and wanting a way to lead herself and others the way her coworker did. She was so curious as to why her coworker seemed effortless in the way she approached her teams and tasks. Susie tried to imitate all of the things her coworker did, only to become more frustrated and fatigued.

When I begin a typical coaching appointment with new clients, I unpack their personality assessment results to get a sense of the way they're wired. We call the best of our wiring our "balconies" and the worst of our wiring our "basements." To set an encouraging tone, I start by looking at the client's balconies. However, each time I began discussing one of Susie's balconies, she would counter with all the reasons that were actually a weakness.

For example, she was highly organized with the capacity to implement vision, keep a myriad of details straight, and deliver projects on time and on budget with excellence. But in her mind, none of that was a gift. *Doesn't everyone do this? Isn't this how responsible women live?* Susie saw those characteristics as unimportant and her words showed she devalued them. In her mind, gifted leaders were charismatic, extroverted, and super conversational. She was a contemplative and deep thinker. As I figuratively held the mirror up to her, what God had given as beautiful skills she disregarded as ugly, small, and unimportant.

As we worked together, we explored how spending time trying to manufacture parts of her personality that were not naturally strong left her drained, just like her iPhone at the end of the day. When she could spend time thinking, planning, organizing, and implementing, she found her battery recharged quickly. She was naturally wired for executing tasks, implementing vision, and project management. But, somewhere along the way, she told herself none of that was special, needed, or even useful. In short, she didn't recognize her own strengths, and so instead of capitalizing on them, she dismissed them and focused all of her attention on trying to be someone she wasn't.

As we worked together, not only did she change how she viewed her strengths, but Susie also began to block her calendar to have increased times of planning, focused working, and implementing. Since those things came naturally to her, she found herself with more energy every day.

What an honor it was to work with her to redefine what a strong, confident woman looked like. And when she looked into the mirror when we were done, she saw one looking back at her. When was the last time *you* took a good, long look at yourself in a mirror? I mean, *really looked*, not just the appraising glance you take before you run out the door.

My guess is it's been a long time.

And it's possible that, like Susie, when you do look, you see yourself through a lens that distorts your true strengths and weaknesses.

Know Thyself

Focusing on yourself first—or at all—might seem counterintuitive in a faith-based coaching book. Shouldn't we be focusing on others and how we can serve them?

Scripture is constantly pointing us toward selflessness and service. For example, Philippians 2:3 (AMP) says, "Do nothing from selfishness or empty conceit [through factional motives, or strife], but with [an attitude of] humility [being neither arrogant nor self-righteous], regard others as more important than yourselves." Doesn't that mean we should focus on others and avoid thinking too much about ourselves?

While the Bible does encourage us to serve others, pouring out to others while ignoring yourself creates physical, emotional, and spiritual deficits. We all know of (or were) the helicopter mom who did everything for her family at the expense of her own needs. Or the corporate executive who gave everything to her supervisor yet ignored her own doctor's appointments, mammograms, and dental checks. Or for you, it may be borderline codependence trying to keep the peace in your home by making up for others' behavior to no avail.

We've all heard the sayings, "*Put your own oxygen mask on before helping others,*" and "*You can't pour from an empty cup.*" They speak to the reality that we have to take care of ourselves first if we're going to be able to serve others well. .

It's also true that when we understand ourselves better, we can be more effective in our service to others. The Body of Christ is designed so that we all use our creative wiring, skills, and gifts to build up the body. How can we be used powerfully within the body if we don't see the uniqueness of our contributions?

> **WE HAVE TO TAKE CARE OF OURSELVES FIRST IF WE'RE GOING TO BE ABLE TO SERVE OTHERS WELL.**

More than thirty years ago when we joined our church, we were asked to consider an area of service. Since I had small kids, it seemed logical to start on Wednesday night nursery duty. It was a very task-focused, crawl-on-the-ground assignment (not to mention it was sticky and messy). I found this draining, overwhelming, and generally uncomfortable. I knew God had given me unique gifts to be used in my local church, so I continued to talk with our women's director, Mary Ann, to find my sweet spot assignment. Since my personality leans more toward motivating, influencing, and leading, I eventually found a much better assignment leading a small Bible study that later allowed me to lead all the mom's studies, managing training for the leaders, and recruiting new leaders. This self-awareness led me away from the hands-on task of rocking babies that left me fatigued and into leadership and training that left me fueled. Even after a long day of training, I was energized by the assignment because it aligned with my creative design. Plus, I did a much better job at training than I did at rocking.

Please note: *Babies still needed to be rocked. I did my parental duty helping in the nursery when needed. I just didn't expect it to fuel me like leading women or recruiting leaders.*

Understanding my strengths and weaknesses allowed me to serve more powerfully and make more of an impact.

You might be worried that too much time looking inward will make you selfish or conceited, but I can assure you that is not true. You can become more self-aware without being selfish, inappropriately ambitious, or vain. Becoming more self-aware will allow you to serve others even more selflessly.

We all need a balance of *self*-focus and *other*-focus. When we combine self-awareness with an awareness of how we interact with others, it leads to emotional intelligence and enables us to discern when and how to use our gifts.

For example, I have the gift of positivity. There are countless times God has used this gift through me to affirm, develop, and motivate others. However, there are just as many times when someone is hurting and processing pain or loss that my positivity and faith that things will work out isn't useful for them to hear at that moment. It diminishes what they're feeling and shuts down their processing. Understanding that about myself allows me to recognize when my strength would be a weakness.

I'll share one more example. I'm an early riser and love mornings. On family vacations, I continue to awaken by 5:30 a.m. each day. By the time my family wakes up, I've had three cups of coffee, quiet time, and scrolled social media finding out the news for the day. I used to greet my night-owl family members with my chatty, playful, enthusiastic morning self, and I would feel irritated when they seemed grumpy or didn't reciprocate. However, as I became more self-aware, I realized what felt fun and friendly to me was inconsiderate to them. They had barely opened their eyes and still needed some time to ease into the day. I learned offering a quiet "good morning" and quick smile was the best way to care for them in these early hours on vacations. This is just one example from my life of how self-awareness has led to richer relationships. Quite the opposite of selfish ambition.

> WE NEED TO AVERT OUR EYES FROM THE WORLD, LOOK UP AND GAZE UPON THE TRUTH GOD SAYS ABOUT US.

The Source of Your Identity

I stumbled on an article once that said when the Kardashians took a selfie, they always kept the iPhone above them because looking up was the most flattering angle. While I was tempted to dismiss this as vain selfie culture, it did make me think about how looking up does give us the best possible perspective of ourselves—only in a different way.

To be a truly confident woman, we need to avert our eyes from the world, look up and gaze upon the truth God says about us. Only God sees us perfectly, and our true identity is found only in Him. We will wrestle with finding our identity in God because we are tempted to find it in the success of our careers, promotions, titles, and salaries. We also want our children to be successful so we can find our identity in that success. If we are single, sometimes we want our identity to be in getting married. If we are married, we will be tempted to find our identity in our husbands. But none of these pursuits give lasting confidence.

In fact, when our identity is found is God, we can navigate being passed over for that promotion. We can stay single when all our friends are getting married. We can let our husbands be who they are and not try to form them into a version that makes us look good. And we can allow our kids to find their own identity through the changing seasons of their lives . . . the good, the bad, and the ugly. This kind of confidence reveals a woman who can be content in her present reality and still ambitious for the dreams God has laid on her heart.

Who are you giving permission to define you? Social media accounts? Maybe it's time to unfollow or mute a couple that tempts or discourages you. Your mom? No matter how wonderful your momma is, her plans for you may not align with your God-given purpose. Your boss? She can be the best boss in the world, growing you, developing you, and promoting you, but she is not your plumb line for confidence. Who is it for you? Your siblings? A gym teacher from thirty years ago? Your Bible study friends?

Look up, my friend. Decide now to look away from the horizontal mirrors that falsely promise to give us confidence. Instead, look into God's vertical mirror and allow Him to show you who He dreamed you to be. Trust Him to arm you with strength for the pieces of your life that turned out to be the opposite of what you thought. Let Him have the messy and undefined circumstances and believe He will strengthen and define you as you walk forward.

If the SHOE Fits

If we don't know who we are, we waste our energy trying to be someone we're not. We look to others we admire for an example of who we should be. While it is wise to have godly examples, we often misread how unique their wiring and experiences are. We seek to replicate what we admire in others only to find ourselves exhausted and competitive because being "them" doesn't fit us.

The story of David and Goliath illustrates the importance of knowing ourselves and trusting our unique identity. 1 Samuel 17:38-40 reads:

CHAPTER 1: WHO AM I?

> "Then Saul dressed David in his own tunic. He put a coat of armor on him and a bronze helmet on his head. David fastened on his sword over the tunic and tried walking around, because he was not used to them. "I cannot go in these," he said to Saul, "because I am not used to them." So he took them off. Then he took his staff in his hand, chose five smooth stones from the stream, put them in the pouch of his shepherd's bag and, with his sling in his hand, approached the Philistine."

David understood that when he tried on Saul's tunic and armor, they made him uncomfortable. David preferred to go in his own style to fight the giant, using a shepherd's bag and slingshot.

The same is true for us when we try to mimic others' styles. We walk around in a suit that wasn't designed for us. The sleeves are dragging on the ground, the buttons are about to pop, or the pants are high-waters. We become uncomfortable and exhausted.

We each come into this world bent a certain way or leaning in the direction of our natural wiring. Of course, over time, we are influenced by people, experiences, and peer pressure. However, a reflection of Christ that is unique to each of us is etched deep inside.

Yet, when it comes to being ourselves in front of others, we often get self-conscious. We feel like we have to conform to the world or be like other people instead of just being who God made us to be. We're afraid they might think we're weird, even *peculiar*.

Even though we might use it as an insult, the word "peculiar" actually means "belonging solely to." As Christ-followers, Hebrews 10:10 says we are holy and set apart, and this definition of peculiar confirms that we have been wired, created, fashioned, and equipped to stand apart. (That makes a lot of sense now that you think of the family member you've always considered as peculiar, right?) Seriously, I love using the word "peculiar" now that I understand this definition.

GODLY CONFIDENCE IS A PEACEFUL ACCEPTANCE OF WHO I AM AND WHO I AM NOT.

You see each one of us has a unique contribution to make to the Body of Christ and to our families, neighborhoods, churches, communities, and workplaces. Understanding your unique personality allows you to accept who you are and stop trying to be who you are *not*.

It takes an incredible amount of humility expressed as confidence to simply be who we are without giving too much unnecessary energy to thinking of ourselves or what others think of us. This is the confidence with which we should steward our God-given personalities.

I like to call it "godly swagger." The difference between worldly arrogance and godly confidence is seeing who God created us to be. Worldly arrogance is more of the end zone dance begging for attention. Godly confidence is a peaceful acceptance of who I am and who I am not—and willingly letting others be who God created them to be.

This chapter will reveal your unique personality in a playful way by identifying you as one of four different types of SHOEs: Workboot, Stiletto, Mary Jane, or Flip Flop. (What girl doesn't like to think of a pair of shoes?) Each type has unique strengths and weaknesses. When you take that personality style and consider your spiritual gifts, skill set, birth order, the generation you've been born into, and other unique experiences, you will be able to name exactly who you were designed to be.

For example, my husband and I are very different than one another. Bill is a Workboot, which means he's the strong, silent type. I, on the other hand, am a verbal processor which is a classic characteristic of the Stiletto personality type. One of my husband's favorite sayings (kiddingly . . . kind of) is, "I think people should only speak if they can improve upon the silence." Yes, deep down all Workboots love the bottom line and periods of silence. Whenever Bill has that look on his face, I remind him that, as a Stiletto, I *always* think my speaking improves upon the silence. I love the sound of my voice, and I often talk to the dog . . . even when no one else is home. Almost thirty-six years later, Bill and I are learning how "peculiar" we both are. The SHOE Model helps us to understand the ways we are different so we can allow ourselves the space to be who God created us to be.

Understanding your SHOE, both the strengths and weaknesses, will allow you to be in more meaningful relationships, pursue a career that uses your unique wiring, and have more focus as you serve in your community, all because you learn to be in the comfort of your own skin. That comfort doesn't mean we won't get tired or the projects we focus on won't be difficult. It simply means it will be the best tired we have ever felt, because we are aiming for the best of who God created us to be as we engage the people and projects around us.

A Word About Bias

Back when I first started studying personalities, I mistakenly and privately believed there were several different personality styles and thanked God I got "the good one." Twenty-plus years later and I've been humbled by the reality that I have some strengths that are super and some weaknesses that are downright irritating to me and to others. Just ask my family, friends, or teammates.

Personality bias or "SHOE bias" means over-valuing or under-valuing your SHOE personality. Or, over-valuing or under-valuing someone else's SHOE personality. As a Stiletto, I am motivated more by people and feelings than by tasks and logic. I recall a teammate I used to work with who said, "Aww, you have all those touchy-feely strengths." I knew immediately in my gut her intention was kind, but her bias was clear as she had strategic wiring and often dismissed relational interactions.

We all have bias. We are human and can never be fully neutral. However, we can become aware of our bias and how it changes our interactions.

Your bias walks into the room with you whether or not you know it. It sits in your team meetings displaying itself as the look on your face, your level of engagement, your body language, and, in more overt cases, your eye rolls. It rears its head when you're detached and prefer to work on emails rather than participate in the conversation. Your spouse, friends and teammates all feel it. This is why learning to look through each other's lenses is so important. We can learn to see things differently. What your bias may have told you is a weakness can actually be an important and productive part of someone else's personality.

When we identify our bias, we can redirect and manage it. I was coaching a client who was incredibly strategic and intellectual. In one of our sessions, he was brave enough to admit, "I usually think I am smarter than most people." That led to a powerful coaching discussion about how he was placing greater value on his intellect than the relational skills some of his coworkers had. As we peeled back the layers of this bias, I asked what impact this had on his coworkers. He obviously never walked into a conference room saying, "You are all less intelligent than I am;" but boy, his coworkers sensed it. We had a great session talking about the impact that bias had on others and how he could learn to see their personality contributions as significant as his.

Bias can also go the other way. We can sometimes see a strength someone else has and compare ourselves to them negatively.

I recall one of my early Executive Team meetings at Proverbs 31 Ministries, where we all had to bring our metrics. One of my teammates, Amy, brought hers on an elaborate and color-coded pie chart spreadsheet. I had no idea you could turn a spreadsheet into a pie chart, let alone color code it. This was a shining example of gifting that was *surely* not mine! Meanwhile, I had my metrics on what felt like Post-it Notes compared to Amy's. I left that meeting determined to bring a shiny spreadsheet to the next meeting. I went so far, I'm ashamed to say, as to Google "spreadsheets for dummies."

It was then I felt a nudge of the Holy Spirit say, "Just go ask Amy how she does that." It was when I asked Amy about her masterful spreadsheets that she quickly and effortlessly prepared a template for me that I could use repeatedly. When I simply leaned into her strengths, the wedge of comparison fell away, and Amy and I became closer. In fact, Amy began to enlist my insights before sending emails that could be too direct or, better yet, needed to be a face-to-face conversation. She leaned into my gift of intuition with people, and I leaned into her gift of thinking strategically.

That is the design God has for us within the Body of Christ. Instead of creating wedges of comparison that keep us distanced from one another, our differences should cause us to lean into one another, if only we'll take the risk to rely on each other.

CHAPTER 1: WHO AM I?

When we compare our wiring with someone else's, whether positively or negatively, we place a wedge between them and us. Competitive comparison creates distance in our relationships, which means we always end up losing. Instead, we must try to view the differences between us and those around us as opportunities to connect like two puzzle pieces interlocking. They have what we need and we can share what they need.

The Four SHOEs

Now it's time to take your SHOE Assessment. I am a Certified Behavioral Specialist in the DISC Personality Profile, and I created the SHOE Assessment to provide a fun and brief way for you to gain insights on your creative wiring.

When you're looking at the descriptions, don't get bogged down with what you disagree with, but focus on what you can relate to. What strengths does it confirm and what areas of improvement does it highlight for you? Ask yourself, "What is this assessment confirming and what is it shedding light on? How can it help me become more self-aware?"

Stop and take the SHOE Assessment now. Flip to the Appendix to access the assessment.

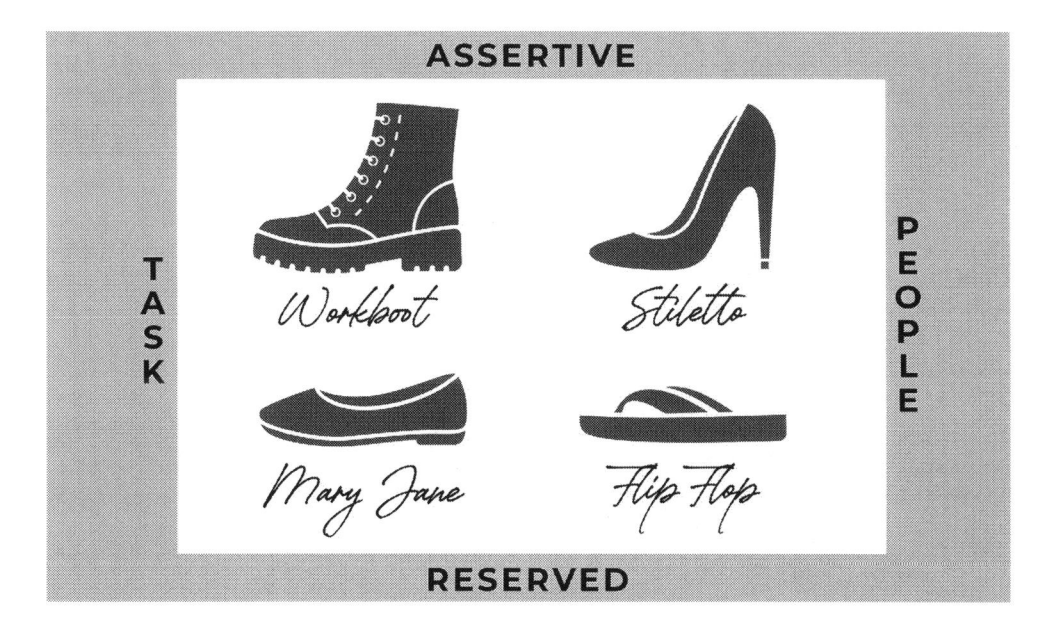

ASSERTIVE

TASK — Workboot | Stiletto — PEOPLE

Mary Jane | Flip Flop

RESERVED

YOUR CONFIDENCE COMPASS

You should now have your top two SHOEs. You might be more dominant in one or fairly balanced between the two.

As you can see on the graphic above, the SHOE system organizes personalities according to their attitude (assertive vs. reserved) and their motivation (tasks vs. people).

The Workboot and Stiletto are more assertive by nature, which means they will most likely initiate conversation or commentary, whereas the Mary Jane and Flip Flop are more reserved. They will likely wait until someone initiates conversation with them. Workboots and Mary Janes are more motivated by tasks, while Stilettos and Flip Flops are more motivated by relationships and people.

Remember, our goal here is not only to understand ourselves better. It's also to understand others better, including how we're different. So, I encourage you to get to know all the SHOE types, not just your own.

Let's look at the strengths and weaknesses of each of our SHOEs, shall we?

Wanda Workboot

Workboots are task-oriented and assertive, which makes them strong, decisive leaders. It won't take you long at the playground to figure out which toddlers are Workboots. They are taking charge, deciding what game to play, choosing what positions all the other toddlers will play in, and determining how long to play the game.

If you want to motivate a Workboot, give them a challenge or goal to meet. They love to win and are highly competitive, though that can also make them sore losers.

Workboots make quick and accurate decisions and like to take action. They have a strong work ethic with a high tendency to overwork if they aren't careful. They get bored sitting in endless meetings. If you want to make a Workboot mad, have a meeting that should have been an email. They like to keep a fast pace without getting bogged down by details.

Because Workboots prefer tasks, action, and metrics, it can feel that they care more about the business side of things than the people.

Strengths

Impartial – Workboots have the advantage of being unemotional. That may not sound like a strength, but being able to make decisions outside of emotion is a gift. (But, like any strength, if carried to an extreme, it will become a weakness.) Workboots can make logical decisions under pressure without getting swayed by others, but they can also stomp on other's feelings unintentionally.

Visionary – Workboots will venture into new territory. They can figure things out along the way as they focus their strategic thinking and visionary gifts. So many entrepreneurs are Workboots who have created new and fresh innovative products and processes.

Discerning – Workboots have a strong gut instinct and discernment. When they are healthy, their instincts are strong and can be trusted.

Hardworking – As their name implies, Workboots enjoy working and like to stay busy, which often means they work longer and harder than everyone else. My husband serves our family tirelessly beyond just his profession. You can always find him on the weekends helping fix, create, or begin something in the garage to help his family. He has more energy than the rest of us combined! If you need to get something done, you want a Workboot in your corner.

Weaknesses

Confrontational – Workboots tend to thrive on opposition. They enjoy a good debate, and they genuinely don't mean any harm because they love to spar with others. However, this can feel like constant bickering or fighting to other personalities. I have seen this in Bible studies through the years that a Workboot will challenge interpretations of Scripture and other people's comments. When misunderstood, this can feel like a fight; in reality, Workboots enjoy engaging things from different angles. This reminds me of our English saying, *devil's advocate*. Now, this phrase has nothing to do with the Evil One, but the Cambridge Dictionary defines it as:

"someone who pretends, in an argument or discussion, to be against an idea or plan that a lot of people support, in order to make people discuss and consider it in more detail."

Bossy – Another possible weakness a Workboot is probably used to hearing is that they can be quite bossy. They are great leaders, but they can often come across as just downright commanding, barking orders right and left. A healthy Workboot is a snowplow making the way ahead safe for others. An unhealthy Workboot is a bulldozer leaving a trail of exhausted and upset bodies.

Impatient – Workboots love action and will often become agitated when others take longer to arrive at a decision or discuss a project. This impatience can often result in them quickly losing their tempers with others. They are so visionary and trust their guts that even though they often ask people's opinions, they don't allow others to arrive at their own conclusions. If a Workboot can be patient enough, others will most likely agree with the Workboot's initial instinct, but they need to arrive at that conclusion in their own time, rather than being dragged there too quickly.

Unsympathetic – Since Workboots are such hard workers and "get 'er done" people, they will work remotely with a 103-degree fever and wonder why you don't too. They love phrases like "buck up, buttercup!" and can appear unsympathetic to someone else's needs. One Workboot told me she literally had the tip of her finger cut off at her job and promptly had it put on ice so she could work through to the end of her shift before going to the ER. She could not have been prouder of that story of perseverance, and it's a classic example of why Workboots don't have much sympathy for others.

One note here for women who are Workboots: many of the Workboot's characteristics are often considered in our society to be "male" traits. For that reason, many female Workboots find they are often misunderstood. Men can have these same characteristics and are applauded, yet when women demonstrate these strengths, they are labeled . . . *you know what*. If you are a misunderstood female Workboot, sit and soak up how which God sees you. Work on your weak areas, but don't shy away from being the strong vessel you are. Allow your strengths to be used for God's glory and walk in the assurance that you are a reflection of Him.

CHAPTER 1: WHO AM I?

Stacey Stiletto

Stilettos are people-oriented and assertive, which makes them people magnets. Others are naturally drawn to their joy and playful passion. They have a wonderful sense of humor, and their laugh can be heard long before they arrive in a room. People will often say yes to their invitations because they know their Stiletto friend is always on the cutting edge of something worthwhile.

If you've given birth to a Stiletto, you may have noticed that they are the class clown. They use your fireplace hearth as a stage to perform all sorts of acts for your enjoyment. They're comfortable in front of a crowd and love being the center of attention.

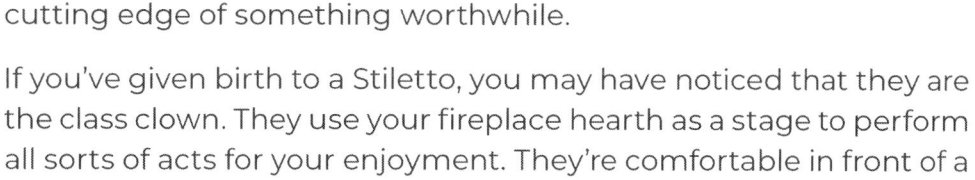

They are bent toward influencing and moving others to action through authentic motivation and affirmation. Encouragement is a powerful characteristic in any family, church, or business.

Strengths

Friendly – Because they are assertive and social by nature, Stilettos can make BFFs in any location. If they are in a grocery line for more than five minutes, they've managed to chat with every person behind them and in front of them, and have traded contact info with at least three people.

Positive – Stilettos are incredibly positive and their passion is contagious. Stacey Stiletto is a cheerleader, using encouragement and authentic motivation to spur others on. They can always find a silver lining and don't give up easily.

Inspiring – People look to Stilettos as influencers and trendsetters. This influence can be something as small as sparking the latest fashion trend or as impactful as bringing friends to church services, conferences, and Bible studies. They inspire people and are often found as upfront presenters for the PTA, at church, and at work.

Engaging – Stilettos tell great stories and are strong communicators. They are selected as vision casters in their church and organizations because they can communicate in a way that connects a person's heart to a mission, project, or initiative.

Weaknesses

Too talkative – As a Stiletto myself, this is my number one weakness. As I mentioned earlier, I love the sound of my own voice. When I worked towards my coaching certification, we learned the acronym that I have shared many times: WAIT (*Why am I talking?*). It's designed to help us think before we talk. This acronym can be especially useful to Stilettos, because we often speak before thinking and scramble to put words back in that are insensitive, ill-timed, or inappropriate. Stilettos are genuine verbal processors. It is important they feel heard and have the opportunity to talk through their decisions, conclusions, and insights. However, Stilettos need to learn that not every situation requires this verbal processing and that they can also process via journaling or even voice memos rather than lengthy discussions that can exhaust others.

Toxic Positivity – Though positivity is a strength, Stilettos can be overly positive. Why is that a bad thing? Because Stilettos are glass-half-full people, they can often avoid sitting with people in pain or overuse their positivity to gloss over someone's suffering, rather than just being present and listening to someone who is hurting.

Unscheduled – Because the Stiletto is suppressed rather than comforted by a schedule, they often run late. It is common for a Stiletto's family to tell (a.k.a. lie) Stacy Stiletto that Thanksgiving dinner will start earlier than usual to trick her into being on time. Stilettos also enjoy being spontaneous and love to make last-minute plans. But this can be frustrating to other types who like to have a plan and stick to it. Then, Stilettos also wonder why others can't just relax and have fun.

Easily Distracted – A Stiletto can have the best of intentions to stay home Saturday and finish their laundry only to reply "Yes!" to their friend's text to meet for coffee and shop. They're like the dog in the movie *Up* who would stop talking mid-sentence to chase a squirrel. That's why reducing distractions is crucial for Stilettos. Social media can be particularly distracting since that social pull is so strong for them.

CHAPTER 1: WHO AM I?

Merry Mary Jane

Mary Janes are reserved and task-oriented, which means they love to work behind the scenes to make sure everything runs according to plan. Quality, excellence, and consistency are Mary Jane's core values.

They are low-risk individuals. They deliberate over options and outcomes. Questions like "Can we afford it?", "Can we insure it?", and "How have others done it?" help them assess risks before making a decision or taking action. They create, follow, and guard processes, systems, and forms. And Heaven help you if you don't follow their ordered process! Our daughter is a strong Mary Jane who works in corporate America analyzing risk and return. She was a cautious toddler who seemed to be assessing risks from a very young age. We love seeing how this trait matured and enables her to benefit others. HR tends to attract a lot of Mary Janes because of the nature of needing to follow a procedure and manage risk.

They are the most prayerful of our four SHOEs because they don't just say they will pray . . . they actually do it. Mary Janes typically have a system for praying each day of the week. Monday, they pray for Africa. Tuesday is for work teams, projects, and coworkers. Wednesday is for meetings with the pastor, Bible study leaders, etc. You get the idea.

If you've given birth to a Mary Jane, you're probably impressed with your parenting skills. Why? Mary Janes seem parent themselves. They are excellent students, follow the rules, and even tend to be tidy in their rooms because they innately love order.

Strengths

Thoughtful – Mary Janes are thoughtful in two ways. First, they will remember you like your coffee black or are allergic to seafood. They're also contemplative, often enjoying times of silence to ponder. Unlike our Stiletto, a Mary Jane always thinks before speaking. This gives them a chance to pray, identify what they are trying to communicate, and time their comments in a way others will receive it well. They also like space alone to ponder thoughts privately. Our daughter (who would be a Mary Jane in the SHOE Assessment) used to come home during her early elementary school days and need ten minutes on the swing playing quietly before she engaged in homework or conversation.

Loyal – Mary Janes are self-sacrificing friends, though it may take you a while to get close to them because they are reserved and more guarded until they get to know you. Once you develop a friendship with a Mary Jane, they are faithful and loving.

Organized – Mary Janes love to organize things. (I would suspect Marie Kondo is a Mary Jane.) They love the Container Store because they want their lives in clear plastic boxes with white labels on the outside. Organizing is a form of self-care for a Mary Jane.

Detail-Oriented – Mary Janes are capable of juggling more details in an accurate and organized fashion than the other three SHOEs combined. They seem like they have six hands and an expanded brain to hold all the varying responsibilities, commitments, and itemized action steps associated with each task. They pair well with Workboots, because Workboots like the tasks but not the details. Thus, Mary Janes can implement vision and create the process to bring it forth on budget, on deadline, and with excellence. When our daughter was in kindergarten, she would tell us she could see patterns and detail in the ceiling tiles, but she couldn't tell where they began and ended. A Mary Jane notices details and seeks to strategically analyze them.

Weaknesses

Perfectionistic – If you're a Mary Jane, your standards for yourself and others are always so high (and often unattainable) that you and others close to you consistently know they fall short of your perfect standard. Over time, this weighs on your spouse, children, and teammates. No matter what they bring to the table, there is always something that could be done better. Instead of appreciating that your kids cleaned the kitchen (yay!), you're keenly aware there is still maple syrup on the counter. Perfectionism creates a wedge in any relationship because it leads to unattainable expectations, causing others to give up, avoid the Mary Jane, and feel insecure when they understandably fall short of perfection.

Overly Detailed – Because you typically have a memory like an elephant and enjoy accuracy, you may find yourself correcting others on things that just don't matter. Like when your husband shares that a story happened in the Fall, and you correct him because it occurred in the Spring. I witnessed this with a friend who interrupted her husband to clarify, "Honey, it couldn't have been in the Fall, because I remember wearing a sundress and I wouldn't have worn that while it was cold." Does it really matter? One of my mentors told me a long time ago, "Do you want to be right or do you want to be well?" Mary Janes might need to lighten up on things that can slide so they can focus on the non-negotiables that must be accurate, like your income taxes, budget, etc.

Overly Scheduled – As a Mary Jane, one of your strengths is discipline, focus, and routine. However, this can lead to a lack of novelty, and you may want to try something fresh and spontaneous. Heck, even parking in a new location or using a different workout machine at your gym reminds you to shake it up a bit. This is especially important if you're in a relationship with a Stiletto who loves spontaneity. Regardless, it's important to be able to roll with the punches when life happens and plans need adjusting. If nothing else, try to schedule some unstructured time to just "be" once in a while. When you experience the tension that arises within you when your plans are interrupted, take deep breaths and accept your revised limitations.

Overly Prepared – While Mary Janes think before speaking, they may also ruminate too long or wrestle too much with a problem, conversation, or situation. They often spend too much time preparing to do a project, running the numbers one more time, or waiting until the timing is perfect. Rarely will there be a "perfect time" to have every possible outcome examined and thoroughly covered. Sometimes, in the fast-paced world we live in, we just have to think through a few scenarios, then jump and figure it out as we go.

Critical – Mary Janes can be very critical, both of themselves and of others. God has wired them as critical thinkers and problem solvers, which are powerful strengths. However, when used to criticize or judge someone else, this can be so damaging. If you're a Mary Jane, you may not always say your critical thoughts out loud, but you may still entertain them in your head like, "I cannot believe she wore that dress to church." Be careful not to encourage this critical spirit in yourself and instead remember we're all imperfect.

Pessimistic – Mary Janes are realistic and bring much needed logic to various situations. But they also like to spot potential problems and point out all the ways things could go wrong. This can be misunderstood as pessimism, particularly if the timing and tone are off. For example, during a church event team meeting, someone (maybe a Stiletto) has an exciting idea and says, "I think we can release 10,000 balloons at the end of our conference in order to create a marked moment of what the women are releasing to Jesus." Before she can even get the words out of her mouth, the Mary Jane shoots it down saying, "We tried that in 2004 and we all got muddy from the field and cited from the city for not having a permit." *Womp, womp.* Instead, try framing it differently: "This has a lot of potential, Stacy. Thanks for this great idea. Let me check the permit and weather so we can make sure our guests and city have a great experience."

Frannie Flip Flop

Flip Flops are laid-back and people-oriented, which makes them easy-going and reliable peacemakers. They genuinely love people and enjoy face-to-face, one-on-one quality time listening and pondering all that is going on around them. They are observers, taking things in without inserting themselves much. They genuinely enjoy and appreciate others' way of doing things.

The Flip Flop is a peacemaker who brings harmony to relationships just like an orchestra conductor brings together all the notes of varying instruments into a lovely melody. At their healthiest, the Flip Flop can be a strong voice in conflict, building bridges, pointing out common ground, and seeing two sides of an issue objectively.

Flip Flops possess a unique wit, but not the laugh-out-loud humor of a Stiletto. It's more the quiet wit of a schoolmate who tells a joke in the back of the room, but then you are the one who gets in trouble with the teacher.

One of the single biggest characteristics of the Flip Flop is that they avoid conflict at all costs. While this helps them mediate harmony among others, and while they will stick up for others if they see injustice, they avoid causing conflict when it involves them personally. That can lead to resentment and, eventually, explosions from a Flip Flop who has stuffed her feelings too long.

If you are in a relationship with a Flip Flop, take a moment to write or text them, and share how grateful you are for their life and apologize if you've taken them for granted. They are the most invisible of the SHOEs preferring to work behind the scenes rather than center stage. What a gift they are!

Strengths

Laid-back – Relaxing with a Flip Flop is easy because they seek comfort in all they do, whether it's their yoga pants, casual posture, or hospitable style. Because they are never in a hurry, you can sense their patient attentiveness. They're also happy to go along with the preferences of others and rarely have strong opinions. Instead of having conditions and requirements, they just want to be together.

Loyal – Other personality assessments might call our Flip Flop "The Golden Retriever," capturing their core characteristic of loyalty. Our son shares this trait as we've observed his loyalty to relationships, sports teams, and even hobbies. What he loves, he loves completely. Flip Flops are extremely loyal to family and friends, and one powerful way to see them face conflict is when they are defending their family from those who have done them wrong. You don't mess with the people a Flip Flop loves. Suddenly, the laid-back Flip Flop becomes a fierce protector.

Accepting – Also like a golden retriever, Flip Flops are warm and safe. Flip Flops make space for others and accept them where they are without expectations. They can compassionately sit with someone in pain and create space for processing without the need to fix them.

Caring – Because of their loyalty, they are often the glue that holds a family together. Our son, who is a Flip Flops is always pulling the family together and focusing on the family's connections, often checking on others and creating ways to connect through arranging meals, watching movies, and being attentive.

Weaknesses

Unmotivated – Flip Flops are always *fixin'* to do something (*insert Southern accent*). They intend to do something, but they never actually get around to doing it. I had a Flip Flop friend years ago who received lovely, framed prints for Christmas. I visited her home in February (her Christmas tree was still up . . . thought there were no more needles on it, just a stick full of bare branches and ornaments), and her lovely prints were leaned up against the wall which would become their home. Sitting on the table next to them was a hammer and nails, but my Flip Flop friend was still *fixin'* to get to it. Procrastination can be a huge source of frustration for family, friends, and workmates. As a Flip Flop, you need to create some motivation for work projects, perhaps by drawing motivation from the relationships associated with the task.

Passive – Akin to lacking motivation, a Flip Flop tends to do bare minimum in any setting. While this can be wise in some situations, it may keep them from progressing in others. Flip Flop moms attend school functions, but never join the PTA. They attend Sunday services yet never venture into a Life Group. They respond to invitations, but are never the pursuer of others or the maker of plans. Flip Flops often enjoy observing situations rather than actually participating in them. For example, while on a mission trip with a Flip Flop, I noticed they did a lot of fun talking but almost no work. It created a lot of frustration for our other teammates who were sweating it out in a strange culture and stifling hot weather. Which leads to the next possible weakness . . .

Lazy – Flip Flops remain so laid-back and comfortable that they are actually, *dare I say it*, lazy in their weakest state. I knew a toddler who had learned how to tie his shoes, but his parents couldn't get him to ever do it, so they purchased Velcro shoes only to find their lazy

Flip Flop toddler thought it was too taxing to bend over to apply the Velcro. The toddler's solution was to jam their feet into their shoes from a standing position, thus turning them into Velcro clogs.

Indecisive – Flip Flops want anyone other than themselves to make their decisions. They frequently ask, "What do you think I should do?" When our son was two, his grandparents had Friday night sleepovers which meant a trip to the local Dollar Store to choose one prize. Long after his sister had selected her book or crayons, Connor would still be in the truck aisle with Papa, holding two trucks and agonizing over which one he should choose.

A Masterpiece in the Making

When I work with clients on personality behaviors, I often hear, "Well, that isn't so special. All I do is create spreadsheets. Doesn't everyone?" No. Those spreadsheets are an indication of a skill of creating order, systems, and processes, and not everyone can do that. Whatever that skill is for you, it is special and valuable, even if it doesn't seem that way to you.

The verse at the beginning of this chapter (Ephesians 2:10) refers to us as *God's masterpiece*. What would happen if we really believed that we were created in the image of God and trusted that what He placed within us is part of His mark on our world? The Greek word in that verse for masterpiece is the word *poeima*, from which we get our English word "poem." What would be different if we lived our lives like a poem written to our families, neighbors, churches, schools, and workplaces?

> **WHAT WOULD BE DIFFERENT IF WE LIVED OUR LIVES LIKE A POEM WRITTEN TO OUR FAMILIES, NEIGHBORS, CHURCHES, SCHOOLS, AND WORKPLACES?**

That kind of confidence is rooted in knowing who we are in Christ. Godly confidence accepts and uses the traits God has placed within us, but also accepts and releases the traits God has left out of us. We are puzzle pieces within the Body of Christ. As each of us does our own part, we find that we have what others need and others have what we lack.

We are made to be masterpieces. But we are all still under construction and will be until we stand before Jesus in Heaven. We should participate with God in the process of polishing our strengths and chipping away at our weaknesses. As we do, we'll fit even better with the puzzle pieces around us.

There is no one else like you. I love the phrase "Be you . . . everyone else is taken." The Message translation of Romans 12:4-5 says, "In this way we are like the various parts of a human body. Each part gets its meaning from the body as a whole, not the other way around. The body we're talking about is Christ's body of chosen people. Each of us finds our meaning and function as a part of his body." Bring your strengths before God with gratitude for how He's gifted you and is using you in your family, church, community, workplace, and the Body of Christ.

Offer your strengths back to God. Own and appreciate what He's placed within you, your ability to organize, lead, listen, influence, etc. and ask Him how to use His gifts to bring Him glory. In the same way, bring your weaknesses to Him and, if they have become sinful, confess them. Ask Him to remove them and tell Him that you're wanting to change. "God, I'm tired of running late, being judgmental, talking too much, being bossy . . . " If you could have removed them in your own strength, you would have by now. Most of the weak areas that frustrate you have likely done so since early childhood. 2 Corinthians 12:9 says, "My grace is sufficient for you, for my power is made perfect in weakness."

Let God do His work in both your strengths and weakness. Consider the statue of David. There's a story that when Michaelangelo was asked, "How did you take a block of marble and turn it into that masterpiece.", he replied, "It was easy. You just chip away the stone that doesn't look like David." Friends, when God does His deep work in you, He's polishing your strengths and chipping away your weaknesses, working to make you into a reflection of Jesus. Because when people look at you, He wants them to see Him, not you. Let God do His work.

The Layers of You

You are more than just your SHOE personality. Yes, it is wise to identify your personality, but you are also your spiritual gifts, your birth order, your love language, your life's experiences, the generation you've been born into, and more. It is the combination of all these elements that creates the masterpiece God created you to be. That is why you can sit next to someone who has the exact same "SHOE combination" as you do and yet behave very differently. It's like when you combine hydrogen and oxygen, both powerful on their own but combined, you create something altogether different depending on the proportions. One form is water, and another is hydrogen peroxide.

Also, remember that our personalities answer to us. We don't answer to them. The purpose of learning about our wiring is so that we can use that knowledge to make better decisions, rather than running on autopilot. We have the Holy Spirit to temper our actions and responses.

The self-awareness you're developing in this chapter is the beginning of emotional intelligence: the ability to recognize your emotions and those of others, and to decide how to respond, rather than being controlled by them. The Flip Flop, for example, has the desire for peace, which can lead to people-pleasing. However, when asked for an opinion, a self-aware Flip Flop must not lie or give in for the sake of perceived peace. The Flip Flop personality may be your natural inclination, but it is up to you to say something that you know will lead to healthy and needed conflict.

Let's not use our personalities as an excuse for poor behavior. Even the good things that are tucked inside our strengths can become weaknesses if they're carried too far. As the saying goes, "Strengths carried to extremes become weaknesses." A leadership strength carried to an extreme can lead to someone becoming a dictator. The strength of mercy carried to the extreme can lead to someone being a doormat. Ecclesiastes 7:18 says, "Whoever fears God will avoid all extremes." So, to be wise, we need to make sure we are operating within the best of our wiring, not our worst.

We can use secular assessments to get a glimpse of how God sees us. We should ask God, "What do you want me to see about myself here?" I like to envision God taking my face in His hands and turning it away from the world's view of me and lifting my face to Him causing me to gaze into His vertical mirror. It's a wonderful opportunity to see what HE sees, instead of what I see.

There are a lot of horizontal mirrors that try to tell us who we are, often in hurtful ways that make us feel less than. I have a vivid memory of my middle school art teacher looking at me during project day, curling his lip and asking, "Lisa, why are you always so loud?" *Ouch*. As much as I loved (love) attention, it was embarrassing and I felt inferior. Admittedly, it was my raw, unrefined Stiletto personality probably chatting too much, too loudly, or out of turn. But I will never forget the way that made me feel.

What is it for you? The horizontal mirrors from your past could be the comments a sports coach or family member made to you. Social media is a horizontal mirror that is constantly sending messages of who we should be, most of which are filtered and unrealistic. Take a moment to ask God to show you the woman He created you to be. Let the world's distorted reflections fall away. When you begin to examine yourself, the best and the worst of yourself, you allow God's perfect mirror to help you see rightly.

Now that you understand your SHOE personality, my hope is you've seen the beauty of who God created you to be.

Next, it's time to extend into full circle self-awareness by not just evaluating, "Who am I?", but "Who am I alongside of *you*?" What happens when my SHOE interacts with your SHOE? How do we complement each other, and how do we complicate one another?

Reflect & Respond

1. What combination of SHOEs are you based on your SHOE Assessment? What is your initial reaction to that discovery?

2. Human nature is to focus on everything that we do not love about our wiring. Let's instead start with things you can celebrate about your SHOE personality. What do you like about the description of your SHOE? How has your SHOE personality helped you succeed?

3. What are a few warnings you see that will help you avoid the weaknesses of your SHOE?

4. Can you see any bias that you prefer certain SHOES more than others? Is it your own SHOE that you prefer? Is it someone else's wiring you prefer? Write down what comes up for you as the "best" ways to be. Then, can you release that bias in order to accept what is in you and what has been left out of you? Who would benefit knowing more about what you've learned about yourself? Your spouse? A friend? Your mother-in-law? The team you work with? Committee members at church? Your supervisor?

Chapter 2
Who Am I Alongside Others?

"If it is possible, as far as it depends on you, live at peace with all men."

Romans 12:18

Like I said, I am a verbal processor, but clarity for me comes in knowing when it is appropriate to verbally process with someone and when it is time to keep that inside. I always have a thought, idea, or response when I'm engaging in conversation, Bible studies, coaching appointments, and ministry meetings. However, overusing my voice can be just as unhealthy as someone who suppresses their voice. I have to continually read the room I am in and gauge whether my comment is crucial, needed or important to the discussion at hand. Because my strength of coming up with comments and having a ready response can also inadvertently cause others not to speak up or annoy them, I have asked myself questions like, "Am I oversharing? Have I already spoken often? Have others in the room had enough silence to have a chance to share themselves?" There are important times when I need to verbally process, so I can advocate for myself and say, "I would love to have some time to process this a little more. I don't want to take all the group time right now. Would it be possible for me to get some time with you to go deeper?" I also try to find appropriate ways in significant relationships to share the insight I have about myself that I am a verbal processor and it helps me absorb information and make decisions. That way, those who are closest to me will know that about me.

So often, what we find annoying in someone else is a God-given strength that we misunderstand simply because it's different than our own strengths.

Full Circle Self-Awareness

People ask me all the time how their weaknesses hinder their growth. While understanding our weaknesses is important, often an overuse of one of our strengths is inappropriate in a given situation. As we grow in our clarity and become more emotionally intelligent, we realize that sometimes we complement others with our personalities and sometimes we complicate each other. Not every personality trait, no matter how good it is, complements our relationships or certain circumstances.

Full circle self-awareness takes into account the relationships around us in our homes, our work teams, boss and direct reports, in our church Bible study, and beyond. This full circle clarity leads to emotional intelligence by removing barriers, uncovering bias, and identifying blind spots.

For example, my Stiletto personality is very positive and expressive by nature. However, there are times when expressing my positivity isn't helpful. If someone is going through a particularly hard time, it isn't helpful for me to say, "Chin up, friend. God's got this." (Even though I believe that to be true.) Those well-intentioned words dismiss the person's pain and makes them feel unseen. Full-circle self-awareness in this situation tells my positivity to zip it and just listen. When I feel positivity rising inside my head knocking on the door to be expressed, I ask myself this question: "What is needed in this situation?" If I am with someone processing frustration or grief, I need to self-lead my behavior to tell my positivity to stay put and not be expressed. Even though I have faith that things will indeed work out for my friend, it isn't always helpful for my positive perspective to be spoken. I essentially tell my positivity, "You're not needed right now. You can sit and I'll call you in when appropriate."

> AS WE GROW IN OUR CLARITY AND BECOME MORE EMOTIONALLY INTELLIGENT, WE REALIZE THAT SOMETIMES WE COMPLEMENT OTHERS WITH OUR PERSONALITIES AND SOMETIMES WE COMPLICATE EACH OTHER.

We must manage our personalities instead of giving in to every tempting thought, feeling, or knee-jerk response we have. It doesn't mean those qualities of ours are bad—it just may not be the right time or the right person to display them. Every strength can become a weakness if it's used in the wrong way.

I like to use three basic self-awareness questions to help us consider how we can bring the best of ourselves in any given situation and relationship:

1. Who am I?
2. Who are they?
3. Who am I alongside of them?

Let's break it down a little further. The first question asks us to understand ourselves. Who am I at my best and at my worst? How am I often misunderstood? How do I tend to misunderstand others? What do I need and how do I complicate it when I'm unhealthy? Knowing ourselves is the first step.

But we can't stop there. The next step is to move on to examining who others are. What can I learn about other people? Who did God create them to be? How can I learn more about their wiring and improve our relationship? It can be your spouse, sister, brother, mother-in-law, boss, or neighbor—anyone you interact with regularly. I highly recommend that you take your SHOE Assessment with those in your family, your Life Group at church, or even your coworkers. It will help you learn more about them and what motivates them. But even with people who haven't taken the assessment, you can still seek to understand them better through the lens of a different SHOE.

The third question asks you to use the knowledge you have about yourself and about others in order to make an informed decision about how to act. Ask yourself, "What does this situation require of me in light of who we both are? Given our unique strengths and tendencies, how can we best pursue our goal?"

When you put all three questions into play, you have full-circle self-awareness.

This involves recognizing other people's strengths and allowing them to shine, as well as minimizing the friction that can arise when different types have conflicting ideas about what needs to be done.

When Different SHOEs Interact

We all tend to be irritated when other people do things differently than us. We assume that they're doing it on purpose to bother us or even hurt us, when usually it's mostly unintentional. But by becoming aware of these distinctions, we can take steps to understand our preferences, unearth our blind spots, and remove our biases around personalities in general. This will lead to:

1. A deepened understanding of and appreciation for others.

2. More patience with others whose wiring clashes with ours. It's easy to understand that opposite personalities clash, but even similar personalities can bump into each other.

3. Better management of our personalities and our responses so we don't annoy or offend others as much.

Most conflict is rooted in misunderstanding. So, the solution is often understanding one another better. This chapter will help you do that.

Conflict is an unavoidable part of life, but there are good and bad ways to work through it. As Flip Flops know all too well, when we try to avoid conflict altogether, it always backfires. We can only stuff our feelings down so long before they explode. Instead, we have to learn how to engage in conflict in a healthy way. Healthy conflict will keep your relationships healthy.

When you take the time to learn other people's wiring, you are putting tools in your relationship toolbox to be at peace with them, as the verse (Romans 12:18) at the beginning of this chapter says. It's important to understand what real peace is, though. Peace doesn't mean the absence of fighting while you're quietly simmering with resentment. Real peace means genuine understanding, acceptance, and love. It means working through misunderstandings and disagreements with kindness and respect. It means making sure everyone's emotional needs are met.

This chapter will help you learn how to meet the needs of others while not denying your own needs, so you can be at peace in your relationships and work together to achieve your goals.

CHAPTER 2: WHO AM I ALONGSIDE OTHERS?

When you learn to love others the way they need to be loved, rather than the way you want to be loved, you'll make lots of emotional "deposits" in the "bank account" of your relationship. This will create trust and goodwill, reducing conflict and paving the way for healthy conflict. It's a little like the parenting philosophy that you need to put chips in your kids' bank so that when you need to make a withdrawal, it comes from a place of them feeling full already.

Be intentional about pouring into relationships enough with listening, serving, affirming, and uplifting so that there is room for conflict when it happens. Don't "Oreo" them . . . "You're such a Godly friend. I wish you weren't scattered and forgetful about your commitments, but you're a great sister in Christ." People can see right through those "compliment sandwiches" and sense your lack of authenticity. Instead, build the kinds of relationships that don't need an Oreo approach.

Knowing what tends to bother your SHOE type and how your type can accidentally bug others reflects the full-circle self-awareness that builds true confidence. By recognizing your own needs and the needs of each type, you'll be able to see them more clearly and meet the needs underneath their difficult behaviors.

This chapter will also help you to understand how each type behaves during conflict, which usually brings out the worst in us. You'll know what to watch out for, both in yourself and in others, and that knowledge can help you stay calm even if the other person starts to become upset.

Please remember that this is a dance. It's give and take. It can't always be you bending to another style, nor can it always be them bending to yours. That's why I strongly encourage you to share this chapter and the previous one with those closest to you and invite them along on this journey of self-discovery.

Let's consider how the different SHOEs interact, how each SHOE can be misunderstood, and how we can handle such interactions better.

For each SHOE, we'll look at:

1. Why others bug them.
2. Why they bug others.
3. What they need.
4. How they behave in conflict.

Note: *I strongly encourage you to read all four SHOE descriptions. Read your SHOE type from the perspective of how you behave and how you impact others. And read the other types from the perspective of how they behave differently and might impact you. Remember, the goal is full-circle self-awareness, so we need to understand all four types.*

The Workboot Alongside Others

Workboots are driven, visionary, and highly productive. They like action and control, and they're task-oriented. They can be unemotional, dismissive of others, and possibly aggressive in conflict.

If you regularly interact with a Workboot (and you're not one), they will have certain tendencies that are different from yours that could irritate you in predictable ways and vice versa.

Why Others Bug the Workboot

1. Relationships Over Results

    Workboots perceive that others are only focused on relationships without giving the proper attention to the results. They might become frustrated when people are talking instead of working or when the plan changes because of one person's feelings.

2. Indecisiveness and Inaction

    Workboots are assertive by nature. Workboots are the ones to speak first, dive into the fray, and move quickly, so they get impatient when others (like the Mary Jane and Flip Flop) need longer stretches of time to process and take action. This can complicate relationships.

3. Life in the Slow Lane

    Because the Workboot moves quickly from project to project and conversation to conversation, they may misunderstand others' need to pause and celebrate, or even just take a breather between one project and the next.

Why Workboots Bug Others

1. Intensity That Feels like Intimidation

    There is a definite intensity about a Workboot. They walk with incredible intention and make their way into any conference room, worship center, or living room as a force. Workboots are often unaware that this intensity can actually be intimidating and downright polarizing. My husband is a Workboot who rarely raised his voice in our home. Yet, our kids often felt like their dad was yelling. Because of the intensity of the Workboot's personality, normal conversations can *feel* like yelling. Our daughter interned at my Workboot hubby's office one year and came home saying, "Everyone seems scared of Dad at the office." Of course they were not, but they were aware of the intensity.

    John Trent created a personality assessment and the Workboots in his assessment are lions. Now think about attending a cocktail party and seeing a lion sitting on the couch. You would admire the majestic nature of that lion, but you may not want to sit next to it. Why? Because there is this fear that the lion might roar. This is similar to the intensity of a Workboot. They are typically unaware of it and it will trip them up if they don't understand it. They don't create it or use it intentionally. It just is. This is where it can be helpful for Workboots to ask those close to them to let them know how they come across in discussions, meetings, church committees, etc. It's important for Workboots in significant relationships to be aware they can be intense and let others know that they welcome feedback. Workboots actually enjoy direct feedback.

2. Relentless Competitiveness

    The Workboot's desire to compete and win can cause teammates, friends, and family to feel like nothing is celebrated as the Workboot moves from one win to another. Their temptation is to find their worth in their work, so anyone who seems like they are standing in the way of a Workboot's success can result in the Workboot overcompensating and becoming controlling in order to win. This competitive nature means that Workboots tend to feel they are must always right. Of course, *no* personality is always correct, but Workboots have a strong sense of discernment, which often leads them in the right direction or decision. Workboots get so used to going with their gut that, even if/when they stop to ask their spouse's or coworker's opinion, their family and friends know they have already made up their mind that they're right, so why bother to give another opinion?

3. Bluntness

    Workboots are direct and to the point. However, sometimes they are *too* direct. If you're a Workboot, it's important to consider who you are talking to when adding your insights or direction. Warming up the conversation, using more adjectives, and allowing time for social dialogue will counteract this blunt approach to others. A Workboot can easily take the wind out of someone's new idea. Spouses, children, and teammates feel this over and over. Giving other's ideas a chance before shooting them down is important.

What Workboots Need

1. Independence and Control

    Workboots are free spirits who love autonomy and independence. They resist submitting to others because their fear is losing control. Therefore, when possible, even with the tiniest and youngest Workboots, giving them as much independence and control as is practical (without losing your own boundaries) will improve your relationships.

2. The Bottom Line

    My DISC trainer, Janice, used to teach that the D (the Workboot in the SHOE Assessment) needs you to be brief and be gone.

Whenever you want to have a meaningful conversation with them, plan ahead, bullet point the conversation rather than rambling, and make sure you have thought through their possible questions. They like succinct, direct communication without a lot of processing.

The Workboot in Conflict

First, remember, Workboots *enjoy* a great debate. So, when interacting with them, it's wise to consider, "Is this really a conflict or just a sport kind of debate?" However, if they're feeling threatened, they can become aggressive, volatile, and intimidating.

Workboot Conflict Trigger: Loss of control or looking weak

In Conflict, Workboots:

- Have a goal to win, so they create win/lose outcomes. If you try to beat them at this game, they will dig in and may get mean.

- Can be stubborn or inflexible. They become rigid in conflict and can seem like they are unwilling to find common ground. This is because making peace feels like a lack of control for a Workboot or can even feel like losing.

- Overpower others with force. This is not physical force. Remember the Workboot's intensity we talked about above? Workboots get very logical in conflict and they can be perceived as cold or insensitive.

How to Speak to Workboots in Conflict:

- Be direct and speak up for yourself. They don't like weakness.

- Be brief and to the point, rather than sharing long, drawn-out stories.

- Use facts, not emotion or feeling. Present things logically and pragmatically.

How to De-escalate a Workboot in Conflict:

Their black and white approach to conflict where one person will be a winner and the other a loser would benefit from taking a win/win, shades-of-gray perspective, instead. How can each side win? Where is the middle ground? Remind them you're on the same team and want the same things even though you see the situation differently.

Healthy Workboots in Relationship:

Workboots are gifts in our relationships as they keep us moving to new heights, lead with vision and passion, and are an example of a strong work ethic. Workboots take great joy in protecting and problem-solving on behalf of those they love and lead.

The Stiletto Alongside Others

Stilettos are positive and motivating. They are people-oriented and love to talk, and they have trouble being quiet or alone too long. They want to be liked and love to use their gifts to influence others.

If you regularly interact with a Stiletto (and you're not one), they will have certain tendencies that are different from yours that will tend to irritate you and vice versa.

Why Others Bug Stilettos:

Stilettos want to contribute to brainstorms, projects, and discussions. Others bug Stilettos when they are not allowed to contribute, motivate, or influence. Stilettos are made to get involved, and they feel stifled if they're not able to do so.

1. Rules Over Relationships

    Stilettos do their best in a collaborative environment, so they are frustrated when they have to work alone for long periods of time. Because people are their motivation to achieve goals, enforce priorities, and succeed personally and professionally, they become resentful if their tasks and projects are focused on the rules and outcomes.

CHAPTER 2: WHO AM I ALONGSIDE OTHERS?

2. Stoic Interactions

    Because Stilettos are tempted to find their worth in being the "fun" one, cold interactions are especially threatening to them. The other SHOEs will often grunt out a *"good morning"* without eye contact when a Stiletto comes near to shield themselves from chit-chat (which Stilettos are eager to provide). However, this is disheartening to the highly social Stiletto, who would much prefer a quick "hello" with eye contact and a smile over a brusque "good morning."

Why Stilettos Bug Others:

1. An Endless Social Battery

    Stilettos are verbal processors who are very expressive, conversational, and collaborative. They love teamwork, have multiple BFFs, and gain energy from time with people. When healthy, this is a great gift as they often will draw out the best in others, encourage others to take adventures, and engage others through stories, jokes, and tales. Their motivating style can keep a spouse on course in a hard season as they cheer them toward the finish line. And while being social is an asset, it can become a deficit in business or committee meetings. When the Stiletto lacks emotional intelligence, their chatter can feel intrusive and inappropriate. Consider the Stiletto coworker who arrives to work at 8:00 a.m. on Monday and desires to spend about thirty to forty minutes connecting with teammates to hear all about their fun weekend experiences. Meanwhile, the Workboot and Mary Jane are neck deep in productivity and feel frustrated with the interruption for chit chat. Stilettos need to remember to WAIT *(Why am I talking?)*.

2. Not Reading the Room

    By human nature, we are all self-focused. However, Stilettos sometimes are less aware of the needs of those around them than others. Stilettos often interrupt, not noticing that others are neck deep in a project and that their timing to tell a story is poor. Even if they don't interrupt, they sing. They talk to themselves. In some ways they "demand" verbal processing. This feels especially true in their safest spaces with family and close friends. If you're a Stiletto, remember that not everything needs to be talked about. It is wise for the Stiletto to learn to read a room, consider timing, and save up in-depth interactions for a time that works for both parties.

3. Lack of Discipline

    Getting out of the house is quite a feat for the Stiletto. They often ask themselves, "Where is my purse? What did I do with my diaper bag?" And the most typical question . . . "Where are my keys?" Now, the Mary Janes reading this are thinking, "How hard can it be to put the plaque next to your garage doorway that says "KEYS" or better yet, leave them in your cupholder in the car?" But Stiletto rarely take the time to organize that much. This lack of discipline shows up as a lack of follow-through. Because one of the Stiletto's basic desires is to be accepted, they often say "yes" to baking the brownies for the bake sale, facilitating the next Bible study, or recruiting door prizes for the next event. However, rarely do they write these things down in their calendar or plan for them, so they often lack the follow-through required to deliver on their promises.

What Stilettos Need:

1. To Be Heard and Express Themselves

    As verbal processors, the Stiletto uses a lot of words in order to absorb a new idea, retain information, and make decisions. It is wise for a Stiletto to let others know, "I need some extra time with you to process this." This will allow others to create the space for this processing time.

2. FUN

    Whether it is a brief adventure during a lunch hour, a hobby, or a simple, properly-timed joke, Stilettos want to play, laugh, entertain, and be entertained (even at work).

The Stilettos in Conflict:

As verbal processors, Stilettos want to have time to talk things out and express themselves. In fact, being heard in conflict is as important as being right. Sometimes it's even more important.

Stiletto Conflict Trigger: Being invisible, dismissed or not listened to; not being given recognition or affirmation

In Conflict, Stilettos:

- Have a goal to be acknowledged. You don't have to agree with them, but you do have to let them know you hear and understand their point of view.
- May initially make light of the conflict through jokes or self-deprecation, hoping their positivity can smooth things over. Try not to take this personally.
- May say something mean (and later regret it). Of all the four SHOEs, they are most likely to personally attack and speak without thinking. The Stiletto should remember that words cannot be put back in once they are spoken.

How to Speak to Stilettos in Conflict:

- Remain casual and lighthearted, if possible. Be more friendly than formal.
- Affirm them when possible, but make sure it's genuine. Stilettos can sniff out you trying to spin them and blow sparkles up their dress.
- Consider their feelings as well as the facts. Stilettos are emotionally-driven, so be warm and sympathetic rather than cold and logical.

How to De-escalate a Stiletto in Conflict:

Affirm them with words like, "What I'm hearing you say is_____. Is that correct?" At the end of an argument, ask them, "Is there more you need to say or process?"

Healthy Stilettos in Relationship:

Stilettos bring such encouragement and motivation to their relationships. They see the good in others and bring out their best. During tense or even sad moments, a healthy Stiletto can bring a much-needed chuckle or playful activity.

The Mary Jane Alongside Others

Mary Janes are precise and detailed. Everything they do is something they pride themselves on as accurate, exact, and excellent. Details matter to them (no matter how small). They like organizing, can be perfectionistic, and have a strong sense of fairness and justice.

If you regularly interact with a Mary Jane (and you're not one), they will have certain tendencies that are different from yours that can cause tension.

Why Others Bug Mary Janes:

1. Incomplete Work or Incompetence

    Mary Janes will dot their i's and cross their t's in all areas of life, including in work projects, budgeting, family vacations, and dinner plans with friends. They have the memory of an elephant. It bothers Mary Janes when others submit incomplete projects. At home, it might be their kids cutting the grass but not doing the edging. In the office, someone might submit a report without proofing it causing there to be errors. This kind of shoddy work and lack of attention to detail drives Mary Janes crazy.

2. Requests for Spur of the Moment Feedback

    Mary Janes are thinkers. They ponder. They process. They enjoy having advance notice before being called out during meetings or even in a Bible study. They are capable of immediate feedback, but when possible, it's wise to honor their contemplative side by giving them time to process privately whenever possible. When Mary Janes are put on the spot, they might respond with incorrect information, fulfilling one of their biggest fears—appearing incompetent.

3.   Constant Social Interaction

If you find yourself on vacation with a Mary Jane, don't be offended when they need some privacy in their room or space alone on the beach. They are not being rude, but instead are refueling to bring their best selves later in the day. Spending all day with people, even people they love, causes their battery to drain more than other personalities.

Why Mary Janes Bug Others:

1.   Perfectionism

Mary Janes have high standards for all areas of their lives. From their immaculate and stunningly designed homes to their organized offices, desks, closets, and pantry spaces, they have a keen eye for order and corrections. Living and working alongside of a Mary Jane can feel like an impossible standard to live up to. Though this is not overtly discussed, the Mary Jane can make others feel like they need to constantly improve.

When Mary Jane's fall into this perfectionism, the glass feels half-empty. They are gifted in realism that can quickly slide into either pessimism or perfectionism. When I coach recovering perfectionists, one of my assignments is for them to make the bed, but not to adjust the pillows after that. Believe it or not, this is quite a challenging assignment. The aim is excellence rather than perfection.

2.   Correcting Others and Hypercriticism

The unhealthy side of Mary Jane can be overly-detailed, leading them to correct the smallest detail sometimes impulsively. If it's something on a tax return, this is a strength. But Mary Janes can also want to correct details that don't really matter. They tend to interrupt and interject with correction, causing those around them to feel like the Mary Jane is their school teacher rather than their wife, mother, or coworker. Mary Janes also sometimes try to make others follow their rigid schedules, rather than remembering that other types may prefer more flexibility. They should remind themselves of the people in their lives who are more spontaneous and fluid by nature, and be as flexible as possible with them.

What Mary Janes Need:

1. Order, Structure, Routine and Process

    The joy of being in relationship with a Mary Jane is that they bring much needed order to life. Though often teased that this structure is "anal," it is required for the world, our homes, our communities, and our workplaces to function. Mary Janes parent well because little ones naturally require order and they give them bedtime routines, organized rooms, and even healthy, structured menus. If a system is required, a Mary Jane is the first to be able to strategize how to create a new process that leads to greater efficiency and productivity. Give the Mary Jane advance notice for plans that are changing and show extra patience when life throws a curveball, knocking Mary Jane's plan off kilter.

2. Space

    Our daughter and son both have the Mary Jane personality style. As early as toddler/elementary school, they both expressed the need for time alone. Our daughter was happy to play the piano after school or swing on the backyard swing. When our son started his first job out of college, I excitedly asked him about his cubicle and office set up. My Mary Jane son replied, "It's way in the back at the end of the office." From a Stiletto point of view, his description sounded like a dungeon, so I said, "I'm so sorry." But he immediately piped up, "No, I love it. It's awesome. No one comes back there unless they need me, and I get the space and silence I love." Once the Mary Jane has space, they emerge ready for interactions with family and friends. If you vacation with a Mary Jane, they will like to have these same breaks from the family or the girls' trip just to recharge. The Mary Jane's battery runs low more quickly after lots of people and activities. When possible, it's nice to ask, "Would you like thirty minutes to yourself? I can go upstairs and read."

The Mary Jane in Conflict:

Mary Janes value precision and responsibility, so it's important to them that everyone gets the facts right and takes responsibility for their part. Their goal in conflict is getting justice and making things fair. However, while believing they are seeking justice, they can start to see the other person as an adversary and become combative.

Their secret weapon is overwhelming their opponent with facts and details. For example, a Mary Jane may say, "I emailed you on Monday, 3/3, then followed it up with a text on Wednesday, 3/5. I then took a screen shot of the text and added it to the email and resent it on 3/7." At this point, the Mary Jane's "opponent" may just give in because they are overwhelmed, but that doesn't lead to healthy relationships.

Mary Jane Conflict Trigger: When they are made to look incompetent, are given inaccurate information, or held back from meeting a deadline due to someone else's irresponsibility.

In Conflict, Mary Janes:

- Can come across defensive (think *hand on hip*) and have a slightly superior air. This is because they hate to be wrong and struggle to admit mistakes.

- Strategize like a chess player rehearsing how to make the next move. This can feel like they are constantly correcting others or overthinking minor details that can be let go.

- Can become passive aggressive or make snarky comments. They might make side comments rather than speak directly. For example, perhaps a coworker often misses deadlines. This month, the coworker makes their monthly report deadline, so the Mary Jane inserts a comment like, "Nice you could find the time to meet the deadline this month," rather than talk openly to the coworker about the importance of meeting deadlines.

How to Speak to Mary Janes in Conflict:

- Come prepared and use accurate facts. If you're not sure if a point is accurate, don't use it. Don't embellish or try to fudge your way through something.

- Avoid becoming emotional. They respect logical and pragmatic thinking.

- Keep your chit-chat to a minimum. Don't overtalk—talk straight and plain.

- Avoid emphasizing what they did wrong in an aggressive way because they'll interpret it as accusatory. They desire to be perfect so don't be overly critical.

How to De-escalate a Mary Jane in Conflict:

Acknowledge and even praise their hard work and what they've done well to show them you're on their side. Give them space, time, and resources for them to process their feelings and pursue their goals.

Healthy Mary Janes in Relationship:

Mary Janes bring much needed order to our chaotic lives. Their sensitivity to prayer, details, and others' preferences is a gift, allowing others to feel cared for and seen. Everything they touch becomes better as they move potential risks out of the way and create a pathway to excellence.

The Flip Flop Alongside Others

Flip Flops are laid-back and accommodating. They like peace and resist conflict. Highly social and compliant, they will often stuff their feelings until they build up and eventually explode.

If you regularly interact with a Flip Flop (and you're not one), they will have attributes that are different from yours that will tend to bother you and vice versa.

Why Others Bug Flip Flops:

1. Unnecessary Conflict or Debate for Sport

    Flip Flops feel very uncomfortable around conflict, even around disagreements that other types might not consider real conflict. In contrast, Workboots and sometimes Mary Janes love to debate and enjoy it almost like a sport. This causes a Flip Flop to withdraw, not only because they hate conflict, but they don't see

CHAPTER 2: WHO AM I ALONGSIDE OTHERS?

what outcome the conflict is tied to. Because conflict is hard for them, Flip Flops appreciate people who only engage in it when it's necessary.

2. Decision Overload

   Flip Flops have a laid-back and slower pace and will become overwhelmed if peppered with questions needing to be answered, decisions needing to be made, and boxes that need to be checked on a task list at once. While they do need some gentle pushes to get into action and get things done sometimes, this will be better received if it's done in a calm and leisurely way.

3. Perceived Judgement for Being Laid-back

   Flip Flops live in the present. They don't feel the need to vision-cast, prove anything, accomplish tasks, or fill their days unnecessarily. Personalities like the Workboot and Mary Jane who are highly productive can sometimes judge or even resent the way a Flip Flop pursues and achieves comfort. They will typically do what they have committed to (when healthy), but often won't overwork, overproduce, or over-do. Flip Flops feel hurt and can become resentful if they feel like others are trying to make them something they're not.

Why Flip Flops Bug Others:

1. Procrastination

   When they come together with the other SHOEs, Flip Flops can generate some friction by being so laid-back that they are actually not doing anything their partner, teammate, boss, or kids want them to do. Their family wants the grass cut, that wall painted, and that pile of laundry put away. Flip Flops will sometimes say that they'll take care of it because they want to appease the other person, but then they'll put it off so long that the other person begins to wonder if it will ever get done. Flip Flops need to create reward systems so that once the grass it cut, they can read a chapter of their favorite book, or once the work report is finished, they can watch their favorite Netflix episode.

2. Running From Conflict

    Being a peacemaker is a strength, but unhealthy Flip Flops can resist hard conversations to a fault, giving in and stuffing their real feelings. All relationships need some healthy conflict, and everyone needs to be honest about how they feel. Those close to Flip Flops can be taken by surprise when a Flip Flop suddenly bursts out with a flood of negative emotions and complaints that they'd been holding inside for weeks or months. The Flip Flop thought they were being kind by overlooking things, but the other person didn't have a chance to change their behavior because they didn't know it bothered them. If you're a Flip Flop, it's important to remember that those feelings you don't express stay inside of you and lead to an unhealthy release. For example, maybe you are feeling taken advantage of by your husband not pulling his portion of the housework. You fume. You stew. But you don't speak. And then, you explode over a fork being left in the sink rather than being placed in the dishwasher. Instead, create an agreed-upon list a week or more ahead of time to express your needs and expectations with your husband or coworkers.

What Flip Flops Need:

1. Advance Notice for Change

    Flip Flops are change-averse. They love to drive the same way to work each day. They don't want to move to the new office location because, "Why change when we have a good thing going?" And every family is embarrassed by the old recliner in the family room that is covered with a decorative blanket to hide the tatters. If your kids are Flip Flops, a new school will require a longer adjustment period than the other SHOEs. Even a much-desired promotion could be accompanied by apprehension as the Flip Flop adjusts to new teammates, a new city, and new responsibilities.

    If you are in relationship with a Flip Flop, introduce change as early as possible to allow time for them to try it on for size and kick the tires a bit. Explain the reason for the change (we need an extra bedroom and this will allow you to have your own bedroom). Be sensitive if you are someone who thrives on change. A Flip Flop will become stubborn and dig their heels in if you introduce too much change too often.

2. Motivation and Affirmation

As mentioned in Chapter 1, Flip Flops are always *fixin'* to do something, but never quite get around to it. Yet, pressuring them often backfires. Instead, offer them encouragement, like saying how great the grass will look for the party once they cut it or how much the kids will enjoy a run at the track to train for the football team. Praise the Flip Flop when they accomplish things and tie tasks to either a reward or a why so they can feel appreciated and understand the impact they're making.

The Flip Flop in Conflict:

It is worth repeating that Flip Flops are the most fragile SHOE around conflict, so enter it carefully. It sits on them longer and weighs on them heavier than the other three SHOEs. They seek peace and harmony and will try to avoid conflict at all costs. They will tell you what you want to hear, even if it means lying in some cases to end conflict. They may need to take a break overnight or take a walk around the block to recover.

Flip Flop Conflict Trigger: If they sense someone is being picked on or if one of their closest family or friends is being maligned, their deep loyalty will rise up and take on conflict for those they are loyal to. They will also explode if they've stuffed their feelings too long.

In Conflict, Flip Flops:

- May withdraw. They are like a turtle. Conflict happens and they drop down inside their shell. They may pop their head out occasionally to see if it's safe.
- Can play the role of martyr, savior, or rescuer in a family or team when conflict arises.
- Often give in without buying in to end the conflict. Check on them the next day to make sure they didn't just give in to end it.

- May explode suddenly due to previous complaints that have remained unexpressed and stuffed deep within them.

How to Speak to Flip Flops in Conflict:

- Draw them in gently and carefully. Make sure you don't say things you can't take back or lose your temper.

- Give them time to think it through over a day or two, or take a break during conflict if you can see it's too intense for them.

- Go back gently on the other side of conflict to check on them. They most likely will not bring it up if you don't. Let them know it's important to you that they feel heard and that their needs are met.

How to De-escalate a Flip Flop in Conflict:

Assume a reassuring, gentle tone with Flip Flops to deescalate conflict. Check in and tell them, "I know this is hard and I appreciate you talking it through with me." Ask them, "We have a bit more discussion, but do you need a break to walk around the block?"

Healthy Flip Flops in Relationship:

Flip Flops are amazing peacemakers, listeners, mediators, and empaths, bringing harmony to all their relationships. They are present with you. They are patient and willing to be a Long-Suffering Friend. (*More on that in the next chapter.*) They don't make waves or have huge expectations you will continually fall short of. What a gift to this overstimulated, rushed, and divisive world Flip Flops are. They are so often overlooked, because they demand so little. A healthy Flip Flop, though they won't ever enjoy conflict, can find and use a bold voice for truth, loved ones, or the oppressed.

Step Over Before You Overstep

Hopefully, you have started to see how misunderstanding people who are different from you can lead to unnecessary and unhealthy conflict. Instead, when you seek to understand the needs of others and to consider which parts of yourself you need to bring to a given interaction, you can engage in healthy conflict in order to fulfill your goal of living at peace with one another. The investment in understanding others without losing yourself will lead to exponential gains by avoiding misunderstandings, generating healthy conflict as needed, and deepening communication that leads to stronger relationships.

As we learn about one another, we become better observers of others and understand more of how they are motivated. People are always telling us who they are and sometimes they use words. According to a popular communication theory, we typically communicate seven percent with our words, thirty-eight percent with our tone, and fifty-five percent with our actions. It is wise to observe others in order to learn how to better be at peace with them. We can learn to see things differently when we place ourselves in the posture of wanting to see their perspective. We can never fully understand what their filter looks like; however, simply being willing to look through their lens improves our relationships.

If you live or work with someone who wears glasses, try them on. Seriously, put down this book and put their glasses on. How do you see based on their prescription? I'll bet you realize how differently you see than they do. If your eyeglasses prescription is similar, then you probably see things about the same. However, if their prescription is very different than yours, you can squint and try to focus but will never see clearly through their lenses the way they do. However, it is the act of trying to understand how they see life that is impactful.

PEOPLE ARE ALWAYS TELLING US WHO THEY ARE AND SOMETIMES THEY USE WORDS.

Our human nature is attracted to opposites. We are attracted to our potential spouse who can make quick decisions, mediate tension, plan every detail, or is always the life of the party. However, after a period of time the things that we thought "completed" us become complications to us.

This is normal, and it requires us to be intentional about seeing things from others' point of view. We have to stop and ask ourselves, "What needs are the other person trying to meet through their behavior right now?" and "How can I communicate in a way that respects how they are wired while also honoring my own needs and wiring?" This is the heart of full-circle self-awareness.

One of the phrases I've developed as I seek to allow others to be who God created them to be while maintaining my unique personality bent is "Learn to step over before you overstep." Being in relationship is kind of like dancing. I need to step over my need to always be loved the way I want to be and learn to love others the way they need to be loved.

The most perfect example of this is with my husband, who is a Workboot, bottom-line kind of guy. I'm a Stiletto, which means I tend to be a chatterbox. When I step over my need to have constant dialogue, I pull out my laptop and sit quietly with him on the couch as he watches the History channel. I step *over* my preference for dialogue and learn to dance with his need for quiet space. When he wants to love me the way I'm wired, he asks me questions that require detailed answers, engaging me in deeper conversation. Those questions represent him stepping over his preferences to dance with me in dialogue.

Remember the importance of trying on other people's glasses. You won't completely be able to see their world like they do, but compassion is the act of trying to. When you seek to understand them, you can learn to see things differently. Try on the glasses of all four types, look through their lenses, and you will gain insight as to how they see their world. It will help you speak in a way they can hear and avoid tripping over obstacles that can become unhealthy conflict.

Of course, the dance means a give and take. You can't always be the one who is stepping over your preferences or only have someone else stepping over theirs for you. You cannot always be cognizant of others and be the consistent adjuster of your behavior while they do anything they feel like. In any relationship, both people are equals and both people need to be practicing full-circle self-awareness for the relationship to be healthy. Relationships should be reciprocal. That's why I encourage you to share the SHOE Assessment with anyone close to you. If you sense your spouse, mother-in-law, or coworker won't be receptive to taking the assessment and learning more, please pray about this and possibly talk to your Bible study leader or pastor. It may be minor or it may reveal a larger relational issue that requires more attention.

True confidence allows us to lean into others and let their strengths shine. This is how God created the Body of Christ to fit together as puzzle pieces. Where one is weak, the other is strong.

Full-circle self-awareness allow us to appreciate the variety of people God has placed in our lives and all the ways they can support, complement, and sharpen us. We have been created as masterpieces. And part of being those masterpieces is that awareness that He hasn't made us everything—He's given us some strengths, and He's left some out of us.

LEARN TO STEP OVER BEFORE YOU OVERSTEP

For example, I've never been able to do math. I can't think strategically. I've never had an original thought in my life, but I can take your thoughts and make them amazing. He intentionally has left some strengths out of me, because I need people. It's how the Body of Christ operates.

The ultimate confidence is seeing ourselves through the lens of God's purpose and trusting His design.

Reflect & Respond

1. Make a list of five or six relationships that you want to enrich with what you've learned in these past two chapters. Consider asking these people to take the SHOE Assessment in this book. If they won't, spend some time observing and reflecting on their behavior to make an educated guess about which type they are.

2. For each person, consider how your SHOE complements their SHOE and vice versa. What strengths do you each bring to your relationship? Now, note how your SHOE complicates their SHOE. I encourage you to think about how you might bug them first (consider the plank in your own eye), and then you can move on to consider how they bug you and why. What needs are they trying to meet through those behaviors?

3. Create a conversation with each person to discuss what you've learned, but make sure the other person is ready and open to it. Begin by acknowledging their strengths and the ways you might bug them.

Chapter 3
Who Is with Me?

> *"Two are better than one, because they have a good return for their labor. If either of them falls down, one can help the other up. But, pity anyone who falls and has no one to help them up. Also, if two lie down together, they will keep warm. But how can one keep warm alone? Though one may be overpowered, two can defend themselves. A cord of three strands is not quickly broken."*
>
> Ecclesiastes 4:9-12

God's design for our lives is for us to live in meaningful community. Jim Rohn's famous quote "You are the average of the five people you spend the most time with" shows that the people we do life with influence us immensely. God will continually provide relationships for our various needs and seasons as we submit to Him, remain open to new relationships, and place value on relationships instead of isolating ourselves.

There is an African proverb which says, "*If you want to go fast, go alone. If you want to go far, go together.*" While people are important in helping us reach our goals, we must resist viewing people as a means to an end. All relationships require reciprocity as iron sharpening iron.

In this chapter, we will talk about the varying relationships that will keep us moving forward to our preferred lives. God uses people around us to reveal Himself to us, to provide fellowship in good and hard seasons, and to keep us growing in self-awareness so that we improve our relationships and encourage those around us. Going alone might be faster as the proverb above implies, but it will be a lonely, boring journey.

Wired for Relationship

It's essential to start with yourself if you want to grow in your confidence. However, now that you understand yourself better, including how to interact in healthy ways with people who are different from you, it's time to focus on your travel companions. Having a diverse and dedicated support system in life is crucial.

God designed us for relationship. Even though Adam had perfect fellowship with God in the Garden, he still needed a human companion because it was not good for him to be alone (see Genesis 2). Relationships surround us from the day we are born as our mom nurses us, our dad sings to us, our daycare workers comfort us, and our siblings taunt us and play with us. Even in the womb, we are not alone. This is the same reflection of community found in the Trinity: the Father, the Son, and the Holy Spirit.

As we mature, our primary relationships shift from our immediate family to friendships, sports teammates, college roommates, boyfriends or girlfriends, and eventually, for many people, a spouse or partner. However, once we leave the structured social environments of school, it often becomes more difficult to make new friends and maintain relationships, especially in today's world of social media and online interaction.

As many of us learned first-hand during the Covid-19 shutdown, social isolation takes a toll on mental health, even for the less social among us (like Workboots and Mary Janes). In May 2023, the U.S. Surgeon General called loneliness a public health epidemic. A 2024 poll from the American Psychiatric Association (APA) found that 30% of adults say they have experienced feeling lonely every week.

Gallup even says that one of the twelve questions they ask organizations to assess employee engagement is "do you have a best friend at work?" Camaraderie makes life easier. Their data concludes that employees who have a friend at work are more engaged and look forward to coming to work.

It's easy to get distracted by the glittering accomplishments that our culture tells us will bring satisfaction, but the truth is that those things bring much less satisfaction than we expect them to. At the end of your life, will your books, podcasts, accomplishments, degrees, bonuses, possessions, hobbies, or trips surround your deathbed? No. Those who have traveled with you to the end of your life will be.

This chapter is about helping you think about how to develop deep, lasting relationships that build you up and challenge you to be the best version of yourself you can be. This is different from the superficial relationships you might have where you send a Christmas card or exchange small talk at church and not much else. True companions celebrate with us. Cry with us. Hold us accountable. Help us see our blind spots. Clear the way ahead of us. Walk behind us to make sure we are covered.

Beyond just the richness that relationships add to our lives, the horizontal mirrors provided by trusted friends are the best complement to God's vertical mirror and help us see ourselves clearly. These kinds of relationships require trust that can only be built over time. And they require the courage to be vulnerable, to open up, and to be our true selves.

> **TRUE CONFIDENCE REQUIRES YOU TO BE WILLING TO ALLOW OTHERS TO KNOW YOU THROUGH VULNERABLE CONVERSATION AND TIME SPENT TOGETHER.**

True confidence requires you to be willing to allow others to know you through vulnerable conversation and time spent together. Those relationships will then strengthen your confidence even more so that you can go deeper, allowing your connection to build strong roots that will support you for a lifetime.

For some who have been betrayed, rejected, or abused, being alone with yourself feels safer than risking authentic community. If that's you, I get it. I've been there. Some of my deepest betrayal wounds have been given in the tightest Christian circles, and it was hard for me to learn to trust again. But it's so worth it.

I encourage you to seek wise counsel (possibly including a professional counselor) to help you move through your pain and start to open up to relationships again. That's what I did. As I was in the process of working with a counselor in order to heal from a wound, my counselor wisely started with the role I played in this painful ending. As I began confessing, forgiving, and applying what she gave me, I had a realization. You see, I like things to move quickly, especially when there is pain involved. God was so sweet in this season as He slowed me down to process what I was feeling and to let this healing process thicken my skin without hardening my heart. It was in this same process that three of my best and long-term friends sat with me. Cried with me. Corrected me when or if I remembered things wrong. Challenged me. Held up a mirror up to hold me responsible for my own wrongs in this relationship. Without these three precious souls, I would have surrounded myself with an echo chamber of others who would confirm how I was the only one wronged. But these three precious travel companions would not allow it. They did it in love. They did it with the proper timing. And they would not allow me to squirm my way out of seeing both sides.

> **LET THIS HEALING PROCESS THICKEN MY SKIN WITHOUT HARDENING MY HEART.**

The gang you travel through life with changes based on seasons, states, and life-stages. Some people have friends from elementary school. Others have friends based on their place of employment. Still others find their people through church or hobbies. As you work through this chapter, you will learn how to create the space you need to have varying styles of friendships that complement your different seasons of life. Whether you're starting out with a wealth of close friends, just one or two, or none you feel you can really trust right now, there's room for you to grow and develop the kind of relationships that will help you go far in this life.

A Note on Virtual Connection: *One of the greatest impacts of the 2020 pandemic is the advent of virtual Zoom meetings. I am truly grateful that Zoom enabled business meetings to continue, small* *groups to gather, and gyms to help us workout together during that isolating time. But I am also deeply aware that the kind of meaningful community God intends for us requires face-to-face interaction. Studies show that virtual meetings, while better than nothing, are simply not the same as being with someone face-to-face. If you spend a great deal of time connecting with teammates, family, and friends digitally, that's ok. Not all relationships need or even can be face-to-face. I coach about 75% of my clients on Zoom. However, the closest relationships must be face-to-face. I encourage you to prioritize gathering with your people in person whenever possible.*

The Six Kinds of Relationships You Need

The impact of your relationships on your trip of a lifetime cannot be overstated. Below are the six different types of relationships that keep your life grounded and become a foundation for the confidence you seek.

1. Spouse, Partner, or Significant Other
2. Family (Parents, Siblings, Children, Aunts, Uncles, and Cousins)
3. Friendships
4. Personal "Board of Directors"
5. Networking Relationships
6. Mentor (Pastor, Counselor, or Coach)

Spouse, Partner, or Significant Other

If you have a spouse or partner, how do you stay connected throughout busy seasons of life? Just like the analogy that a shoemaker's kids often have holes in their shoes, you might neglect the most important relationships in your life, like your marriage. While it is important to nurture your love connection, as you grow and age, the original passions you felt dating are replaced with deep love and respect for the person you journey with throughout your lifetime.

Please Note: *You do not need a spouse or partner to have a well-rounded and fulfilling life as a single woman, divorcee, or widow.*

All relationships and marriages are different. Neither Bill nor I are quality time people. We can stay connected well by adding short bursts of togetherness and communication. However, during the pandemic, I learned to tap into my less extroverted side by enjoying slow and uninterrupted time together. I was so sick and quite frightened as the sickness lingered for over three weeks. (Grateful for a full recovery!) As empty-nesters, being sheltered in was a lovely way for us to slow down and reconnect. I can also see how it prepared me to lean into Bill during the hardest professional transition I have faced. It was so comforting to feel Bill's support throughout a transition season as I let go of my executive director role to prepare to relaunch my coaching business and speaking ministry, while others my age were retiring. As Bill and I have aged together in our marriage, we have supported one another beyond just sickness and health, but in career transitions, dark seasons, and joyful celebrations.

As I ponder my parent's marriage of over sixty-six years, it is an illustrative reminder that romance remains through practical acts of serving one another as our bodies age. What was once youthful passion remains passion in the heart, but turns into caring for one another through hearing loss, health crises, and simple tasks like clasping a bracelet.

Tips for a Healthy Dynamic with Your Spouse, Partner, or Significant Other:

- How do you complement each other? Compare your SHOE personalities together. Appreciate the strengths your partner has that you lack.

- What are the ways you complicate each other? Review the descriptions of how your SHOE types interact in Chapter 2. Talk about the ways you bug one another and how you could minimize those behaviors.

- Consider your unique dynamic as a couple. What kind of "couple" are you? Don't try to be like some other couple you admire or see on TV. Try to be the best version of "you together" that you can be.

- Determine your love language (you can find a free test online) and determine to express love in the other person's love language more often: Words of Affirmation, Acts of Service, Gifts, Quality Time, or Physical Touch.

Family

Our family includes our small children, adult kids, aging parents, siblings, and beyond. Cultivating healthy family relationships allows us to prioritize time together through knowing one another, respecting different seasons of our lives, and staying connected in our hearts, even if time or miles tempt us to drift apart.

Families come in all different shapes and sizes, and each family has its own personality. I have a friend who has a highly interactive, social family. They have coffee with their adult kids at least twice a month. Other families are more spontaneous, because some kids can feel like a rigid structure is too restrictive or suffocating. Some families are big and loud, while others are more reserved and appreciate quiet. It's important to understand the "personality" of your family and not try to make it be something it's not.

Tips for a Healthy Dynamic with Family:

- Make a list of the family members you are in close contact with. Then compare your SHOE personalities together. How do you complement and complicate each other?

- What unpleasant or unhealthy patterns of interaction can you identify? How could understanding your different SHOE types help you change those patterns? Consider asking others what they need and expressing what you need more clearly.

- What kind of family are you? Take a moment to describe your family's "personality." What do you love about your unique family dynamic? Remember, no two families are exactly alike, so don't try to match some ideal you saw in a movie or even compare it the one you grew up in. Try to appreciate the family you have and build on what you do well together.

- Prioritize time to connect, but stay flexible as you navigate new seasons. For example, the older I get, the more aware I am of the limited time I have with my mom. I am more grateful for the investments of time I had made with my dad before he died. I am open-handed with the schedules of our adult children and their spouses and enjoy every moment we share together. Bill and I make ourselves available to be part of every significant (and small detail) of their lives that they invite us into. We have crafted strong and appropriate boundaries with each one and remain grateful for the privilege of parenting. I also have two older siblings who live in Pennsylvania. Honestly, when we were young, we used to fight with one another. But now, especially after the loss of our precious dad, we have leaned into one another more than ever and truly appreciate the ability to have siblings. We consistently make time for our relationships in this season of our lives. As we seek increased self-awareness, it is important that we remain aware of our limited time during seasons of growing babies and aging parents, yet remain flexible during the seasons of our growing kids and adult children's lives.

Friendships

Friendship is easily overlooked in our family-centric and individualistic culture, but strong, close friendships are absolutely essential for a fulfilling life. Without vibrant friendships, we are prone to loneliness and isolation. According to an AP poll in 2023, loneliness is as deadly as smoking fifteen cigarettes a day. Having a variety of friendships adds flavor to our lives just like spices enhance your favorite recipe. Without them, we can become isolated and overly self-focused.

In our disconnected, busy society, we have to be intentional about nurturing our friendships. Advances in technology have helped us grow in productivity, but have replaced face-to-face conversations with screen interactions. Social media can be used as a fun way to stay connected to friends on the other side of the country, but it is a poor imitation for the relational equity gained from face-to-face friendships. It's too easy to let weeks and months go by without seeing or talking with even our closest friends. But having regular interaction is crucial for strong friendships. Most people find they have to put it on their calendar, even if they're a Flip Flop and hate scheduling things.

That's what my BFF, Janet, challenged me to do a few years ago. Janet challenged us to meet for one and a half hours every other Thursday. We did it for one year. Then another and now, well into our third or fourth year, we both have seen the benefits of creating space for this coffee time. We've prayed. We've coached one another. We've cried. We've listened to God. We've read books. We've celebrated children and welcomed grandchildren together. We've laughed. We've prioritized this relationship in a way that has impacted every part of my life. I would not be the woman, coach, mom, or wife I am today without Janet's influence in my life.

> GOD PROVIDES DIFFERENT FRIENDS TO MEET DIFFERENT NEEDS JUST LIKE BASKIN ROBBINS MAKES THIRTY-ONE FLAVORS OF ICE CREAM.

Another thing we have to be intentional about is having honest, deep conversations with our friends. It's possible to see our friends a lot but never talk about anything real. Surface chit-chat rises to the surface, but it takes self-control to intentionally go deeper with our conversations. When I meet with my close friends, I find myself using a note so that I don't forget the things I would love to update them on or receive updates on from them. This helps keep our interactions from being shallow and grow deeper roots of connection with one another.

It is best to resist asking one friend to be all things to you. God provides different friends to meet different needs just like Baskin Robbins makes thirty-one flavors of ice cream. Below are fourteen types of friends that I've had through the years that have been a foundation that I rely on. Having this foundation has given me firm footing for the confidence that comes from a variety of relationships. You've heard the saying that variety is the spice of life.

As you look through this list, make note of which role you play in various relationships and consider which of your friends plays this role for you. This becomes a wonderful way to acknowledge (and possibly pause to thank) the friends who contribute to your life and to recognize any lonely places you feel so you can ask God to provide this kind of friend in the future.

1. A Long-Term Friend

   A friend who knows you long-term, has been through thick and thin with you, and who still loves you is more precious than gold. Long-term friendships bring health to all areas of your life. Someone who has walked with you for years has probably butted heads a couple times with you and weathered the storms. Long-term friends have also seen you grow and change, so they know you in a deeper way than others can. Having long-term friendships can anchor you. If you currently have shorter term friendships, pray for long-term ones and make it a priority to spend time to develop longer term friendships.

2. A Wise Friend

   Everyone needs a friend who gives great advice, brings clarity, challenges you, and has good discernment. This is not to say your other friends aren't wise, but someone who is The Wise Friend may have the spiritual gift of knowledge or wisdom and consistently has insights that protect and guide you. This person also has to be willing to speak into your life, and you have to be willing to listen. Their wisdom increases your confidence as you problem-solve and brainstorm together, leading to decisions and action steps.

3. A Fun Friend

   This is someone playful (maybe a Stiletto or a Flip Flop) that may pull the fun out of you. They call you to adventures, have a keen sense of humor, tell you great stories, jokes, and memes, and just generally lighten things up. This kind of friend balances the loads of responsibility you carry by creating playful confidence in your life.

4. A Calling Friend

   This is someone who encourages your calling and holds you accountable to it. They offer insights, make networking connections, and cheer you on, but they also check on you if you seem to be getting off track or distracted from your calling by other commitments. This friend recognizes your talents and gifts, believes in your dreams, and won't let you forget it. A Calling Friend understands the importance of knowing your purpose, leading to increased confidence in your life.

5. A Celebrate-With-You Friend

   Everyone needs a friend with whom you can celebrate your achievements without jealousy or feeling arrogant. My friend Janet and I call this "permission to brag." This friend gives you permission to celebrate work accomplishments, parenting victories, boundaries you've set, or even conversations you've been avoiding. If you have an exceptionally stellar week of ministry, work, parenting, etc. you share those things with one another and celebrate these special endeavors. Affirmation and celebration boost confidence.

6. A Prayer Warrior

   Most (if not all) of our Christian friends should pray for us on occasion. However, this kind of friend is an intercessor. My friend Wendy puts my speaking engagements on her calendar and notes the specific times I'm speaking (and my speaking topics) and prays for me. She has prayed my children into marriage, houses, colleges, and more. Another friend of mine who lives in another state showed me her home office and I was blown away to see my family's photo on her wall alongside Scripture verses. Her wall is filled with photos of those she prays for, along with a kneeling pillow on the floor beneath them. Knowing I am covered in prayer leads to confidence throughout my personal and professional seasons of life. One great way to find a friend like this is by developing your own prayer life for your friends and asking God to connect you to someone who can be your intercessor.

7. A Peaceful Friend

   Especially since I can be high-strung, having a Peaceful Friend who can speak one sentence and calm me down when I have my knickers in a wad is essential. They often offer perspective and pause that diffuses chaotic seasons and helps you re-center. Flip Flops are often great at this. Peaceful Friends have boosted your confidence by helping you avoid ill-spoken words or rash decisions.

8. A Hobby Friend

   Do you golf? Play pickleball? Attend a book club? Even a friend you work out with can be a Hobby Friend. I joke that my hobby is fashion. I love poring over trends and the next season's colors and styles. Years ago, my friend Wendy and I attended the grand opening of a department store and literally walked the red carpet together (and bought matching shoes)! Whatever you do for fun or are particularly interested in, try to find a friend who shares that passion. Having a hobby helps us be productive in our professional roles, marriage, and even parenting.

9. A Strategic Friend

   These friends love solving problems. My friend Amy can help me talk through large, complicated seasons, projects, and problems and break them down practically and strategically. Mary Janes are usually amazing at this. They often offer solutions even when you aren't asking, so let them know when you need their help and they will be eager to ponder solutions to whatever you face. It's easy to get overwhelmed with the details of your life, so having someone else to sort through the chaos gives you confidence to solve the problems that hold you back.

10. An Advocate

    This is someone who speaks about and for you when you aren't around. My friend, Wendy, has a way of introducing me that makes me feel like the best thing since sliced bread. It could be bragging what a great mom you are or it could be opening a professional door by way of an introduction. I love the meme that is going around social media that says, "Be the kind of woman that speaks positively about another woman who is not seated at the table." Another way to say it is "Be the woman that straightens another woman's crown." With so much division in the world today, everyone needs to be, and have, an authentic advocate. You never know the confidence boost your advocacy can bring to another.

11. An Initiator

    While relationships need to be reciprocal and it takes two to keep a friendship healthy, your natural wiring will make some people more prone to initiate conversations, connections, and outings. Especially if you're more reserved and might just stay home in your PJs if left to your own devices, having an Initiator friend is essential. However, make sure you reach out first sometimes and be sure to respond positively when your friend initiates. It can wear on friends (even Initiators) if it's too one-sided. They can often feel used if they are always the ones reaching out.

12. A Helper

    This friend is always ready to help in small and large ways, from running to the store to pick up the birthday present you forgot to helping you set up for the party itself. This is the person who will bring extra dishes to your potluck just in case or watch your kids when your babysitter falls through. Just like with the Initiator, be careful not to take advantage of this friend. They love to help, but they also appreciate being thanked sincerely, and it's important to them that you help them as well when they need it.

13. A Long-Suffering Friend

    I have nicknamed these friends my "Couch Friends" because they will sit on the couch next to me while I cry and talk through hard things. They are willing to walk with you through longer seasons of pain, confusion, or the dark night of the soul. They are incredibly patient and good listeners who offer God's Word and insights when they discern it's appropriate. They are perfectly comfortable with not offering answers, providing times of silence, and simply meeting you where you are. When I went through a dark night of the soul, my Long-Suffering Friend reminded me that she had enough faith for both of us in that moment.

14. A Challenger Friend

    Need to stick to a workout routine or walk through Whole 30? This friend will keep you moving forward, but won't allow you to use unnecessary excuses. They will hold you accountable to that new job interview, the hard conversation you need to have, and more. They won't let you feel sorry for yourself or throw a pity party. They'll cheer you on and give you a good kick in the rear if you need it. Just like a trainer gives you confidence in your physical strength, our Challenger Friends help grow our confidence by helping us cross the finish line of our goals.

These are the fourteen different types of friends that provide a diverse support system for the different challenges and seasons of our lives. Sometimes one person can fill two or three roles. It's not that you have to have all fifteen in order to reach your destination, but the more kinds of friends you have, the more balanced life you will live. Think of it as relational wealth diversification. We are told in our finances that we need to diversify to remain financially stable. The same is true in our friendships.

Who are the friendships God has provided for you that are foundational to strong confidence?

Tips for a Healthy Dynamic with Friends:

- Think about your friends and consider which of the above roles they fill in your life. Take a moment to text or call them and tell them how grateful you are that they are a Long-Term Friend, Initiator, Fun Friend, etc.

- Consider your SHOE type and those of your friends. Have them take the assessment with you if possible. How do you complement and complicate each other? How can you use this information to strengthen your friendship?

- Which of the friend types do you crave but don't have yet? Which one do you feel like is most lacking in your life right now? Turn that into a prayer that God would provide this for you.

- It's also essential to remember that you have to be a great friend if you want to have great friends. You can't be every kind of friend on the list above, but which roles do you fulfill for others? How could you do that even better?

Personal Board of Directors

This is more for those who are entrepreneurial or run their own business. My business does not have a formal board. However, I have three smart, wise, business-minded, and ministry-minded guides who I share all my business prayer needs with and run ideas past from time to time. They have permission to speak directly to me and hold me accountable to things we've all discussed. I trust them and each one of them believes in the work I do as a coach.

Tips for Finding and Keeping a Personal Board of Directors:

- Reflect on the people in your life you reach out to for advice, encouragement, direction, or guidance. Pray that God would open a door for them to continue to guide you as you grow your ministry or small business, or seek to deepen your calling, whatever it may be. (More on that in Chapter 5.)

- Who are other entrepreneurs in your life who might need or want to be on your Personal Board of Directors because they uniquely understand these needs?

Networking Relationships

Ok, some of you are rolling your eyes because you dislike networking. Perhaps you find it draining because it is outside of your wiring. (*Hello, Mary Janes and Flip Flops!*) However, if you have your own ministry, business, or passion (which means everyone!), you should allow God to highlight partnerships and relationships that will provide shared passions, unique perspectives, and much-needed introductions to clients, donors, partners, and like-minded peers.

I do this in Charlotte, North Carolina, every Thursday morning at my WIN (Women in Networking) Group. This group has sharpened me so much professionally. They have provided referrals for my various coaching and speaking needs. They are now trusted friends beyond just our professional context.

These relationships usually start out a bit more professionally than others and may begin as acquaintances rather than close friendships. But they fill an essential role by advocating for us and even challenging us to stay the course. In our networking group, we do a sixty-second "commercial" for our calling every week. That boosts my confidence because it is a weekly review of my "why" and passion for coaching and speaking.

Do you need to journey with a networking group in your area or niche?

Tips for Finding and Maintaining Networking Relationships:

- Do a quick city-wide search for the kind of networking groups in your community. Then think about what would be most beneficial for you and your business or calling. Do you need a female-only group? Industry-specific? Faith-based? Commit to visit one of these groups each month for six months to find your fit.

- You might also be surprised by how many connections you can make simply by getting to know people at random social events. Strike up conversations with people and find out what they do and what they see as their calling. Then share yours. You never know who might know someone that could one day help you out. Also, always be looking for a way you might help someone else, even in a small way. Your generosity in sharing your expertise or resources will come back to you three-fold.

- ⊘ As with all relationships, it could be fun to add the SHOE Assessment with your networking group to understand and maintain healthy dynamics.

Mentor/Coach/Counselor

In addition to peers who can commiserate and encourage us in our callings, we also need someone who's a few steps ahead and who can provide more explicit guidance. I have a mentor, great pastors, a gifted counselor, and dynamic coaches. I don't engage these relationships all the time, but I have in the past and continue to do so throughout various seasons of my life.

Proverbs 20:5 says, "The purposes of a person's heart are deep waters, but one who has insight draws them out." A mentor or coach has practice and possibly training in helping draw out deep insight from those they work with. They have acquired wisdom through their own struggles and experiences, and now they can pass it on to you. They've been where you are now, so they can help you see the path forward.

Mentors may be free (like an older friend from church), but professionals like pastors, coaches, or counselors are held to ethical professional standards and confidentiality in order to protect and guide you. They are neutral and are trained to facilitate discussions that will give you fresh insight. I encourage you to seek all kinds of mentorship as you are able and as you are led. Different specialties will provide different kinds of support to meet your needs in various seasons. But don't underestimate how much a mentor can do to catapult you into the future you desire for yourself.

Also, look for opportunities to be a mentor to someone younger than you or who is going through something you've been through before. You might think you don't have much wisdom to offer, but just sharing your experience and how you survived it can be powerful for them. It will also boost your confidence as you see how much you have to offer.

Tips for Finding and Maintaining a Healthy Mentor, Coach, or Counselor Relationship:

- Your church is a wonderful place to consider finding a mentor. Almost all my mentors originated in my local church. Ask your pastor or other people in your church if they know anyone who's walked through something similar or if they can point you to counseling resources.

- Look at professional directories that are in your local area or online. Starting with ICF Certified Coaches will give you trained and certified coaches in your state or city.

- As you do life with others, pray that God will reveal mentors and coaches. Ask questions about other people's journeys to learn about their stories. Be open to receiving advice even as you also run it through the filter of God's Word and what you know about yourself and your purpose.

- Be realistic with what you expect out of these relationships considering the time and energy you commit to them. Set a time limit like once a month for six months and then evaluate. Come prepared for these conversations rather than expecting the other person to carry all the weight. Try to bring a question or struggle that you want to explore with them.

P.S. *I know a fun coach!*

The Spice of Life

Relationships give our lives flavor. They affirm us, challenge us, make us laugh, reveal our blind spots, and, most importantly, they are biblical. We have been designed to connect with others like puzzle pieces. Where we are weak, others are strong and vice versa, as highlighted in Romans 12:4: "For just as each of us has one body with many members, and these members do not all have the same function."

True self-discovery begins with looking inside ourselves, but continues by understanding ourselves in the context of others. Who brings out the best in us? Who brings out the worst (and why)? How do we bring out the best in others?

Just like our lives have seasons, so do our relationships. You may have lifelong friendships from your childhood; however, it is not uncommon to have seasonal relationships. I wish I had learned early on that it is not a critique on a relationship that ends because season ends. Perhaps you were close to others only during a season, like when your kids went to school, you worked with a specific team, or attended a certain Bible study. All of these have taken place in my life. There was not a large declaration where we said, "Our relationship is over." It was more like the season ended and we just saw less and less of one another. While this can feel sad, rest assured it's normal. Allow friendships to wax and wane like the moon, trusting that God is in control.

AUTHENTIC RELATIONSHIPS HELP US REMOVE BLIND SPOTS, BARRIERS, AND BIASES, LEADING US TO INCREASED SELF-AWARENESS.

We need others in order to have the confidence we desire. Left to our own devices, we will not be affirmed or challenged as we need to be. Authentic relationships help us remove blind spots, barriers, and biases, leading us to increased self-awareness.

Reflect & Respond

1. Evaluate the strength and health of each of the six relationship types in your life. Which ones do you feel are strong or going well? Which of the six relationship types are missing in your life that you can pray about?

2. What strengths do you have to offer your friends and family? Consider the fourteen kinds of friends. Which one(s) are you?

3. How would you describe your current relationships? Do you see any patterns that you need to address? Consider how the SHOE types might help you change those dynamics.

4. Using what you've learned about yourself, how can you be more intentional about investing in relationships?

Chapter 4
What Do I Value?

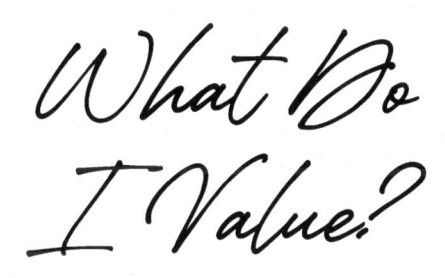

"Mary has chosen what is better."
Luke 10:41

In 2009, Los Angeles widow Elsie Poncher arranged for the remains of her businessman husband, Richard, to be exhumed, so that she could sell his burial plot on eBay and raise enough money to pay off the mortgage of her Beverly Hills home. The unique selling point of this eBay lot? Richard Poncher's burial plot was directly above Marilyn Monroe's in LA's Westwood Village Cemetery.

At auctions all over the world, people bid on things that often seem meaningless or even silly to others. To the bidders and eventual winner, however, these things have value and worth. The answer lies in what the purchaser values. In the case of Richard Poncher's burial plot, people found value in spending "eternity" buried near Marilyn Monroe (with bids rising above $4.5 million).

As bizarre as some of this may sound to you, human behavior indicates that we each have a different set of values. Our values are what make us who we are, driving our decisions consciously or subconsciously.

A search of the word "values" will yield several of the following definitions:

- Something (as a principle or quality) intrinsically valuable or desirable.
- The importance or preciousness of something.

- Principles, standards or qualities that an individual or group of people hold in high regard.
- A commonly formed belief about something's worth.
- Beliefs that guide behavior/actions.
- A central and foundational part of what we place worth upon in our lives.

Our values are the compass we use as we navigate life. In this chapter, you will learn how to identify your top values, what they mean, and how they influence your behavior and decisions.

Why Should I Identify My Values?

Our values determine our behavior whether we recognize it or not. Our values drive our preferences, our potential bias and blind spots, our motivations, and our decisions.

Just like our body has a core that supports our limbs, our values are the core that guides our lives. Values help us arrange the things that are important to us as we pursue our purpose, goals, and priorities. They bring self-awareness and clarity to our actions and interactions with others. Naming and understanding our values helps us know where we have like-minded relationships with others who value similar things. It also helps be curious instead of judging people who value different things than we do. Even if we have the same SHOE type as someone else, if we value different things, we might easily come into conflict.

> **VALUES HELP US ARRANGE THE THINGS THAT ARE IMPORTANT TO US AS WE PURSUE OUR PURPOSE, GOALS, AND PRIORITIES.**

When your values are identified, you can then understand and reflect on how your responses to various circumstances have been driven by your values.

We often thrive when a value of ours that has been validated. For instance, if you have a high value for "unique qualities" (the ability to see each person's gifts, talents, skills, and offerings as individual and

CHAPTER 4: WHAT DO I VALUE?

unique) and your boss seeks to craft projects and assignments that allow you to use your gifts and operate primarily in your strengths, then your value has been validated.

However, if you work for someone who feels that it's "my way or the highway" and provides little room for other people's skills, insights, or expressions of personal identity, then you may experience stress, tension, and potential conflict. This stems from your value for "unique qualities" being overlooked.

I encountered this several years ago during a hard season of transition on the large church staff I was working on. Our entire staff was being taken through a season of pruning to gain focus. Jobs were reassigned, redefined, combined, or eliminated altogether. I was excited to be assigned a new, young leader who was exceptionally strategic. I learned so much working for this young leader. He was kind to me but pushed me harder than I had previously experienced.

Week after week, I began to absorb his bold leadership style. One thing I noticed almost immediately is that he had a slightly irreverent side to him. When he would privately make flippant comments to me about some senior leaders within our organization, I chalked it up to him just being immature and outspoken. I tend to believe the best in others, so I assumed he was trusting me to process things out loud. I trusted his heart even though his words seemed borderline disrespectful and judgmental toward leaders that I had history with and whom I deeply respected. Fast forward through a long and challenging year under his leadership and I had experienced:

- Frustration at his refusal to consider other opinions.

- Naïve surprise that he seemed to believe only his preferences were the correct ones in everything from worship style, music, leadership style, blogs, writers, and mentors.

- Futility giving him my insights and thoughts and realizing, over time, that they were being requested in word only, but not fully weighed into decisions or outcomes.

- Deep discontentedness when I saw how he wrote off other leaders and teammates and disrespected them under the guise of humor.

After much private pondering with God, my husband, and one or two trusted companions, I removed myself from the paid staff role and instead volunteered. Upon deeper reflection, I could not reconcile knowing that there was a gap between the way I felt the Bible taught me to respect and submit to my leaders and the way this leader was disrespecting and not submitting to his leaders. The paycheck was not worth continuing to bridge this gap.

At the time, I couldn't understand why I was experiencing an almost physical type of gut-wrenching pain inside but not knowing what was causing it. I now know that because I so deeply value authenticity, integrity, and truth, I was undergoing such a tremendous amount of processing in my heart and mind that I physically felt the strain of it. At the time, I had no words to articulate how my personal values clashed with his values. However, I have since learned it was simply varied values that led to me resigning from my role. My top values of Authenticity and Integrity/Truth were in conflict with the conversations that I witnessed behind the backs of my senior leaders.

I remember thinking, "Why is no one else on my team concerned about this style of leadership?" While I knew others were not in total agreement with the intensity associated with this leader's style, they were also not led to ultimately reposition themselves like I was.

You see, my teammates held different personal values. And, although, we could all agree that disrespecting senior leadership behind their backs was wrong and each of us tried to speak directly about this, no one else felt it so distressing that they resigned. Only me.

Years later, when I did a personal core values exercise with my own coach, we discussed how my top value of Authenticity had been violated by a leader who was one way in front of senior leadership and another way with his own people. That disrespect violated my intense need for authenticity. In addition, my value of Integrity/Truth was violated by the fact that my leader was not honest in the way he led me, causing me to see a breach in his integrity. I simply could not ride this leadership wave.

The ending of this story goes like this. I had spoken respectfully about my concerns and insights to both my immediate leader and to my

CHAPTER 4: WHAT DO I VALUE?

senior leaders. At the time, the issues I raised were not considered a serious concern to the organization. However, the root of this disrespect for senior leadership grew and resulted in the leader and a few others exiting the organization within a year.

Now that I am decades away from this season, I wonder, if I had known my values at the time, if I could have navigated the situation differently and better expressed myself to my direct leader and others. I trust that God used every bit of that season and I continue to use what I learned in my own leadership. But with the gift of maturity and hindsight, knowing and understanding what my values are would have served me greatly in that situation.

I share this to show how powerful our values can be in determining our actions. Knowing my top five values has helped me with my own self-reflection in personal and professional relationships. Now when I feel anxious, frustration, or unsettled, I ask myself, "Is one of my highest values being challenged right now?"

Throughout this chapter, you will learn to observe your internal and external behaviors and responses to situations. In the moment when you are experiencing tension, you will learn to pause and ask yourself, "Is there a value of mine being either validated or violated? If so, how can I adjust my response?"

> WHEN CONFLICT OR PRESSURE ENTERS OUR DAY THAT OUR TOP VALUES GET SQUEEZED OUT, JUST LIKE WHEN A TOOTHPASTE TUBE EXPERIENCES PRESSURE.

Like any self-assessment tool, identifying your values deepens your self-awareness which, when applied, leads to emotional intelligence. But stopping at only using this information to know yourself better is short sighted. Understanding your values will also help you relate better to others.

When things are going well in our day, we can tap into many of our values at once. I can be compassionate, generous, maintain a strong work ethic, and make time for people, instead of just focusing on completing tasks. However, it's when conflict or pressure enters our day that our top values get squeezed out, just like when a toothpaste tube experiences pressure ... out comes the toothpaste at the top of the tube.

In my home, when my family experiences pressure together, my values are pushed out of my toothpaste tube, but so are my husband's top values (which are different than mine) and my son's and daughter's. Before you know it, we are all seeking resolution based on the things we individually value but not what we collectively value.

Where Do My Values Come From?

We all carry layers of values arranged in a hierarchy of importance.

As people of faith, we know that our most important values, our largest "umbrella" values that span over everything else, ought to come from Christ and God's Word. However, since we are a work in progress, our behavior and internal motivations don't always mirror Christian values. In reality, our values are mostly formed subconsciously during our childhood, so they don't necessarily follow what we know we *should* value.

The good news is that our values can change as we have new experiences and learn about ourselves, about others, and about our purpose. So even if we learned to value something that we later recognize is not aligning with what we want for our lives, the fact that we realize this means we've already started to change that value.

The first step is to identify the values we actually have now and to recognize where those values came from. Once we become aware of them, it becomes much easier to replace a value that no longer supports the person we want to be.

We typically form our values from the following eight sources:

1. Our Faith (Church, Pastor, Scripture Teachings)//
2. Our Family of Origin (How We Were Raised, Parents, Family, Traditions)
3. Our Society (Culture, Hollywood, Wall Street, Media, Government)

4. Our Education
5. Our Generation
6. Our Geography (Country, State, City, Hometown)
7. Our Wiring
8. Our Organization or Workplace

Remember, each of these areas can give us values that are good or that are not helpful to us.

Let's look at each source a bit more carefully. As you read, consider how each one might have influenced you. What values have you picked up from each source?

Faith: What is your faith? Consider the denomination(s) you grew up with and which one you align with now. A mainline denomination? Non-denominational? Do you attend a large church or a small church? Who are the pastors, mentors, Sunday school teachers, small group leaders, and others who have shaped your values? What are the Christian values that you come naturally to you, and which ones do not?

Truth be told, though I would like to say I value all those things all the time, I don't. Some of those things I obey (like being generous), though they do not all come naturally to me. For example, my two lowest spiritual gifts are Serving and Giving. But, as a Christ-follower, I cannot dismiss those because they do not come naturally to me. Still, they are not my natural values, and they will rank lower for me than the others.

Family of Origin: What are the things you can identify that were valued in your upbringing?

In our home, as preacher's kids, we were always on time. To this day, neither my siblings nor I are ever late. In fact, on any given Sunday, we are ready to go five to ten minutes before it's time to leave for church. Our spouses are more on the dot or even a few minutes late.

What did your parents value? A strong work ethic? Education? Manners? Creativity? Are there any of your family traditions that are clues to what your family of origin valued? Do you still value them today as an adult or have you left them behind as you've matured?

What values do you honor from your family of origin?

Society: Within our society, we are shaped by Hollywood, Wall Street, social media, our government, and politics. Whether we realize it or not, we are influenced by the culture around us. Sometimes, we embrace society's values while we reject others. Regardless, society directly impacts our values.

What values have you gotten from society? What values do you reject and embrace instead?

Education: This could also go back to our families of origin, but sometimes, we value education because one or both of our parents were not educated past high school. Sometimes we value a prestigious art school or have a leaning toward an Ivy League school.

Different schools can also teach various values. A private prep school might teach the value of Excellence or Competition. A public school might teach Equality or Self-Sufficiency. A liberal university might teach Inclusion and Diversity.

How have your values been shaped by your view on education and the institutions you've attended?

Generation: Compare baby boomers with Gen Z. Boomers had traditional long-term work experiences and remembered the impact of the Great Depression, so they tend to value stability and loyalty. Gen Z likes a more independent approach to their career and will find the best opportunity ahead even if it means switching organizations or creating a side hustle. We tend to be blind to the bias of our own generation until we consider the way another generation views things.

What has the generation you've been born into taught you to value?

Geography: Where is your corner of the world? This can be the country you live in or the region of the country (for example, if you live in the United States, do you live on the East Coast or the West Coast)? Are you in the Northern states, the Southern states, or the Midwest?

Each region has different values. Are you in a large city or in a more rural area? This will impact your values too.

What has your geography taught you to value?

Wiring: Now, we are heading back to our SHOE personality. (*Check out Chapter 1 if you need a refresher on the SHOEs.*) We've been hard wired with a preference for certain things based on our strengths and the way we process information. Workboots and Mary Janes value Productivity while Stilettos and Flip Flops are more reserved and focus more on being than doing. Mary Janes and Workboots naturally prefer tasks, and Stilettos and Flip Flops prefer relationships. Mary Janes tend to value Justice, while Flip Flops value Peace. Workboots value a Strong Work Ethic and Stilettos value Fun and Playfulness.

What bias has your wiring given you that may clue you in to your values?

Organization: If you are employed by an organization, you will want to include another layer for the organizational values that your company asks you to uphold. These may not be values you would choose to prioritize on your own, but when you're at work, they take on significant importance, so it's worth considering them.

The Values Assessment

It's time to take your Values Assessment. The Values Assessment does not replace other types of personal assessments, but is intended to enhance your self-awareness. You can find the Values Assessment in the Appendix.

Once you have completed this exercise and have your top five values, pay attention for the next two to three weeks as to *how* you see them play out in your life. What decisions are being affected by these values? When have these values been violated and what is your reaction?

Sometimes, upon observation and reflection, we find we might need to reconsider our top five values.

Stepping Over Our Values

Have you ever traveled abroad on vacation or on a mission trip? Often, we prepare for the trip by learning about a new culture. While I was preparing for an upcoming trip to Burundi, Africa, to serve local pastors, I attended several sessions on cross-cultural training. One of the consistent teachings we were instructed to implement was to be willing to lay down our "Western mindset" around time and hospitality to honor our hosts by adopting the way they prioritize these values differently.

An African pastor shared a proverb that says, *"We don't ask the clock permission to start the meeting. We start the meeting when everyone arrives."* My Western upbringing combined with my Family of Origin value of Punctuality made this a tension point that I had to manage throughout the trip. While in Burundi, I respected my hosts by deliberately choosing to place my personal values of Time Management and Punctuality down in order to honor my host's values for Relationships and Living in the Present.

This experience reminded me I am in control of understanding my values, yet I have a choice in appropriate circumstances to honor another's values over my own to enrich relationships.

In Luke 10, we find a powerful illustration of the way we need to keep our values in perspective and determine how best to show up in a given situation.

In Luke 10:38-42, Jesus visited the home of Mary and Martha and, upon His arrival, was met with Martha complaining about her sister, Mary:

> *"As Jesus and his disciples were on their way, he came to a village where a woman named Martha opened her home to him. She had a sister called Mary, who sat at the Lord's feet listening to what he said. But Martha was distracted by all the preparations that had to be made. She came to him and asked, 'Lord, don't you care that my sister has left me to do the work by myself? Tell her to help me!' 'Martha, Martha,' the Lord answered, "you are worried and upset about many things, but only one thing is needed. Mary has chosen what is better, and it will not be taken away from her.'"*

Martha seemed ticked that she was working hard while her sister, Mary was relaxing, lounging at Jesus' feet. Martha was protecting a significant cultural value of Hospitality. In the ancient culture, Hospitality was a highly regarded and collectively assumed value.

I would also speculate that Martha had the spiritual gift of Hospitality. (*See 1 Peter 4:8-10.*) Those who are Christ-followers are given a set of spiritual gifts to edify and build the Body of Christ. Hospitality was one of those gifts and Martha was, no doubt, using hers to make her guests welcomed and comfortable in her home. So why would Jesus encourage Martha to choose a better thing, especially since this better thing went against cultural appropriateness and against her giftedness with hospitality?

Jesus was not saying, "Martha, don't be hospitable." In essence He was saying, "In this particular situation, please choose one thing . . . this better thing (sitting at the feet of Jesus) over a good thing (being hospitable)."

This is a key lesson in understanding what to do when our personal values seem to come into conflict with cultural norms or our own giftedness in a given situation. Like Martha, there will be times when we will be called to "step over" our natural wiring and values to choose a better thing.

> **WE CAN LEARN TO CONTROL THE WAY OUR VALUES INFLUENCE OUR BEHAVIOR—BUT ONLY IF WE BECOME AWARE OF THEM.**

If you have the value of Work Ethic and your spouse has the value of Life Balance, there will be times you will need to step over your value in order to relax with your spouse. Perhaps it means not taking business calls on the beach while on vacation. If Work Ethic is a high value of yours, taking calls on the beach will not *feel* like work to you. It will bring you fun, inspiration, and energy. But to your spouse or family, it feels like an interruption. Choosing to step over your personal value preferences to honor your spouse's shows situational awareness and embracing *the better thing*.

If you have a high value for Independence yet your organization highly values Collaboration, you will have to step over your preference to work independently in order to uphold the value of Collaboration.

At the same time, we also need to communicate our values and make choices that align with them. It's about finding a good balance. We have to recognize when a situation requires us to put aside a top value, but also speak up when we feel a top value is being violated.

Just like our personalities report to us, not the other way around, we can learn to control the way our values influence our behavior—but only if we become aware of them.

What You Value is Valuable

Naming and owning your personal core values is an opportunity to deepen your full-circle self-awareness and understand why you do what you do, why things bug you, and how you might bug others with different or even opposite values.

Knowing your values can help you see through your reactions to the deeper motivations underneath. For example, if you attend a meeting about a new company initiative and you have the value of Being Heard, but this meeting was more of a lecture-style with little to no opportunity for input or questions, then you may leave the meeting not liking the initiative at all. You might be tempted to say the initiative is a bad idea, when in reality, it could be that your value to be heard was violated and you were confusing that unpleasantness with your opinion of the initiative.

KNOWING YOUR VALUES CAN HELP YOU SEE THROUGH YOUR REACTIONS TO THE DEEPER MOTIVATIONS UNDERNEATH.

Recognizing that others may hold different core values than you helps you understand their behaviors and forgive them when they step on your toes. As with the SHOE types, I encourage you to have those close to you take the Values Assessment so that you can understand each other better and learn to make space for each other's values.

As you reflect on your values, remain curious. Become an observer of yourself in various situations. What environments support your values? Are there certain relationships that have similar or different values than you? Again, remain curious about why others value the things they do.

Knowing your values can also help you make choices about how to spend your time, what causes to support, and what goals to pursue—something we'll explore in the next chapter.

Reflect & Respond

1. What surprised you about your values? What was something you already knew?

2. How do your values intersect with what you learned about your SHOE personality?

3. Are there certain people, environments, or organizations that align better with your values than others? Which are particularly challenging and why?

4. How could you communicate your values more clearly and give people a chance to support them?

5. If you're able to learn the values of someone close to you, how can you support their values that are different than yours?

I AM IN CONTROL OF UNDERSTANDING MY VALUES, YET I HAVE A CHOICE IN APPROPRIATE CIRCUMSTANCES TO HONOR ANOTHER'S VALUES OVER MY OWN TO ENRICH RELATIONSHIPS.

PART 2

Self-Leadership Through Self-Reflection

> *"Pay close attention to yourself [concentrate on your personal development] and to your teaching;"*
>
> 1 Timothy 4:16 AMP

In Part I, you dove into self-discovery and began seeing yourself with fresh eyes. You were able to illuminate aspects of who you are that you hadn't ever really seen before and gained a deeper understanding of the unique way God made you.

You also learned to recognize that others are made differently from you—not better or worse, just different—and you are starting to understand how to more effectively interact with people who approach the world differently. You've identified ways you *complement* others in a relationship, but also how you *complicate* your relationships—and how you can use your new understanding to navigate those relationships in a healthier way.

You gained a deeper understanding of who is with you on this journey toward a more confident you and how to better judge the health of those relationships. You also identified the kinds of companions and support you're lacking so you can look and pray for them to come into your life.

Finally, you took time to name your values: the unchanging yet often unseen priorities that guide you through life. You've started to see how your values drive your behavior and how contrasting values can cause relational conflict

These are all important facets of the reality of your life. While some of these elements might change in small ways, they are, for the most part, pretty set at this point in your life. You can't change the way you're wired, just like you can't change who your family is or the formative events of your early life. Those are things we each have to acknowledge and accept—and then learn to make the most of.

INFORMATION WITHOUT APPLICATION CAN'T LEAD TO TRANSFORMATION.

What you *can* change is what you do now—how you leverage your unique strengths and weaknesses to help you move toward your goals. That's what we'll be focusing on in the rest of this book.

As we have been learning, it is crucial to develop full-circle self-awareness, but we can't stop there. We have to use what we've learned about ourselves and others to change our behavior. I always tell my clients, *information* without *application* can't lead to *transformation*. Our goal is to be more emotionally intelligent in varied circumstances, relationships, and conversations, so we can bring the best of ourselves to whatever situation we're in. This is what we mean by self-leadership.

The ability to lead yourself well requires self-reflection, which means constantly evaluating how we are behaving compared to how we want to behave and considering what factors are impacting our ability to show up as our best selves.

True confidence comes when we're consistently (though not perfectly) able to bring the best of ourselves in the situations we find ourselves in. Closing the gap between how we want to show up and how we actually do show up requires self-reflection in order to develop self-leadership.

One of the most impactful lessons I use with my coaching clients is when I ask them to consider the environments that bring out the best of their personalities (what I refer to as our "balconies"). What is happening around them? Who are they with? Why is it an edifying circumstance for them? Are they well-rested? Do they feel safe? Are they with like-minded friends or teammates?

Now the inverse of that question takes it to another level. When they are at their worst (their basements), what is happening around them? Are you H.A.L.T. (*Hungry, Angry, Lonely or Tired*)? Is it "that Tuesday" morning meeting that they dread? What is happening in that meeting that brings out the worst in them? Are they being misunderstood? Not able to use their voice? Are they rushed? Are they asked to present data and are not a data kind of person? Or perhaps what brings out their worst is a certain personality that is the opposite of theirs, like how Workboot is the opposite of Flip Flop and the Stiletto is the opposite of Mary Jane. Or maybe it's an actual person. It's ok to name them here in the margins.

We want to be aware so that we can reflect and actually change our behavior. We might not be able to change one thing about our Tuesday morning meeting or *that person* who attends it each week, but we can be forewarned and thus not be tempted to be drawn into the worst of ourselves by our behavior or mindset.

By reflecting, you're able to manage yourself like a good basketball coach might manage his team. If they're up against a particularly tall team, he might put in his tallest players, while if they're playing a team with shorter, quicker players, he might put in his best ball-handlers even if they're not as tall. In a similar way, self-leadership requires you to know your strengths and weaknesses, anticipate what brings out the best and the worst in you, and then make informed decisions about how to navigate any given situation in order to reach your goals.

An important next step is getting clearer on what those goals are. What is the destination you want to move toward on this trip of a lifetime? What is your target? If you don't know where you're aiming, you have next to no chance of hitting it, or worse yet, you have the chance of hitting the wrong target altogether, requiring you to backtrack on your journey.

A useful tool for setting meaningful goals is the Life Wheel. It shows seven important areas of life so we can evaluate our fulfillment in each area. Go ahead and rate each area on a scale of one to ten now, with one being "completely dissatisfied" and ten being "completely satisfied."

Diagram

- FINANCES
- CAREER
- PHYSICAL EMOTIONAL HELP
- SPIRITUAL
- RELATIONSHIPS
- LIFESTYLE PACING MARGIN
- HOBBIES RECREATION TRAVEL

Place a number 1-10 next to each area of your life. 1 meaning you are completely dissatisfied and 10 meaning you are completely satisfied.

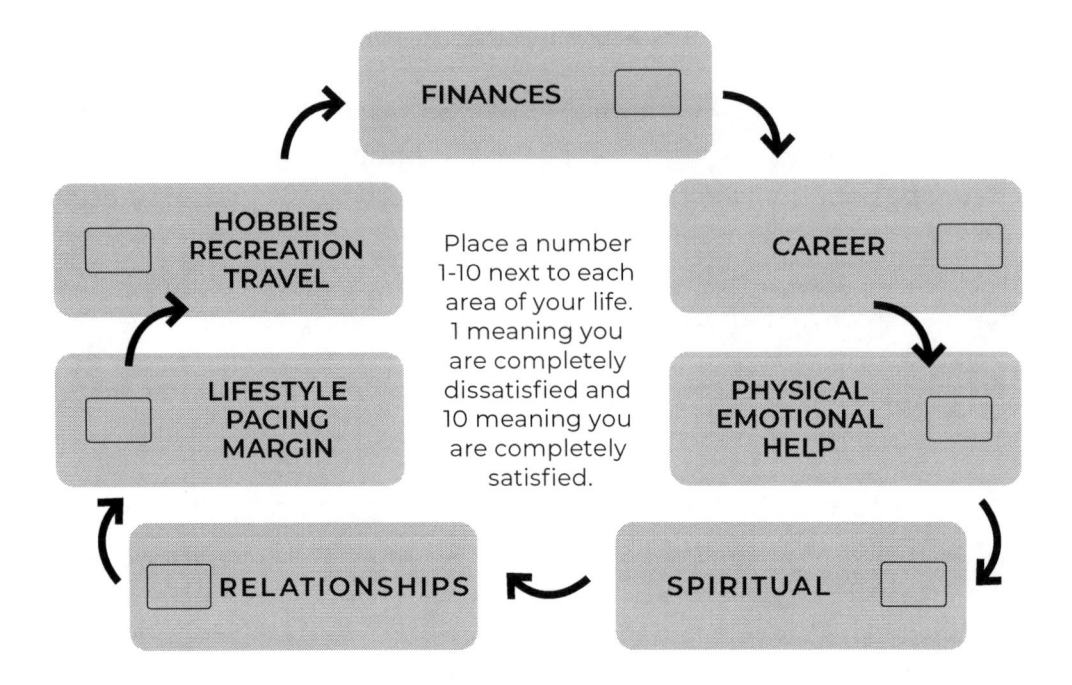

Based on your level of satisfaction in each area, what are one to three areas that you want to improve? This will highlight which goals you should prioritize. Write your score next to each category above.

Part II is all about defining your target destination—where you want to go next on this adventure of a lifetime. Once you know where you want to go, you can chart a course to get you there.

Well-meaning people are constantly charting out the course for us, whether it's the expectation that you get married and have kids, the assumption you will work for the bank since you come from a family of bankers, or the unspoken belief that you will volunteer in your community. But unless you reflect on your values, gifts, and sense of calling, you can't be sure that they're not directing your life to arrive at *their* destination, not the one that God has for your life. Don't let others chart your course for you.

Part II will help you create a map for your unique journey. Your values will serve as a compass, and your sense of calling will be your road signs.

It's time to turn off the GPS you've been following blindly and ask God to help you make your own map.

Chapter 5
What Is My Calling?

"There are different kinds of gifts, but the same Spirit distributes them."

1 Corinthians 12:4

Matt Emmons was a marksman in the 2004 Olympics. He pulled back his rifle, fixed his eyes on the target through the scope, lined up his stance, and slowed his breathing to make it imperceptible. He squeezed the trigger and . . . *bullseye*! The bullet landed dead center. Surely, he had done it. No one could, or would, get closer than this. It was the perfect shot. Yet, he was disqualified from Olympic gold. Why? Because he'd hit the bullseye of the wrong target.

My heart skips a beat when I consider the depth of application this marksman's target faux paus means if I don't heed its warnings in my own life. What if I live my life without aim? What if the target I'm fixed upon in this lifetime is actually the wrong target? Perhaps it's a target the world, social media, Hollywood, a professor, well-meaning parents, or a pastor has set for me? How tragic it would be to get to the end of my life and realize I'd worked so hard to hit the bullseye, but I'd been aiming at the wrong target all along?

This story illustrates how important it is to reflect not only on who we are and how we can excel, but also where we want to end up. What destination do we want to use our strengths and skills to reach? True success is hitting the target that God has prepared in advance for us, which is unique and different from the target anyone else has. This chapter will help us discern what that target is.

YOUR CONFIDENCE COMPASS

Matt Emmons made the mistake of aiming at the wrong target, but he did at least aim carefully. Another mistake we can make is not to aim at all. Imagine someone shooting a bow and arrow blindfolded. How likely are they to hit their target? Yet, often, we approach our lives without taking aim. We don't focus our decisions to guard the things that matter the most and make room for the work God has called us to do.

> ONLY WHEN YOU KNOW YOUR DESTINATION CAN YOU BEGIN TO CHART YOUR COURSE.

So often we walk through our lives robotically responding or reacting, rather than strategically aiming at where we want to end up. As a coach, I have noticed an alarming trend in my life and the lives of so many women I coach. We go through each day managing adrenaline, but not living a life. We go from task to task, commitment to commitment, and responsibility to responsibility without taking the time to pause and evaluate our season, priorities, and goals. Then we hope that a week-long vacation will make up for it all.

Close your eyes for a moment and imagine what it would feel like to live a focused life instead of a life on autopilot. You can learn to live a life on purpose rather than a life on impulse.

Imagine everything God wants you to accomplish for one year, one decade, or by the end of our one life. Now imagine those things as targets on the wall that an arrow can launch into. Often, at the beginning of each season, we take all the things we want to accomplish in our calendars, projects, and free time, and slap them onto the wall and draw a bullseye around it, hoping we hit the target God wants for us. Instead, we need to reverse engineer our lives, getting clear on our target first and then determining how to hit it.

Only when you know your destination can you begin to chart your course.

This chapter will help you roll up your sleeves to create a succinct statement that will serve as a filter for your decisions, activities, and schedule. Let's learn to make no-regret decisions designed to protect our calling and shift from vague awareness to a clear statement of purpose.

This could be something so impactful for you that it is what is remembered about you at your funeral. It may seem morbid, but what do you want to be remembered for? If we don't aim our lives toward our purpose, we will get to the end of this quarter, year or the end of our life without having fully invested ourselves in God's best for us.

Let's start with being intentional with what God is asking of us. Let's create time and space to sit before Him and listen. As we begin to identify what our unique calling is for the season ahead, then we can put it on the wall and consistently spend our year, decade, or life tweaking our aim to ensure we hit the right target.

This chapter will provide a series of practical exercises that will help you aim closer and closer to your life's bulls-eye. First, you will define your purpose and write a Calling Statement that will act as an overarching target to guide your major life decisions. Then, we'll list some smaller targets you want to hit along the way, specific goals that will help you move toward your larger purpose.

Defining Your Purpose

Imagine you're on an elevator riding up to the forty-sixth floor and you find yourself sharing the space with a genie. He tells you he'll make sure your life looks exactly the way you want it to look ten years from now, *but only if you can tell him what that life is before the elevator doors open.* You've got maybe thirty seconds to articulate the overarching vision of your life including your specific, big-picture goals.

What are you going to say?

This imaginative exercise based on the popular marketing term "elevator pitch" is meant to help you realize just how clear you *could be* about your purpose. If you're like most women I coach, and most people more broadly, you probably don't have a great answer on the tip of your tongue.

It's not an easy question. In fact, is probably the most difficult question there is—and the most important.

In his book *Start with Why*, Simon Sinek says*:* "Very few people or companies can clearly articulate *Why* they do *what* they do. By *why*, I mean, your purpose, cause or belief—*why* does your company exist? *Why* do you get out of bed every morning? And *why* should anyone care?"

Identifying your "why" is stating your intentions. The definition of intention is "An act of determining mentally upon some action or result." It's starting on purpose and with the end in mind.

Do you know why you exist? Do you know the purpose for your life? If you're like most people, you have a vague sense of purpose, but it feels overwhelming to try to clarify it into a succinct statement. We've never stopped to envision a purpose in our lives and then that drill down into actions steps so we can walk out our calling. What will I be doing as I live a purposeful life? Why will I be doing it, who will I do it with or for, and what will be different because I did it?

Proverbs 29:18 (NKJV) says, "Where *there is* no vision, the people perish." When we cannot see where we are aiming our lives, there is a piece of us that dies inside. God will give us each a vision for our lives if we take the time to ask and listen carefully for the answer.

Not only will God give us the vision He wants us to aim for, but the provision to accomplish it. The word "provision" comes from two Latin words: *pro*, which means "forward or ahead," and *video*, which means "to see." Therefore, God provides what He sees ahead and gives us what we need to accomplish this calling.

Let's look at Ephesians 2:10 again, but this time in the Amplified version: "For we are His workmanship [His own master work, a work of art], created in Christ Jesus [reborn from above--spiritually transformed, renewed, ready to be used] for good works, which God prepared [for us] beforehand [taking paths which He set], so that we would walk in them [living the good life which He prearranged and made ready for us]."

I love the words "taking the paths which He set so that we would walk in them living the good life which He prearranged and made ready for us." You can be assured that God has already marked out the pathway for you and that nudging in your heart, that bubbling under the surface, that excited and scared feeling you have is one of the ways the Holy Spirit gives you clues for the path ahead.

This is also the invitation to join God in this work He has prepared in advance for us. As I'm writing this, I am reflecting on the coronation of King Charles. Did you watch it? Now, imagine you were invited to that ceremony. Would you RSVP "yes" to reserve your spot and do whatever you needed to do to save up for the airfare, book an Airbnb, and determine what to wear? Well, the God of the universe has sent you an invitation to an even greater event: fulfilling His purpose for your life.

Rick Warren reminds us to keep our lives in perspective of the bigger story God is telling through the world: "It's not about you. The purpose of your life is far greater than your own personal fulfillment, your peace of mind, or even your happiness. It's far greater than your family, your career, or even your wildest dreams and ambitions. If you want to know why you were placed on this planet, you must begin with God. You were born by his purpose and for his purpose."

The only way to accurately determine our true purpose in life—to clarify the target we should be aiming to hit—is to start by asking God, "What is the unique calling you have placed on my life?"

Called by Someone to Something

The idea of crafting a statement of purpose is by no means unique to me. Some people call it a mission statement, others refer to is as a vision statement or a five-year plan. The vocabulary I want to use in this section of the book, however, doesn't use any of those words. The words I use for my life aim is a *"Calling Statement."* This is very intentional.

A CALLING REQUIRES A CALLER.

I use the term Calling Statement because a calling requires a caller. The Latin word *vocāre,* meaning "to call," is where we get our English word, "voice." The question is, "Who is calling us?" Whose voice are we crafting our life work after?

Voices that have historically guided our "calling" include our parents, teachers, professors, pastors, and mentors. However, in the last decades of the internet, we have added other voices from Google, Hollywood, politics, Instagram influencers, Facebook, TikTok, X, and more. There are so many voices that listening to the right one is hard. If we aren't careful, we find ourselves being influenced to be famous, known, and validated by platforms, likes, and shares. Even well-meaning family members, mothers-in-law, Bible study leaders, PTA presidents, and pastors have voices that ask us to aim parts of our lives. Just because these are amazing people, we still must go back to the Caller and ask Him, "Is this where You want me to aim?" We want to be confident in our calling, not striving for a worldly why.

In his book *The Call*, Os Guinness says, "We are not primarily called to do something or go somewhere; we are called to Someone. We are not called first to special work but to God. The key to answering the call is to be devoted to no one and to nothing above God Himself."

Let's silence the other voices for a second and go back to the Caller. For me, that voice is Jesus. Now, when I say "voice," I don't mean I actually hear an audible voice. It is an impression of my direction that my gifts, wiring, experiences, and God's Word affirm for me. I have been uniquely designed to leave a mark that only Lisa Allen can leave on the world. I don't say that because I'm any more special than anyone else. I say that because I have strengths, gifts, leanings, and experiences that are unique to me, just like you do. God doesn't need me to accomplish any of His plans, but He invites me. It's the most precious invitation that the God Who created the universe trusts each of us to be His representative.

Ephesians 4:1 says, "As a prisoner for the Lord, then, I urge you to live a life worthy of the *calling* you have received" (*emphasis added*). The word "calling" in this verse is the Greek word *klésis***,** which means "a calling—a summons or an invitation like to a banquet." It's a divine call. Our dream is God's divine call. The initial invitation is to everlasting life by accepting Christ as our Savior, admitting we are sinners and have fallen short of His righteousness, accepting the atoning work Jesus did on our behalf by shedding His blood on the cross. If you have not done this yet, I urge you to talk to your Bible study leader or pastor.

If we want to live focused on the work God has called us to do, we need to remain connected to Him alone as our source of passion, encouragement, and direction. If you are reading this and have no idea the direction your calling should be aimed, it can be tempting to cling to time with God before any doing any work. However, as soon as you have a sense of where He's guiding you, it is quite common to get ahead of God and move straight into the work.

There are so many reasons this happens. First, we are doers. We genuinely want to impact the people or causes God is calling us to. We are so used to being busy that it's hard to stop and spend time with God. Kingdom causes, social justice, and ministry often result in chaos in other areas of our lives and eventual burnout. It requires discipline to let our head hit the pillow when there is work unfinished.

Let's look to Jesus' example of how He sought His Father above all even as He walked unswervingly toward His calling to the Cross. Jesus was busy fulfilling His mission as he preached and healed others. However, in Luke 5:16, we read "But Jesus often withdrew to lonely places and prayed." There was a rhythm to Him allowing His Father to give Him rest and fuel Him to carry out His calling.

We too need to find a rhythm of connecting with God as we pursue our calling. Psalm 42:1-2 offers two comforting yet challenging verses: "As the deer pants for streams of water, so my soul pants for you, my God. My soul thirsts for God, for the living God. When can I go and meet with God?"

If we pursue our calling without receiving refreshment from God, we will get so busy with the work of our calling we will be tempted to cry out, "When do you expect me to be with God?" rather than experiencing the holy anticipation of just being with the Father. Human Beings are prone to take action. We get clarity around our calling and then start doing it in our own strength, instead of continually going to God for direction, affirmation, correction, and guidance.

Our calling begins and ends with God. So, before we jump into it, let's take some time and pull up our calendar (either our physical or digital ones) and book a few dates with our Father (the Caller) to focus on our calling. This could mean extending your normal time of Bible study and journaling to focus specifically on talking to and listening to Him about your calling. It could mean blocking out a few lunch hours in a quiet spot or arriving early to carpool and sitting quietly with Him in your car.

When my son was little, I would arrive at carpool as much as forty-five minutes to an hour early to do Bible study or have focused time, because I knew my son would sleep in his car seat until his sister was dismissed from school.

When and where will you spend some time with God listening to His call?

Your Role vs. Your Calling

Before we roll up our sleeves to write our Calling Statement, I would like to address something that I have encountered in my life and in the lives of women I coach. It is the confusion between our callings and our roles.

> **Our Time-Stamped Seasons
> (Ecclesiastes 3:1-8 and 3:11)**
>
> *"There is a time for everything,*
> *and a season for every activity under the heavens:*
> *a time to be born and a time to die,*
> *a time to plant and a time to uproot,*
> *a time to kill and a time to heal,*
> *a time to tear down and a time to build,*
> *a time to weep and a time to laugh,*
> *a time to mourn and a time to dance,*
> *a time to scatter stones and a time to gather them,*

a time to embrace and a time to refrain from embracing,

a time to search and a time to give up,

a time to keep and a time to throw away,

a time to tear and a time to mend,

a time to be silent and a time to speak,

a time to love and a time to hate,

a time for war and a time for peace . . .

He has made everything beautiful in its time."

These verses punctuate how cyclical our lives are. Depending on the season, we will have different roles and responsibilities assigned to us. Some seasons can be done any time; however, other seasons are time-stamped, like when we need to be rocking babies or caring for our aging parents. As we consider our callings, we must ask the Lord to be clear about which of our roles are time-stamped.

Just like the milk in our fridge has a date of expiration, some of our seasons do, as well. If we miss them, we will not have a chance to make them up later. I was stopped dead in my tracks when I realized that no one ever records the last time they rock their babies. We honestly never know and we surely don't want to miss it.

> JUST LIKE THE MILK IN OUR FRIDGE HAS A DATE OF EXPIRATION, SOME OF OUR SEASONS DO, AS WELL. IF WE MISS THEM, WE WILL NOT HAVE A CHANCE TO MAKE THEM UP LATER.

Some of us have the role of a wife, mother, grandmother, student, or caregiver for aging parents. Is there a role you would add? Because of the role we've been assigned, certain seasons of life will require more of our time and attention, like caring for our babies who will someday go to kindergarten; tending to aging parents who will someday be in Heaven; finishing a master's degree that will someday lead to graduation; or tending to a difficult season of marriage that *could* someday lead to divorce if we don't work on our marriage now. These are our roles, but they aren't our callings. Let me explain why.

107

If our calling is to be a mom, then what happens when our kids go to college? Our calling is done in our early-to-mid forties. If our calling is to care for our parents, then when they are no longer in need of our care, does our calling end? Even our marriage that requires commitment and attention isn't our calling, because if something happen to our spouse, our calling stops too. No, those are all examples of roles. Our calling, however, is something that God designs to work in tandem with our roles. Our calling will complement our roles. Also, our calling can often span many different seasons of our lives.

So, *as* we rock our babies, we may have a calling to do mission work or build wells in Africa for God's glory. God in His divine economy is preparing us for that work *while* we rock our babies. Sometimes, we may have great childcare and we can actually do both. There are only so many hours in a day and we have to pay attention to both our current role and life's calling.

Sometimes your role will require more from you and your calling has to wait a bit. Your calling waits for you as you sit on a marriage counselor's couch and work on your marriage. Your calling waits for you as you finish your degree.

I like to think of the wait times like "Calling School." As you walk out each role you've been assigned, you can still spark the passion within you even if you only can work on your calling by taking a webinar, doing research on that book you want to write, or networking with others who have a similar calling. Even if you do those things for an hour a week or an hour a month, you are still honoring your God-given role while pursuing a heart-driven calling. You are in Calling School. I heard a pastor say that "God's provision awaits your preparation. Don't expect the classroom to look like the calling. God is putting you in CLASS for your CALLING."

Take a moment to write down every role that you are in right now. Make special note for roles or seasons that are time-stamped. Here are some common roles to help get you started:

Rocking Babies ⊘ Caring for Aging Parents ⊘ A Tough Marriage

A Significant School Year (Senior) ⊘ Finishing School

A Career/Being the Breadwinner for Your Family

What Is a Calling?

Because your calling is based in something that you are passionate about, it creates fresh energy in you. You will find that energy becomes fuel for you to be more engaged to each of your roles. One hour of work or research in your calling will fuel you with passionate energy for other areas of your life.

Let's break down what a calling *is* and what a calling *isn't*.

A Calling is:

- Something that fuels you. It gives you energy. My friend Shari sat in church for many months thinking about her calling to become a Christian Image Consultant. It fueled her to eventually become one of the most prominent Christian Image Consultants in the world at StylebyColor.com

- Something you've been wired for. Your SHOE personality we discussed in Chapter 1 aligns with and will equip you for your calling. God doesn't need you to be different for your calling. If you are assertive, He will use that. If you are more reserved, He intends to use that.

- Energy producing. It isn't always easy, but it gives you energy. Doing a four-hour task in your calling feels like two hours. You will have that moment when you look at the clock and say, "Where did the time go? I totally missed lunch."

- What you do when you're tired. It can pull you off the couch without much prep time. You love talking about it with others. I say that I can accomplish a great deal if I have eight hours of sleep and good pair of shoes. However, my true calling doesn't need either of those things.

- What you would do if you won the lottery. If you find yourself with a windfall profit, or an inheritance from dear old Aunt Betty, you will still do your calling because it doesn't feel like work to you. You may eventually be paid to do your calling, but a true calling is something you can volunteer to do happily. I used to joke with my teams that if I came into an unexpected amount of cash, I would still arrive at work because it was a calling to me. I would also add that I would be dragging Louis Vuitton luggage.

- Something you can do as a side hustle that pairs well with your role and seasons of life. You might be working in corporate American as your family breadwinner. Your calling can be done on the side. In fact, if you cannot do something you are passionate about eight hours a day in your job, it is even more important to identify and carve out time for your calling on the weekends and in the evenings.

Your Calling isn't:

- Necessarily something huge or public. It can be mentoring one married couple or investing in one teen instead of starting an entire non-profit for married couples or teens.

- Something you dread. You can be a little intimated or scared of your calling, but you won't dread it. It is tied to something you are passionately intrigued about.

- Something that you want to do in your own strength. Because you are seeking your Caller to direct your life, you need to trust Him to supply the energy, resources, and time to walk out your calling.

- Something you can rush. Some of you don't want to be in your current role (work at a bank, finish your degree), because you want to jump right into our calling now. But, learning, growing into, and developing your calling takes time.

- Something tied to a specific role, especially a time-stamped one, as discussed above. A calling may take different forms throughout your life, but it will last beyond any particular role.

- Something unbiblical, unhealthy, or illegal.

The callings God gives us are as unlimited as our unlimited God.

Anything can be a calling as long as it's not unbiblical or illegal. We often think of a calling as Kingdom work, and it is, but Kingdom work isn't limited to ministry or missionary work. I don't want to lose you here if you think the only work God would call you into is a structured ministry. Kingdom work is also being the reflection of God in a corporate setting, leading teams, or volunteering in your local shelter. Let's look at the New Living Translation of Ephesians 4:16: "He makes the whole body fit together perfectly. As each part does its own special work, it helps the other parts grow, so that the whole body is healthy and growing and full of love." We need all kinds of people working in all kinds of ways.

> **THE CALLINGS GOD GIVES US ARE AS UNLIMITED AS OUR UNLIMITED GOD.**

When you participate in Kingdom work where you are, you are operating as a fully-functioning part of the Body of Christ as you do your own special work.

I worked with someone once who loved all things data because data was black-and-white, reliable, and could prove or disprove things. But, she didn't think it was part of her calling. It was scientific, mathematic, and corporate. She had predetermined that God couldn't use her amazing brain to guide corporations, organizations, nonprofits, and ministry endeavors. Yet, boy did He ever use it.

What is it for you that doesn't feel like your calling? Art? Music? Creativity? Organizing? I want to encourage you not to put God or your calling in a box.

Within the word "work" in Ephesians 4:16, we find another layer of how our calling impacts us. This word in the Greek is *enérgeia* from which we get our word "energy." It is God's divine empowerment for our work. When we operate in our calling even for short periods of time during any given day or week, we are filled, fueled, and energized. It is the best tired we will ever feel. And it helps us balance the other areas of our lives' responsibilities that may be profound and important yet more fatiguing.

A calling is anything that lights you up, uses your gifts and strengths, and aligns with what you discern to be God's purpose for your life.

Let's look now at how to discern that purpose.

Calling Clues

Below are a series of coaching exercises to help you brainstorm your calling. Each one asks you to look for clues from your life that might reveal your purpose. As much as I wish God would say, "Lisa, thus saith the Lord, this is your calling," it is often that the Holy Spirit gives impressions and experiences that I can use as clues sewn together into a directed calling for my life. It's the same for you.

Since my desire is for this chapter to feel like a one-on-one coaching appointment where we are sitting across the table from each other at a coffee shop, I will incorporate the questions and assignments I would give you if we were face-to-face. Throughout this section, I will have Coaching Questions for you to ponder and write your answers to.

Of course, like you, I am always tempted to skip any of the application portions of the books I read, but I want to encourage you to pause and reflect on each question and record your answer either on the page of this book or in your journal. Remember that information without *application* can't lead to transformation.

What Others Have Seen

Think back to childhood, middle school, college, etc. Consider those words spoken prophetically over you either from your family or some meaningful teacher, pastor, or professor. Think about neighbors, coaches, or mentors you've had that have spoken words of affirmation and guidance based on what they see in you.

Keep in mind that some people may have said things about you that were not accurate and were not prophetic at all. Some of these words may have stung or even caused deep pain or shame. That's not what I want you to look at now. If the words made you feel small or discouraged, or if they simply did not fit with what you know to be true in your heart about yourself, you should disregard them. Of course, sometimes we hear necessary rebukes that doesn't feel great, but that's different from words that cut us down.

Instead, I want you to think about words that felt like they named something true about yourself or that made you feel a sense of passion, confidence, and purpose. Here are some examples to get your wheels turning:

- You're going to be a great leader someday.
- You're an example of hard work and perseverance.
- You have a flare for art.
- No one tells a better story than you.
- How do you consistently keep everything organized in the midst of chaos?
- You are a problem-solver, always thinking strategically and analytically.
- Thank you for being a peace-making mediator in so many relationships.

For me, when I was looking into becoming a coach, I made an appointment with an executive coach from our church to discuss it with her. After I shared my heart about coaching, her words blessed me: "You're already a coach. You just don't have the training or certification yet." You see, as she listened to my leadership journey, she was wise enough to observe that I had a coaching leadership style that pulled out the best in others and created purpose, self-awareness, and confidence in those I was responsible for. This gave me the courage and confidence to pursue getting my coaching certification and launch my coaching business.

A friend of mine began her writing career all because of a thank you note. She had written a beautifully worded note to a friend for a birthday gift. Upon reading it, her friend promptly rang her doorbell and said, "This is the most beautiful note I've ever received. If this is what you can do with a thank you note, you need to pursue writing." And she did. She started writing Bible studies in our church and is now a best-selling author.

What are some of the things people say you are good at? What do people often thank you for doing or ask you to help them with?

_____

_____

_____

_____

_____

_____

_____

_____

_____

_____

_____

_____

What You Loved as a Kid

Think about what you dreamed of being as a child. It is not always the case, but sometimes, there are clues to our calling from our childhood.

I always wanted to be Cher. I would swing my long, straight hair behind my shoulder while lip-syncing into a hairbrush. It's not lost on me that several weekends a year, you find me on a stage holding a microphone as I speak to groups of women (and thankfully, *not* singing).

My friend Shari, the Christian Image Consultant, was the only girl in her second-grade photo with a matching purse for her outfit.

One little girl from our playgroup thirty years ago was kind of the play-group "boss," though sometimes it tipped into being a "bully." She meant no harm, but she just had unrefined, immature leadership skills that expressed themselves in stealing toys, slugging kids who got in her way, and deciding all the games that were played. I heard recently she was high up in the Navy. That totally makes sense because she's sought leadership positions.

Your calling will most likely not look exactly the same as what you did as a child, but your childhood interests and tendencies can reveal your gifts. Looking at the things you enjoyed and did easily as a kid can provide valuable clues to the nature of your calling.

What did you enjoy as a child? What came naturally to you? Consider asking a parent or childhood friend what you were like. Even if you "grew out of it," write down anything you spent a lot of time or energy doing or dreaming of doing.

_____

_____

_____

_____

_____

_____

_____

_____

_____

_____

_____

_____

Your "Used To's"

When I work with coaching clients, I have become attuned to listening for the words "I used to," especially if they are said with a hint of regret. We then explore what made them stop and if they wanted to pick that hobby back up again. I would encourage you to pay attention to your "used to's" as well.

- I used to sing in the choir.
- I used to play the piano.
- I used to paint
- I used to lead a Bible study.
- I used to teach in Young Life.

CHAPTER 5: WHAT IS MY CALLING?

This is similar to the previous segment about what you liked to do as a child, but now you're considering things you did as a young(er) adult as well. What did you do in high school and/or college? What did you do before you got married or before you had kids?

Is there a clue to your calling from your past "used to's?" Write down everything you can think of that you used to do (and enjoyed), but stopped doing for one reason or another.

_____

_____

_____

_____

_____

_____

_____

_____

_____

_____

Your Spiritual Gifts

Spiritual gifts are an important calling clue. Everyone is gifted in one or two areas.

Here's what the Bible says about spiritual gifts in 1 Corinthians 12:7-11:

> *"Now to each one the manifestation of the Spirit is given for the common good. To one there is given through the Spirit a message of wisdom, to another a message of knowledge by means of the same Spirit, to another faith by the same Spirit, to another gifts of healing by that one Spirit, to another miraculous powers, to another prophecy, to another distinguishing between spirits, to another speaking in different kinds of tongues, and to still another the interpretation of tongues. All these are the work of one and the same Spirit, and he distributes them to each one, just as he determines."*

There are seven gifts as commonly described:

- **Teaching:** The joy of researching and learning the Bible in order to teach and instruct others in truth.
- **Mercy:** Compassion for and unique discernment of suffering in others, along with the desire to help them.
- **Prophecy:** Bold and direct delivery of truth rooted in Scripture
- **Serving:** Blessing others through practical and tangible service.
- **Giving:** Serious about and motivated around financial generosity.
- **Exhortation:** Exhorting others through encouragement and advice centered around God's Word.
- **Leadership:** Gathers and moves others toward common a vision and goals.

If you've never determined your spiritual gifts, you can access a free quiz in the Appendix.

What are your spiritual gifts? What clues do they show for your calling?

What Gets You Fired Up

What makes you mad? What makes you say, "It shouldn't be like this?" This can be a powerful clue to your calling.

Another clue might be subjects that get you excited and energized, or topics that you want to spend hours learning about or practicing. For example, one of my first ever speaking assignments was a breakout session at a women's retreat. I was doing a session on the personalities of our children based on Florence Littauer's book, *Personality Plus*. The women were so amazed to learn about personalities and the uniqueness of their kids that they wanted to apply the same thing to their personalities as moms. I realized that I had a passion for personalities and began to pursue reading and studying them and attaining certifications. Why? Because it helps women appreciate who God created them to be and builds their confidence. It is part of my calling to empower and equip women by helping them glimpse their creative design in God's vertical mirror.

What issues get you fired up and full of righteous indignation? What topics get you buzzing with energy because you find them so fascinating or motivating?

_____

_____

_____

_____

_____

_____

CHAPTER 5: WHAT IS MY CALLING?

_____

_____

_____

_____

_____

_____

_____

_____

Consider:

- The pain you've experienced in your life. Though we don't like to travel through painful seasons like divorce, the death of a loved one, forced early retirement, being fired, a prodigal child, being a cancer survivor and beyond, we often find our deepest pain becomes our greatest calling.

- News stories and articles that grab your attention.

- Social media accounts and posts you like, share, and save— or that you want to block or otherwise work against.

- The people groups that you have a soft spot for, or that you think don't get the help or protection that they need.

- Subjects you've spent a lot of time researching or learning about, or that you could talk about for hours without getting bored.

Your Pain

I also find that your deepest aim can often come from your life's greatest pain. The word "passion" actually comes from the root word for suffering!

In 2012, I was working with African Initiatives at our church and involved with groups traveling back and forth to Burundi and Rwanda, Africa. There was an amazing gentleman I met through this experience named Celestin. His life had been ravaged by the Rwandan genocide decades prior and he had lost most, if not all, of his immediate family. Over the years, Celestin had learned forgiveness, became a pastor, and spent his life helping tribes reconcile their conflict according to the Gospel. His deepest pain became his life's greatest aim. During our last connection, he was not only training pastors on this but also military, police, and government officials on the importance of forgiveness from past trauma. God has used his pain to become his passion and change the climate of these areas in Africa.

How has your life been impacted by suffering as you've seen God provide for your healing in areas such as infidelity, addiction, divorce, widowhood, childhood poverty, adoption, or church hurt? What clues to your calling might be found here?

_____

_____

_____

_____

_____

_____

Writing Your Calling Statement

Now it's time to take all those clues, look for patterns and priorities, and then write your personal Calling Statement. Your Calling Statement will act as an overarching target to guide your major life decisions.

Before you begin, I recommend grabbing your Bible, a journal, and perhaps this book or another article that has captured your attention about what God is stirring within you.

I am including my Calling Statement as an example for you. My Calling Statement isn't particularly flashy or creative. However, it has faithfully served to keep me moving toward my God-ordained target for almost twenty-five years.

> My Calling Statement: **To encourage, inspire, empower and equip women to be the unique individuals God created them to be and leave HIS mark on their world through their lives.**

(How cool is it that the writing of this very chapter and this entire book you are reading is me living out that calling? Thank you. My calling is to help you find *your* calling.)

Every Calling Statement has three parts:

1. Action words or verbs
2. A people group or cause
3. A *"so that,"* which is the impact of your calling on others

You need to include action words or verbs because your calling will allow you to *do* something. You will eventually want two to four action words. But, if you end this chapter with ten or more action words or verbs, you are ten words closer to an aimed and purposeful life.

Your Calling Statement highlights a people group or cause because you will do those things *for or to someone*. Yes, your purpose is ultimately to serve God, but we all serve Him by serving "our neighbors." Who are the "neighbors" you've been called to serve? It could be a group of people like widows, orphans, corporate women, abuse survivors, or others. If you're having trouble determining which people group or cause to include, it might help you to revisit some of your painful seasons of life.

Finally, your Calling Statement must have a *"so that."* Your *"so that"* is the impact of you walking out your calling in the world. What will *be different* because you did those things? The impact is usually (though not always) a solution to someone's problem. What will be different in someone's life because of your calling? How will they be changed?

Now, let's go back to my Calling Statement as an example of these three areas:

To encourage, inspire, empower and equip women to be the unique individuals God created them to be and leave HIS mark on their world through their lives.

My Action Words: Encourage, Inspire, Empower, and Equip

My People Group: Women (or, in some areas, ministry leaders)

My "So That:" They can be the unique individuals God created them to be and leave His mark on their world through their lives.

This is the fingerprint I want left from my life long after I am gone. If I have encouraged someone in their calling, purpose, wiring, and habits, I've had a life well lived. If women gain confidence in their unique giftedness, wiring, skillset, and purpose, then I've had a life well lived. If my workshop clients and audiences leave God's mark on their worlds in ministry, the corporate world, at their church, in their families, or in their communities, I've had a life well lived.

My Calling Statement was formed directly out of the clues my life has left me. I worked those clues into the words I've chosen. Decades ago, when I initially wrote my Calling Statement, I had not made this connection, however, over time it became clear.

The word *encourage* is directly tied to my spiritual gift of exhortation.

The word *inspire* is a reflection of my SHOE personality as a Stiletto.

The words *equip* and *empower* are coaching words so naturally, I would be drawn to them as a coach.

YOUR CONFIDENCE COMPASS

It's Your Turn

Take a few minutes to look over your list of clues, pray, and start piecing together your own Calling Statement. This is not a final draft, just a work in progress.

Remember, this is a statement, not a paragraph, so the goal is to keep it short. That said, feel free to make it longer for now. Just get started.

I've provided word banks for your action words and for the people groups or cause to help get you started.

Your Action Words

Use the word bank below as a launch pad, but feel free to use your own words. Google different words. Look at synonyms and even antonyms. Your words should make you feel something.

What do you feel called to *do* with your life?

Dream	Highlight	Eliminate	Train	Restore	Create	Assist
Pursue	Initiate	Simplify	Assert	Invent	Benefit	Assume
Generate	Value	Highlight	Examine	Vision	Encourage
Empower	Lead	Guide	Customize	Develop	Facilitate
Negotiate	Synergize	Complete	Share	Solve	Defend	Heal
Gather	Exemplify	Progress	Capture	Experience	Inspire
Navigate	Build	Leverage	Orchestrate	Fashion	Network
Supply	Continue	Strategize	Resource	Draft	Iluminate
Expose	Maximize	Realize	Educate	Equip	Maneuver
Coordinate	Promote	Foster	Pursue	Utilize	Analyze	Deliver
Validate	Provide Access	Individualize	Revolutionize

Write your action words here _____

CHAPTER 5: WHAT IS MY CALLING?

Your People Group/Cause

Now, let's shift our focus to your people group or cause. There is a word bank for people groups/causes to spur you on. As above, feel free to google, use synonyms, etc.

Who do you want to help with your life?

God Family Women Athletes Marriage Teens College Friendship

Relationships Parents Childhood Single Moms Foster/Adopted

Teachers Poverty Forgotten Addicted Invisible Victimized

Abandoned Global Students Pastors/ Pastors wives Corporate

Write your people group or cause here: _____

Your "So That":

Lastly, what is the result you want your efforts to achieve? What will be the impact because you aimed your life with your action words at your people group?

Below are results of callings that I have experienced with clients and audiences who have done this exercise:

- Water will be clean
- Hunger will be eliminated
- Pornography will be in recovery
- Surviving after infidelity
- Divorced women go from surviving to thriving
- Addicts become sober
- Kids will have beds and food
- Children will be fostered or adopted
- Abuse survivors will heal

- Politics will be civil
- Senior saints will be treasured
- Mental health will be discussed in church
- Civil and racial injustice will be eradicated

Write your "*so that*" or result here: _____

Now, write out your entire Calling Statement below, using this formula to get you started:

"My calling is to _____ [your verbs] _____

_____ [your people group] _____ so that _____

_____[your "*so that*"] _____ ."

Pause and read this statement out loud. Is there anything you want to adjust?

Read it one more time. If you have a spouse, BFF, or teammate near you, say it out loud to them. How does it make you feel?

Living Your Calling

Consider the significance that if you can write this out in probably about forty-five to sixty minutes, how much can you do with it now that you know it?

A Calling Statement can be used as a filter for our lives, similar to a coffee filter. Picture in your mind how you use a coffee filter. I *love* coffee. I am a coffee snob. I don't love fru fru, sweet concoctions—no cream, no syrup, and no sugar for me. I love bold, black coffee. This is one of the only low-maintenance parts of me. When I make coffee, I put dry coffee grounds into the coffee filter and pour cold water over the top. What drips through into my cup is bold, rich, and delicious coffee.

CHAPTER 5: WHAT IS MY CALLING?

The same is true for our Calling Statement. It serves as a filter in which we place our:

`Decisions` `Activities` `Calendar` `Schedule` `Career` `Choices` `Skills` `Spiritual Gifts` `Pacing` `Energy` `Ministry` `Opportunities` `Time` `Invitations`

When we place those things in the filter of our Calling Statement and pour the living water of Jesus' direction over them, what drips forth is a pure, bold, and delicious life.

As you begin to apply this to your life, I want you to be reminded of a few things.

First, this is a starting place. As you walk it out, you may find a clearer word or group of words that summarize what gives your life purpose. Your Calling Statement can and should be updated whenever you discover a new clue to give it even more clarity.

Next, consider researching organizations in your area that serve a similar people group that you are called to. Find another person who has a similar passion and schedule time networking with others who can help guide you, equip you, champion you, encourage you, and instruct you in your calling.

If your work already puts you in contact with the people group you wrote on your Calling Statement, brainstorm ways that you might be able to reach out to those people in new ways. You might set up a series of coffee dates with people who are working in a similar calling. Create a focus group with the people you already know who are in your people group and ask them some strategic questions to learn from their experiences.

Keep in mind that we can pursue our purpose in the form of a side-hustle. Not everyone has the privilege of working full-time in their calling. Many of us need to provide for our family through corporate careers that provide not only a strong

> **WHEN WE PLACE THOSE THINGS IN THE FILTER OF OUR CALLING STATEMENT AND POUR THE LIVING WATER OF JESUS' DIRECTION OVER THEM, WHAT DRIPS FORTH IS A PURE, BOLD, AND DELICIOUS LIFE.**

income, but also health insurance and benefits. We show up every day and do a great job, but that job may not touch upon that craving to live a purposeful life. I have coached several clients into a side hustle of calling and purpose while maintaining what is required in their corporate careers to provide for their families.

Think about how you might be able to engage with your calling in *this* season of your life. It might be within your full-time or part-time job. It might be as a side-hustle entrepreneurial endeavor. Maybe it's in the form of a ministry, either by working with one that already exists or by starting a new one. Maybe it's by working on a personal project like writing a book or designing a course. Or, it could be as simple as leaning into a strength in your existing relationships and no longer being afraid to speak into people's lives.

There's no one "right" way to pursue your calling. Bigger is not necessarily better. Doing something more "official" or public isn't necessarily better either. The way to pursue your calling is as unique as your calling itself. And it will change with the seasons of your life.

We will work on getting specific about how to pursue your calling in your current season in the next chapter. For now, focus on crafting a Calling Statement that resonates with you and brainstorming different ways you might start living out that calling in your life.

Lastly, I want you to put down specific dates on your calendar when you will meet with God to seek more insight on your calling, and think about who can hold you accountable. I want you to tell a good friend about these important dates. I mean it. Put this book down and text your sister, BFF, or husband . . . someone that deeply cares about this pursuit, and tell them, "Hey, I'm spending some time with God working on my calling and I would love two things from you. First, please pray for me. Second, please ask me if I completed these dates with God. I can't wait to tell you how I think He is leading me." This is instant accountability.

For too many years, my calling remained in my head and heart, but I never took any action toward making it happen. I now realize the importance of having some accountability in order to move forward. I also have trusted friends who are cheering me on and lifting my head when I feel like giving up. You could also share your Calling Statement at your next small group. Just don't allow yourself to stall because you are afraid to say it out loud to someone. I know it's scary, but I am right here with you and so are they.

Speaking it out loud gives it more power to be accomplished. When we speak our calling aloud (even in its early stages), the Enemy quakes because he knows we are serious about aiming our lives for Kingdom purposes.

Aiming Your Arrow

As I consider the arrows we've been handed by God to aim our lives toward our Calling Statements, I am reminded of those who have gone before us as examples of a life well lived:

- Martin Luther King, Jr. was handed an arrow which he aimed at civil rights. Although we have a long way to go in this area, I have no doubt that his arrow has been passed along to others to keep his calling going.

- Billy Graham was handed an arrow to aim at evangelism. Though he is in heaven now, his family and organizations continue to pursue that calling.

- Queen Esther was handed an arrow which she aimed to save the Jews. Her calling was so risky, she said, "if I perish, I perish." However, her bravery to accept and aim her life led to the Jews being saved.

- Noah was handed an arrow to build an ark . . . before rain had happened. I imagine he was ridiculed and misunderstood, yet he built and loaded that ark to survive the flood.

- Moses was handed an arrow to free the Israelites from captivity. He felt ill-equipped for this assignment and yet aimed his arrow with passion and courage.

- My precious Dad was handed the arrow of ministry to pastor a church. As I stood at his bedside saying goodbye to him, it was clear he was told the words, "Well done, good and faithful servant" that his life deserved. I feel like the ministry I am pursuing is a continuation of the ministry arrow my precious father was handed.

As you grab ahold of your arrow, you might feel scared, ill-equipped, too old, too young, under educated, time poor, and under resourced. But God. Moses in Exodus 4 told God, "'Pardon your servant, LORD. I have never been eloquent, neither in the past nor since you have spoken to your servant. I am slow of speech and tongue.' The LORD said to him, 'Who gave human beings their mouths? Who makes them deaf or mute? Who gives them sight or makes them blind? Is it not I, the LORD? Now go; I will help you speak and teach you want to say.'" Repeat those words to yourself. God is telling you, "*Go*, I will help you speak and teach you what to say as you pursue your Kingdom calling."

Reflect & Respond

1. Were you able to write a Calling Statement you feel good about? How does it make you feel to read it over or even out loud?

2. Who is going to hold you accountable to living out this calling? What did that person say when you read your Calling Statement to them?

3. What ideas stand out to you about how you might be able to live out your calling in your current roles and season?

4. What is one next step you want to take to begin applying this new vision to your life?

Chapter 6
Where Do I Want to Go Next?

> *"Therefore, do not run like someone running aimlessly."* 1 Corinthians 9:26

Are you familiar with the "One in Sixty Rule"?

According to Randall Turner,

> *". . . the rule is that for every 1° you are off course, you will end up being 1 mile off course after traveling 60 miles. Consequently, getting just 1° off course at the start will result in you becoming farther off course the longer you travel.*
>
> *Imagine you're on a flight from New York's JFK Airport to Tokyo's Narita International Airport. The flight takes about 14 hours. If your plane is just 1° off course from the beginning, after flying 6,755 miles you'd end up 112 miles away from Tokyo! This would put your plane either somewhere over the Sea of Japan or the Pacific Ocean, and you'd be running low on fuel. If that happened to you, I think a little panic would begin setting in. Because neither you nor I think your airplane makes a very good cruise ship."*

All this drama caused by being off course just *one* degree.

The same is true for our lives. If we fail to examine the current trajectory of our habits, decisions, and choices, we can find ourselves, over time, reaching the wrong destination and becoming the wrong person.

What is it for you? It could be that being one percent off on getting your annual checkups allows diseased cells to grow too long and not be cured. If you continue on the trajectory of an over-packed life, you could find stress and burnout requiring you to pause things rather than adjust them to create margin.

> IF I KEEP MY SAME PACE, HABITS, AND DIRECTION IN THESE AREAS OVER THE NEXT YEAR, WILL I BECOME THE PERSON THAT I WANT TO BE?

Let's look at the simple act of flossing your teeth. You've known you needed to for months, years, or decades. You've just never woven the habit into your daily routine. Then, your gums start to bleed and a tooth starts to ache. By the time you head for a root canal, it no longer matters if you start flossing your teeth. You've missed your opportunity. Flossing is a one degree tweak every morning that takes less than a minute. But what a long-term impact ignoring this habit can make on your health.

Now apply that same philosophy to your finances or relationships. You may find the more you remain on your current pathway, the further you get from the things you need and value. Yet, by the time you realize it, it may be too late to make a meaningful course correction.

Of course, as Christians, we ultimately want to become more like Jesus. That requires the spiritual habits of reading His Word, following His example with others, and giving Him access to your heart and mind. You are reading this today for a reason. God is getting your attention about some habit He wants you to course correct.

What do your current choices, pace, and habits lead you into? Are they helping you look more like Jesus? Take a moment to glance back at the Life Wheel work you previously did in the introduction to Part II and ask yourself this question: "If I keep my same pace, habits, and direction in these areas over the next year, will I become the person that I want to be? Who am I becoming?"

What is a one degree change you can make that could significantly change the person you are becoming?

Choosing Your Destination

In the previous chapter, you defined your calling: the overarching purpose of your life. Now it's time to name *how* you will accomplish that overarching purpose.

As I teach about calling to large groups in conferences, one of the hardest things to punctuate for the audience after their Calling Statement is what their first step should be toward that ultimate goal. They know where they want to end up—fulfilling their Calling Statement—but they don't know how to get there from where they are now.

The truth is that there are many paths from where you are now toward your ultimate goal or calling. Some will be easier than others, some are more suited to you than others, but there's no one right way to pursue your calling. After assessing your options, you'll need to pick a path and start walking. Many times, action will lead to greater clarity, so we just have to get moving, stepping out in faith that God will reveal more when the time is right.

For now, your job is to get curious about the paths available to you. You need to become a keen observer of yourself and start researching your calling, networking with others who have similar people groups or causes, and learning the skills for your calling.

Remember, your Calling Statement works like a filter, and now you've got to run all your options through that filter. Every time you do something new, ask yourself, "Does this align with my calling? Does this bring me life? Does this feel like a Kingdom purpose for me?" You'll constantly learn more about how you want to live your calling out, and you will also learn how to adjust your Calling Statement to be an even better filter.

Think of it like this. When you begin to identify your calling, you find your highway and start driving down it, but sometimes there are still a lot of lanes. As you become more certain about your unique calling, you can change lanes until you're in the one that's exactly right for you for the season you're in.

Let's recall that your life is assigned both roles and a calling. As you create detailed goals about your calling, you also need to be very clear about the roles that are required of you in your current season. Please review any roles you noted from the previous chapter and make sure you are being realistic about how much time you have for your calling while you fulfill all of your God-given roles. This will help you determine how much time and energy you can realistically invest in both your roles and your callings. It's easy to overestimate what you can do in a week, yet underestimate what you can accomplish over a year. It also helps to consider how you might move closer to your calling while still staying within your current and necessary roles. If you have several small children at home, for example, you probably can't pursue your calling by being an overseas missionary right now. But maybe you could take one afternoon a month to volunteer locally or research the country you are called to.

Remember, this is a life-long journey, and it may take years to reach your dream goal. That's ok. The important thing is that you're moving closer to your target—the right target for you.

I had to learn this myself. Once I had identified that my passion was to work with, minister to, and help women, I needed to figure out where these women were and how I could best serve them. I had a fairly large jump start because I had volunteered in women's ministry at our church for years and was given the honor to become the women's ministry director. It was then that I ended up speaking to an executive coach from our church, Joan.

I took a brave step to reach out to her and have lunch. I shared that I loved working with the women at our church, yet as the church approached a new direction to eliminate gender-specific ministries, I was given a role as a women's life group director. I was grateful for this role and learned so much in it, but I explained to Joan that I missed the ability to watch women come alive by helping them unwrap their unique personalities and callings like I had done as the women's ministry director.

Joan listened intently and explained to me that I had a "coaching" leadership style. She point blank asked me if I had ever considered coaching. She affirmed me as she said, "Lisa, you are already a coach. Now you need training and certifications." That was when the word "equip" was added to my Calling Statement. As a coach and speaker, I had the ability to equip women to see themselves uniquely and create a life that was purposefully distinctive. Within that same year, I enrolled in the Christian Coach Institute and began the life coaching certification process.

The steps I took after writing my Calling Statement were:

1. Networking with others who could bring clarity to my calling (Joan).

2. Adjusting my Calling Statement to include a word I had not yet considered (equip).

3. Investigating the necessary education required for me to shift from being a women's ministry director and life group director to a Board-Certified Life Coach.

4. Enrolling in coaching certification.

These action steps were all important to keep me moving toward my life destination and calling.

One thing to clarify here is that hindsight is always 20/20. Looking back and seeing the four action steps above is easy. It looks like a straight line, but there were other networking conversations I had that didn't lead me very far. There were starts and stops. But there were not quitting points. I kept praying and pursuing the life I wanted and felt God had for me.

You may go on some detours. You may think you've found a short cut that ends up being a dead-end. Your car may break down and set you back weeks or months. It's all part of the process. If you're prepared for these kinds of obstacles, you don't have to let them discourage you. Just pick yourself up, dust yourself off, reach out to your encouraging friend for support, and keep going.

Looking Back to Plan Forward

My tagline for my coaching business last year was "Turning your dreams into decisions." As a coach, I find clients dream of various results. Some dream of impacting un-homed individuals in their city. Others dream of writing a book, start a ministry, or launching a business of their own. Some dream of having the courage to resign one career in order to pursue another. Some dreams, however, are more practical, like saving money or improving their health. In each case, however, pursuing and reaching a dream involves a decision to make it happen.

> DECISIONS REQUIRE OFFLOADING OPTIONS AND CUTTING THEM OUT OF YOUR PRIORITIES. DECISIONS MEAN SAYING "NO" TO ONE THING IN ORDER TO SAY "YES" TO ANOTHER.

The word decision comes from the prefix *de* meaning "off" or "down" and *caedere* meaning "to cut." Decisions require offloading options and cutting them out of your priorities. Decisions mean saying "no" to one thing in order to say "yes" to another. Often, the "no" we give is to something good in order to make space for the "yes" of something better as we pursue a dream in our lives. If you decide not to decide, I want to remind you of the lyrics of an 80s band, RUSH: "If you choose not to decide, you still have made a choice." So, you can close this chapter and choose to not make a decision that is needed, but you have still made a choice.

In this section, I'll teach you to look back in order to plan ahead. I will give you a series of prompts through five strategic questions. Then, you apply the prompts to watch the story unfold for how to plan for the future.

Let's begin by grabbing your journal, opening a note on your phone, or using your preferred way to record your activity. Write down today's date. Next, go back two years from today. Write that date down and envision where you were in your life at that time. Follow through by writing down everything you accomplished or achieved during the past two years. Go ahead, start documenting all that God has allowed you to achieve. I'll wait. Nothing is too insignificant to record. Our minds tend to go to practical things like "lost ten pounds" or "got promoted at work." But, accomplishments like "staying married," "walking away," "holding my tongue," "used my voice," "set a boundary," etc. are all significant accomplishments, though hard to quantify or measure.

What did you experience during that exercise? If you're like most people, you were encouraged by how much you've actually accomplished. You see, we tend to just plow forward through life without reflecting or documenting all we've accomplished. We need to learn to reflect, celebrate, and respond in gratitude for all God has allowed us to maneuver in our lives.

If you had a hard time identifying accomplishments, here are a few tips. Like I said above, we tend to only view accomplishments as things we can measure like weight loss, muscle gain, clients signed, money saved, workouts completed, etc. But sometimes, our greatest accomplishments are soft skills like holding our tongue, the perseverance to remain in a relationship, the courage to leave a toxic relationship, taking the time required to grieve. These things can't be measured, but they are huge accomplishments.

Second, we tend to view achievements in terms of our professional life, but achievements in our personal life are equally important, if not more important. Holding your temper while parenting toddlers is an achievement. Setting boundaries with a family member is an achievement. Don't dismiss personal accomplishments, either. Last year, my husband and I cleaned out our attic which had over thirty-three years of accumulation within it. It was a huge accomplishment that we had been avoiding and it is a beautiful illustration that I need to remove clutter in other areas of my life (like my desk, my mind, and my calendar).

Take a moment to add to your list if anything came up when you thought about things you can't measure or that are in your personal life.

As you glance over the above list, it represents a life that is already in motion. That is why it's important that we look back to see the momentum we've created in our lives. One of my favorite secular coaches, Mel Robbins, compares it to when our local coffee shop offers us a punch card to get a free coffee after we make ten coffee purchases. Typically, human nature just tosses that into the trash can. However, if two of the punches are already punched, we are likely to keep going and use the card because there is already momentum toward a goal.

This list also allows you to reflect on God's provision and protection. As noted in Joshua 4:20, the Israelites understood the importance of this: "And Joshua set up at Gilgal the twelve stones they had taken out of the Jordan. He said to the Israelites, 'In the future when your descendants ask their parents, *'What do these stones mean?'* tell them, *'Israel crossed the Jordan on dry ground.'*" (Emphasis mine.) By remembering the stones, the Israelites were remembering God's faithful provisions as they participated with him by walking across the Jordan. We must also remember what God has given us. While some of the big things God has done in the past are easier to remember, we have a bad memory when it comes to the smaller things He faithfully provides.

Continue, Begin, Pause, End

You picked up this book because you probably have something—a dream, goal, or vision—that you want to make into a reality. Great! I'm going to help you get there.

But as you've probably started to notice, I'm interested in encouraging a deeper change than simply reaching a goal. (As amazing as that is!) What we're really working toward is helping you become the person God created you to be, which encompasses all areas of your life. So, before we work on naming the specific big goal you will work toward over the next year or two, I want you to take some time to identify some smaller areas for improvement in your life as a whole.

Let's revisit the Life Wheel with the seven areas of life. If you didn't do it before, or if something has changed since then, go ahead and rate your satisfaction in each area now.

CHAPTER 6: WHERE DO I WANT TO GO NEXT?

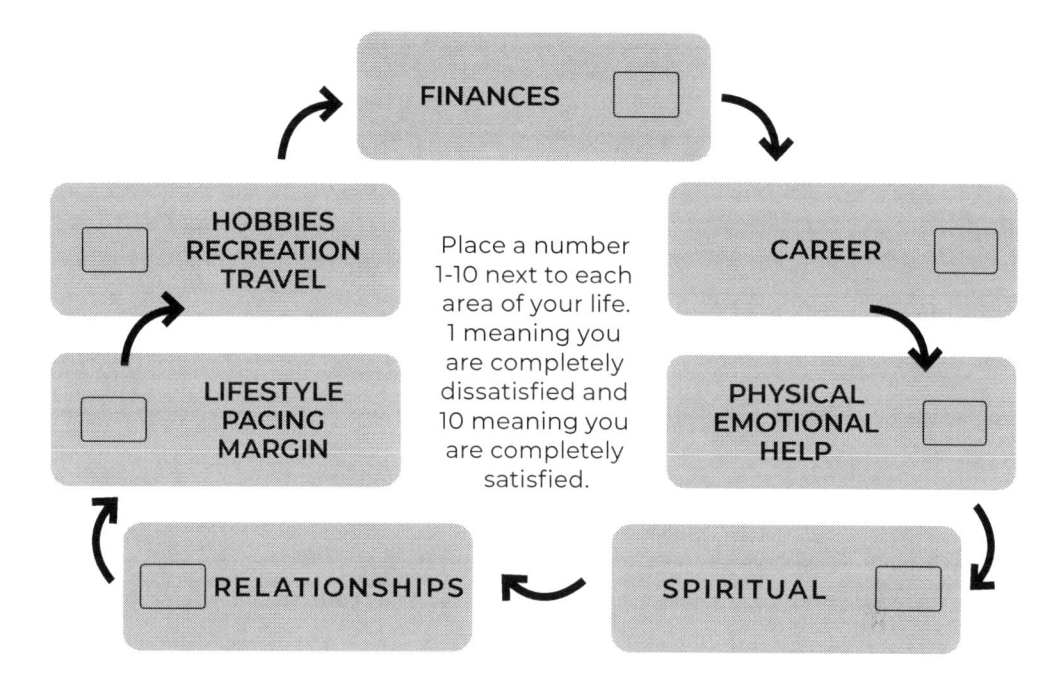

```
                    FINANCES  [ ]
        ↗                              ↘
HOBBIES                                      CAREER  [ ]
RECREATION    Place a number
[ ] TRAVEL    1-10 next to each
              area of your life.
              1 meaning you
              are completely                 PHYSICAL
LIFESTYLE     dissatisfied and               EMOTIONAL  [ ]
[ ] PACING    10 meaning you                 HELP
MARGIN        are completely
              satisfied.
        ↑                              ↘
     [ ] RELATIONSHIPS  ↙       SPIRITUAL  [ ]
```

These areas are all interconnected, and they all have to be in alignment to help you pursue your calling effectively.

Most women I work with know how they want their lives to change in one or two areas, but they will be so much more successful if they take a moment to think about all of these areas and articulate how they want to show up in each one.

To help you do this, we're going to take a moment to look at your life from a bird's eye view and consider how you want it to change in four ways: continue, begin, pause, and end.

- What do you want to *continue* in your life, and why?
- What do you need to *begin* in your life, and why?
- What do you need to *pause* in your life, and why?
- What needs to *end* in your life, and why?

Do not skip over the addition of "why" in each scenario. If you don't know why you need or want something in your life, then you won't be motivated. Your goal will be vague or you will find it easy to give up when moving forward gets hard. Your "why" is very important. It's like a mini Calling Statement for each goal.

For example, at one point, I realized that I needed to stop teaching the weekly Pilates classes that I'd been leading for two years. There were only two classes per week and one class during the weekend each month. But I realized that while I enjoyed it and was good at it, it was a hobby and the same four or five plus hours would have a better ROI if invested in my business or my family. I needed to let teaching those classes end *because* I wanted to spend more time on my business and with my family. Naming my "why" made it easier to say "no" and will help me stick with my decision if I'm asked to return.

For each thing you write down during the exercise, remember that the "why" is the most important part.

Let's start small here and identify only one to three goals to focus on in each of these four categories. If you name too many things to continue, begin, pause, or end, you could get overwhelmed and do nothing at all. Remember, you can always revisit this exercise quarterly.

What Needs to Continue and Why?

What is working in your life? Which of the life areas did you score highly, and what is going particularly well in those areas?

For me, the pace of my life is really good. I feel more in control of my time and energy. Also, though I no longer teach Pilates, I still take about six hours of classes every week. That workout routine is working for my health and my schedule, so that's something I want to continue.

What is it for you?

I am reminded of the passage in Nehemiah 6:3 when Sanballat asked to meet with Nehemiah, and Nehemiah replied, "I am carrying on a great project and cannot go down. Why should the work stop while I leave it and go down to you?" There will always be some person, task, or project tempting you to put something that is serving you well down. But you can draw strength from identifying what is working and why, so that you are prepared to keep going in that area.

Some things I definitely want to continue are:

1. _____
   Why: _____
2. _____
   Why: _____
3. _____
   Why: _____

What Needs to Begin and Why?

When you look over your life areas, which ones need the most attention? What do you need to start doing to increase your satisfaction in those areas? Examples from clients I've worked with include beginning to get up an hour earlier, reclaim their voice, save for retirement, write a book, launch a ministry, make time for friendships, and more.

I know you may have many things you could write down, but try to limit yourself to three for now. Once you've mastered those, you can always add more. Try to pick some that feel like they'll make the biggest impact on your satisfaction but require the least effort. If you achieve them quickly, it will give you momentum to begin something else next.

Some things I want to begin are:

1. _____
   Why: _____
2. _____
   Why: _____
3. _____
   Why: _____

What Needs to Pause and Why?

This is not an ending, but a pause. It's for things that have served you well over the last year, but in the next year, quarter, or season, you need to pause to make room for the things you will begin. It may be evening commitments, the Saturday morning running club, your weekly or monthly book club, or your responsibilities as soccer coach or PTA officer.

Sometimes, we are afraid to pause something because we think we will lose it or not be able to step back into it. So, I will introduce the concept of the shelf. It is an imaginary shelf for ideas, paused commitments, and other engagements, and it is where you will house the things you are pausing. Just like your Christmas décor is housed on a shelf in your attic or basement, and you know exactly where to go to get it when you need it. You can place paused commitments on that shelf, knowing you can return to them when the time is right.

Some things I want to pause are:

1. _____
   Why: _____
2. _____
   Why: _____
3. _____
   Why: _____

What Needs to End and Why?

In his book *Necessary Endings*, Henry Cloud asserts, "Without the ability to end things, people stay stuck, never becoming who they are meant to be, never accomplishing all that their talents and abilities should afford them." Choosing what to let go of is an essential step because that's how you make room for what you want to begin.

This can be something that has been good for a time, but needs to end in order to create space for something great. Or it could be something that used to be really good, but over time, it has stopped serving you well. Or it might be something you never enjoyed but did out of obligation or by default. Look back at the life areas you rated the lowest. What activities or habits are contributing to that low satisfaction?

Is that thing you keep doing CPR on something that God has asked you to lay down? Give yourself time to confirm it with God and time to grieve. Remember the bigger the ending, the more time you will need to grieve it. This step is so important, and often so difficult to fulfill and process, that I devoted the next chapter to helping you through it.

For now, write down anything that you're aware of wanting or needing to end in your life. It could be something that is not bringing you joy, that is taking time away from something more important, or that is actually toxic in your life. Remember to include your "why" for each one.

Often, letting things end is harder than beginning something, so you will need your "why" to help you stay strong! Your "whys" might be the things you already wrote down that you want to begin. It can help to compare the thing you're letting go of to the thing you're grabbing hold of to remind yourself how great the new thing is going to be.

Some things I want or need to end are:

1. _____

    Why: _____

2. _____

    Why: _____

3. _____

    Why: _____

YOUR CONFIDENCE COMPASS

Name Your Mountaintop

Your Calling Statement names what you want to accomplish with your life. Now, it's time to name some goals that you want to reach as part of that bigger calling.

For now, I want you to start with one. This should be something you'd feel really proud of but not necessarily the only or last thing you'll do with your life. It should be something you think you could probably accomplish in a few years, maybe up to five. This is your big goal. You want to end up with your master's degree, you want to launch your own business, or you want to write a book. That is your target goal—the way will you fulfill your purpose.

> THE SAME IS TRUE FOR OUR GOALS. YOU HAVE YOUR MOUNTAINTOP GOAL. THEN, YOU NEED TO CREATE BASECAMPS (MINI-GOALS) ALONG THE WAY.

Once we have a clear target, we can reverse engineer what has to happen strategically to move forward one step at a time. I had the honor to coach someone who successfully climbed Mt. Kilimijaro. Yep, amazing, right? One of the mindset images that came from listening to that experience is that no one climbs straight to the top of the mountain. They prepare for months before they arrive at the foot of the mountain. Then, they create basecamps along the way and when they reach one, they rest, eat, and assess their health and the weather. They sleep and then set out for basecamp two the next day. The same is true for our goals. You have your mountaintop goal. Then, you need to create basecamps (mini-goals) along the way. We'll address basecamps in Chapter 8, but for now, we have to get clear on what your mountaintop is.

Let's get ready to dream. I want you to envision what fully living out your calling would look like. Pretend you have plenty of time, money, education, etc. What do you see?

- A non-profit started to help vulnerable populations or the unhoused.
- Training leaders to minister in Africa
- A counseling center scaled to fit your season of life.

- Staff hired and trained to take your business to the next level.
- Your book getting published.
- Starting a group at your church or community to serve abused women.
- Helping addicts get sober.

So, what is your end goal? Start by writing down a list of possible mountaintop goals you might pursue as part of your calling. Don't be afraid to dream big!

I Would Love to Live Out My Calling By: _____

Next, narrow down your list until one stands out to you, keeping in mind the roles you're occupying in this season.

My Roles in This Season: _____

In light of your list of possible mountaintop goals and your current roles, determine what your first mountaintop goal is.

My First Mountaintop Goal to Pursue My Calling Is: _____

_____

Now, consider the timeframe for your goal. You may or may not reach your goal in that timeframe, but it helps to have one. Deadlines help keep us motivated and plan our time effectively. Be sure to work in a margin of error for things going wrong. Will it take you a year to reach your dream? Six months?

What you envisioned is your end goal, your mountaintop. It's beautiful and I see it with you and for you. But the only way it will become a reality is if you take action to make it happen. This is where self-leadership comes in. You are the only person who can begin to take the steps necessary to reach that dream.

If you have an idea (or even if you don't!), this is a great time to reach out to someone who's done something similar. How long did it take them? What do they recommend you do on your journey? What do they wish they had known at the start?

I Want to Accomplish This Goal By _____

An example of a financial goal for an accountant looks like this:

> **My Roles in This Season:** Accountant, Mother to Adult Children
>
> **My First Mountaintop Goal:** Save $10,000 a year for retirement, so I can be a loving presence and an example of Christ for my grandchildren.
>
> **I Want to Accomplish This Goal By:** The end of this year

It might be a good idea at this point to review the way that God has wired you beautifully for your calling. State out loud: "My SHOE personality is: _____. It will help me achieve this goal by: _____."

I've instructed you to start with just one mountaintop goal, but especially if your goal is fairly modest and feels doable, it's ok if you want to pick a second one as well. Still, I encourage you to keep it simple rather than trying to take on too much at once. Each mountaintop you reach will build your confidence, and each journey will prepare you for the one that follows.

Who is God Calling Me to Become?

You worked hard to clarify your calling: the purpose God has for your life. Now it's time to consider what kind of person does that calling require you to be. Self-awareness that leads to self-reflection represents the self-leadership required to keep growing and evolving. You are never too old or young to grow.

> THE PERSON YOU ARE BECOMING HAS THE STRENGTH TO MAKE SACRIFICES AND THE INSIGHT TO INVEST IN AREAS OF YOUR LIFE THAT HAVE THE LARGEST ROI ON YOU.

The person you are becoming will be the person with the courage to move forward in the midst of a painful job loss, career change, divorce, or even the death of someone significant in your life. The person you are becoming will take risks to network with those who can advise you

CHAPTER 6: WHERE DO I WANT TO GO NEXT?

on your new calling. The person you are becoming is learning new skills and trying things you've never done before. The person you are becoming has the strength to make sacrifices and the insight to invest in areas of your life that have the largest ROI on you.

Remember that God will equip you for the calling He's given you. Likewise, He will sustain you through any challenges or hardship you encounter.

When we consider the season we are in and the cards life has dealt us, we will ask one of the most profound questions we can ask ourselves: "What does this situation require of me?"

- If your marriage is hanging on by a thread, the situation may require counseling and listening more than talking.

- If you've retired early, the situation may require you learning a new skill to launch a part-time side hustle.

- If you want to write a book, the situation will require research, time on your calendar, and connecting to publishers and editors.

- If you want to recreate your life after the loss of a loved one, the situation will require you to learn the new skill of independence.

Remember, we can't control a lot of what happens in life, but we *can* control our response to it. No matter what life has dealt us, we can decide how we want to move forward.

You might be reading this saying, "Lisa, you have no idea what I'm facing. I cannot do this on my own." To which I would reply, "You are right. We can practice self-leadership and even have some success with that. However, if you are facing major life reinvention and adjustment, we must tap into the power of God our Father." Galatians 5:22-23 highlights that fruits of the Spirit we possess as a power greater than ourselves takes our willing obedience and empowers it with the divine Spirit of God. There was an old gospel song that we used to sing that said, "little is much when God is in it." We bring our little and God adds His might.

Everything that happens in your life works together to help you become the person God has called you to be. Trust in His purposes for life, even when the going gets tough. Romans 5:3-5 (NLT) reminds us of this: "We can rejoice, too, when we run into problems and trials, for we know that they help us develop endurance. And endurance develops strength of character, and character strengthens our confident hope of salvation. And this hope will not lead to disappointment."

Ultimately, you're called not just by someone and for something but also to *be* someone—the confident, unique woman God created you to be.

Starting With the End in Mind

Rick Warren says, "Tell me what you're committed to, and I'll tell you what you'll be in twenty years, because we become whatever we're committed to."

Your commitments shape your life more than anything else. Your commitments can develop you or they can destroy you, but either way, they will define you. You get to decide.

In my life and as a Confidence Coach, I have learned the truth that starting with the self-awareness portion of our journey is crucial. Yet, self-awareness and discovery that does not lead to self-leadership is just a lot of information. Looking at this in a different way, awareness without action is just information. On the flip side, action without awareness can be misplaced, at best, or dysfunctional, at worst.

> **SELF-AWARENESS AND DISCOVERY THAT DOES NOT LEAD TO SELF-LEADERSHIP IS JUST A LOT OF INFORMATION.**

James Clear puts it this way, "Every action you take is a vote for the person you want to become." We have to know who we want to become and then take action to make that a reality.

It's going to require commitment. Leadership experts agree that anything worthwhile, valuable, and desirable is hard work. Everyone wants the results, but are you willing to put in the work to get those results? It's like deciding you want to be able to run a 10k race. The only way you're going to reach that goal is by putting in the miles on the treadmill or trail. Intentions are great, but they only matter if you back them up with action.

As we conclude, I want to congratulate you for being honest with yourself. You have self-reflected and identified several areas of your life that you want to change. You also wrote them down, which research show increases your likelihood of accomplishing them. Now, let's take two more steps.

First, read your mountaintop goal out loud to yourself.

> "I want to save $10,000 by the end of this year."
>
> "I want to write a book by this time next year."
>
> "I want to enroll for my master's degree in the fall."

Next, identify one or two trusted people in your life who will support you to achieve this goal. Not your grumpy coworker or discouraging sister. You know who they are. Now, schedule a coffee date or Zoom call to let them know you are serious about turning your self-discovery into self-leadership. Ask them to hold you accountable to the various basecamp mini-goals that will be required to get to the top of your mountain.

My BFFs, Janet and Wendy, are my consistent accountability partners. First, they love me and want me to accomplish the goals I have for my life. We've talked about them, prayed about them, and they have asked me from time to time throughout our discussions, "Do you want me to hold you accountable to this?" When I shifted my tried and true six-days-a-week Pilates workouts at a studio to purchasing my own Reformer at home, I knew I would be tempted to cheat. Janet was the first person I told about this temptation and she was willing to ask me about my in-home workouts. She has made it easy for me to trip and triumph and keep going. Who is that person for you?

In the next chapter, we'll look more carefully at how to let go of the parts of our lives that may be holding us back from pursuing our calling. Endings are just as important as beginnings, so we need to know how to end things well so we can move into the future.

Reflect & Respond

1. How does it feel to have named your mountaintop goal? For most people, it's a mix of exciting and scary. Take a moment to name your feelings, including what feels scary about naming your mountaintop goal. Then, remind yourself that the journey matters more than the destination, because the journey is what shapes you into the person you're meant to be.

2. Think about how you could remind yourself of your mountaintop goal visually. Is there a quote, photo, or object that represents that goal that you could display somewhere prominent? Some people like to make a vision board. Others like to keep it simple with a Post-it Note on the bathroom mirror. What can you do to keep your goal front and center in your mind?

3. Which of your smaller Life Wheel goals feels the most exciting? Which feels the most difficult? Consider what you might do to set yourself up for success for that goal, such as removing temptation, working toward your goal with a friend, or creating a visual way to track your progress.

Chapter 7
How Do I Let Go When Things End?

> *"Forget the former things; do not dwell on the past. See, I am doing a new thing! Now it springs up; do you not perceive it? I am making a way in the wilderness and streams in the wasteland."*
>
> Isaiah 43:18-19

I had enjoyed a decade at Proverbs 31 Ministries as an Executive Director. I loved my Ministry Team that had blossomed to over twenty-two members at that point. I had grown as a leader and I loved leading and developing other leaders through their roles. However, in late 2021, God started to reveal that I should be laying that role down for a myriad of reasons. The strange thing was that I never felt true peace about it. At least not the kind of peace I expected. When I considered laying this role down, I was sad. I had equated sadness with lack of peace.

It was one random day when I was scrolling social media that I was stopped dead in my tracks by a post from Dr. Caroline Leaf: *"It's ok to be sad about the right decision."* I read and re-read that quote. I felt the very peace I was looking for wash over me. In order for my best life to unfold, my calling to grow, and my seasons to shift, I needed to say goodbye to my role at Proverbs 31 Ministries. I will be forever grateful for all the ministry experience I gained throughout those ten years. But it was time for obedience. It was time to let go.

Letting Go

You feel it. God is asking you to end something, to lay something down, to walk away. You have done all you can to hang onto it. You've prayed. You've sought wise counsel. You've gone to your therapist. You have considered all the factors and weighed them carefully. But even if we're sure, that doesn't make letting go easy.

Other times, we are trying to emotionally let go of things that have already ended, not by our choice but because life includes loss. It might be a friendship that drifted into ending, our company forcing early retirement, or the permanent loss of a marriage or loved one. We might be holding on to the memory of something that has long ago ceased to be, or maybe we are still trying to chase a dream that we need to replace with something better.

> YOU CANNOT FACE AN ENDING WITHOUT FACING LOSS. EVEN ENDINGS YOU WANT REQUIRE ACKNOWLEDGING LOSS, CHANGE, AND THE NEED TO GRIEVE.

Whatever it is, whatever the reason, letting go is hard. You cannot face an ending without facing loss. Even endings you want require acknowledging loss, change, and the need to grieve. Have you ever sent a child to kindergarten or college? Have you ever retired from a job? Have you ever left one job to take the next step in your career pathway? Each of these are normal and good things, but they involve the loss of what was. If you haven't spent time actively grieving, you risk bringing something unhealthy into your new season.

I've faced loss many times throughout the last few decades of my life. It never gets easier. But I have learned so much each time I participated in God's plan to move forward. I've found that every time He asks me to lay something down, it's so He can give me something else to pick up.

But that doesn't mean we don't still feel the loss. Endings are always hard, no matter what they make room for. That's why whenever we speak about endings, we must also speak about grief. When good things end in our life, we have to learn to grieve them. Do you

CHAPTER 7: HOW DO I LET GO WHEN THINGS END?

remember when your kids started kindergarten and there was joy about this new season, yet somber awareness that lazy afternoons were over?

Life includes many endings that need to be grieved even when we want them and the endings are good. Of course, we grieve the death of anyone close to us. But we also grieve other things.

- Friendships lost to sudden betrayal or ghosting
- Partners who were unfaithful
- Business associates who took the money and ran
- Church hurt that causes us to be hardened and cynical

Even good endings in our lives need to be grieved:

- Babies too big to rock
- Sending kids to kindergarten
- High school graduation
- Retirement

I have a manifesto of sorts that includes ten habits of a confident woman. One of them is: *The confident woman grieves well so she can move forward with closure.*

This chapter will help you learn how to grieve life transitions well.

The larger the loss that you are facing, the more time it will take to grieve it as you move forward. Grieving is one of the most significant actions required to end well. If we don't take time to feel the grief, process it, pray about it, talk to a counselor about it (if needed), journal about it, or share it with a trusted friend, our unresolved grief can become baggage we drag into our new season. If you are facing a major loss in your life, please connect to your pastor and counselor.

> OUR UNRESOLVED GRIEF CAN BECOME BAGGAGE WE DRAG INTO OUR NEW SEASON.

155

Endings Are Also Beginnings

At my dad's memorial service, we received many lovely floral tributes and one special plant from close friends. I put this plant into a new pot and it sat in my family room in the same spot for over a year. During that entire time, the plant received the same amount of light, shade, and watering. However, it suddenly started to droop and die. I did everything I could think of to keep it alive to no avail. In my quiet time one morning, I sensed an impression from God as I looked over at that drooping plant.

During this season, I sensed God calling me away from a role I had enjoyed for a decade of my life. This role was with people I enjoyed and was in my wheelhouse, yet I knew that I was not called to be part of the next season of the organization. I did my due diligence by appropriately expressing my needs, engaging in honest conversations and more, yet the more I talked, the more I realized it was time to end.

As I looked at the plant that morning, it was as if I heard God whisper, "You are trying to keep something alive that has no more life in it." I knew immediately it was a confirmation from Him to resign my role. Every time I thought about it, I felt sad. It had been ten years of my life. But that is when I saw the following quote by Craig Loundsbrough: "An ending is only a beginning in disguise."

Are you trying to keep something alive that used to be good, but somehow now it's bad? Or maybe it's not bad, but it's no longer for you? Do you know you need to let it go but are resisting? What if God has something better in store for you, if only you will let the old thing end.

Perseverance is celebrated in our society. Underdogs win football games. The unlikely Olympian gets the gold because they didn't quit. And I certainly don't want to ask you to end something that God is showing you to persevere through. However, society gives us mixed messages about when it's time to quit, end, resign, or walk away. Even as I type this, I can hear my early teachers saying, "Quitters never win and winners never quit." But perhaps God has a plan that in order for you to "win" in the next season of your life and quitting is the most courageous action you can take.

CHAPTER 7: HOW DO I LET GO WHEN THINGS END?

Let's revisit Ecclesiastes 3:1-8 (BSV), a Scripture that always comforts and challenges me when facing a transition:

> *"To everything there is a season, and a time for every purpose under heaven: a time to be born* **and a time to** *die, a time to plant* **and a time to** *uproot, a time to kill* **and a time to** *heal, a time to break down* **and a time to** *build, a time to weep* **and a time to** *laugh, a time to mourn* **and a time to** *dance, a time to cast away* **stones and a time to** *gather* **stones together, a time to** *embrace* **and a time to** *refrain from embracing, a time to search* **and a time to** *count as lost, a time to keep* **and a time to** *discard, a time to tear* **and a time to** *mend, a time to be silent* **and a time to** *speak . . . "* *(emphasis added)*

As I read this passage, I am comforted by the contrast of the seasons we face. It is impossible for me to deny that endings, parting, quitting, leaving, and removing ourselves from situations are normal and covered by God's grace in our lives.

The concept of pruning is helpful as we consider stepping away. God allows good branches, dead branches, and unhealthy branches to be pruned so that we can make way for *more* fruit in our lives. Dr. Henry Cloud in *Necessary Endings* writes, "The good cannot begin until the bad ends."

This is where it's important to acknowledge our feelings of sadness, but not use them as an excuse to hang on. Just like our SHOE personality reports to us but we don't report to it, our feelings report to us. We must feel them and acknowledge them, but they do not boss us around. We can move forward even if we are sad, trusting that God has something greater in store for us and is with us in our sadness.

Ending Well

When we face endings, it's important to act in obedience to what God places before you. While endings are inevitable, *ending well is something you can control.* This will involve making sure your heart isn't hard, participating in an authentic grieving process, working through forgiveness, and having honest conversations with everyone involved.

> **WHILE ENDINGS ARE INEVITABLE, ENDING WELL IS SOMETHING YOU CAN CONTROL.**

This is where an understanding of the word "transition" comes in. Transition means "the process or a period of changing from one state or condition to another." If you've ever been the mom in the delivery room or with the mom, you know that the period of transition in labor is known to be a time of irritability, pressure, the desire to give up, need for emotional support, disorientation, self-doubt, and lack of focus for the mom. And the same is true for the seasons of transition we face in our own lives.

As I've journeyed with my mom after my dad's death, she experienced all these feelings as she has learned to move forward without the man she had walked with for sixty-six years in marriage. It was quite a transition and still is. It is one of the bravest journeys I've ever watched her walk. What does this loss or ending make possible? I don't want this to sound insensitive if you have lost a loved one, however, I have watched my mom become a powerful prayer warrior as she has learned to live without her precious husband. She wouldn't have asked for it, nor does it replace my dad in her life, but it is something beautiful that has come from her time without Dad.

For you, it may be the loss of a loved one, a pet, an unexpected ending of a job, a change in career, a move across the country, the death of a dream, the betrayal of a friendship, becoming an empty-nester, or putting that first born on a school bus for kindergarten. These are all moments of transition that represent an ending of one thing and the beginning of the next.

CHAPTER 7: HOW DO I LET GO WHEN THINGS END?

We all face endings differently, and the better we can understand our instincts when we face a transition, the better we can help ourselves through that process.

Your Transition Style

If you've picked up anything about me as a coach, you know I go back to our personality wiring to determine how to face anything new. True to form, below is an overview of how the four SHOEs respond to loss and transition.

Workboots

Workboots will often want to take action too soon. Loss for a Workboot taps into their biggest fear—feeling out of control. Their *can-do* approach to life means they feel like a change is a challenge for them to tackle before *it* tackles them. Another response to loss for a Workboot is to numb the feeling through overwork, working out, and diving into projects that serve as a distraction rather than processing the grief. Of course, these are understandable tactics to avoid the very grief they need to feel and process. As much as a Workboot will want to create a plan of action to move forward, it can be better to let the plan unfold and trust the process of letting go.

Workboot Grief Plan: Plan pause times in your week to just "be" with your feelings and ask a good friend to hold you accountable when you are using activity to avoid your pain.

Stilettos

Our Stilettos will want to avoid the pain of loss because it's just no fun at all. One of their fears is discomfort and pain, so processing loss makes them squirm. It is common for a Stiletto to be in a state of denial and use it as a permission slip to skip the feelings of sadness. Their "girls just wanna have fun" attitude can mean they create numbing strategies like overspending, overdrinking, or over-socializing to avoid the pain.

Stiletto Grief Plan: Acknowledge your desire to numb your sadness and the coping mechanisms that you use to avoid the feelings you need to process. Ask a friend to hold you accountable so that you can face your feelings instead of distracting yourself.

Mary Janes

Mary Janes will want to think their way out of grief. Most likely, the loss they are facing has messed up their perfectly laid-out plans. Grief is messy and Mary Janes don't like a mess. They may want to reason or strategize their way around it, rather than going through their sad feelings. A Mary Jane will numb themselves by pondering, musing, and contemplating so that they can understand this loss. While a portion of this is healthy in grieving, overthinking will keep the Mary Jane shackled.

Mary Jane Grief Plan: Pray for strength to accept what will feel like imperfect plans to you. Enlist a friend who can help you not be too hard on yourself during this loss.

Flip Flops

Flip Flops will isolate themselves when they're grieving and pursue all the comfortable and familiar things they can find. Familiarity is very important to a Flip Flop, so an uncertain road forward can be paralyzing to them. The act of processing the feelings of loss can feel like lifting a heavy weight that their muscles are unprepared for, causing them to give up without ever trying. They numb themselves through binging movies, oversleeping, taking naps, and procrastinating even the simplest tasks.

Flip Flop Grief Plan: Resume your routines as soon as possible. Ask a friend to help you stay engaged in getting out of the house like taking short walks, seeing a movie, or even cooking a meal together.

No matter your personality, it's always good to talk to people as you walk through hard seasons. This could include talking to your pastor, counselor, or good friend. Asking a trusted companion to hold you accountable when your grief-avoidance behaviors are tempting you is also a good idea.

CHAPTER 7: HOW DO I LET GO WHEN THINGS END?

Transitions are always hard, especially if they involve letting go of something that's been a big part of your life. Be gentle with yourself. God's power is perfected in your weakness and He is close to the brokenhearted.

The 7 R's of Transition

It can help to understand more about what we all go through when we're navigating a transition. Knowing what to expect can make it a little less scary because it's less confusing and bewildering.

Let's look at seven steps you will move through if you are struggling to end something in your life or if it's already been ended for you. Please note, again, that the greater this loss is for you, the longer these steps will take, but I do believe they all apply.

1. *Recognize* the Loss.
2. *Resist* Taking on Too Much.
3. See *Reliance* as a Gift.
4. Cultivate *Resilience*.
5. *Release* Your Expectations.
6. *Regroup* With Intention.
7. *Reinvent* Yourself.

Recognize

This is the time to be honest with yourself and recognize the transition you have or are about to walk through. As you recognize it, you move closer to accepting this transition. Acknowledge it. Journal about it. Talk to a close friend or counselor (or both).

Even though it might be hard, try not to be rigid and fight the transition. I remember years ago riding a new and challenging roller coaster with our kids. I was nervous about the uncertainty of the ride ahead. I was stiff as a board riding the coaster and got jostled around pretty badly. However, the next time I rode it, I decided to take the turns as they came without resistance. Although the ride was still scary, it was smooth as I leaned into the twists and turns.

When I work with clients facing the grief of transitions, we identify a grieving chair for them to spend time in as they process this grief. (again, the bigger the loss, the longer it takes the grieve.) It may be ten minutes a day, thirty minutes a day, or an hour a week. This will help keep them from stuffing the loss and grief showing up out of nowhere in an unhealthy way in the future. When my friend Janet lost her sister, her grief counselor reminded her that grief is a gentleman. If we don't process it, it will wait for us and show itself in the future.

Grief will demand that we recognize it sooner or later, so the sooner you face it, the sooner you can move through it and past it.

Coaching Questions: What specific transition are you in? Is it a change in career, like retirement or a new position? Is it a change in your family situation (marrying off a child, your youngest going to kindergarten, etc.)? Is it the death of a marriage or the actual death of a loved one? Find a way to sit with this loss in a way that allows you to recognize and feel it. This could be mean journaling or going to counseling. Identify a grief chair where you can sit for five to twenty-five minutes a day acknowledging this season of loss, transition, and grief.

Resist

In our transitions, it is wise to resist the urge to take on too much. Don't fall prey to the lie that this transition doesn't impact you emotionally, spiritually, physically, and mentally.

When my dad died, my counselor called it a "Big T Trauma." At the same time, I experienced a very hurtful ministry challenge and a friendship betrayal at the same time I was processing my dad's death. The counselor called those things "Little t Traumas." When combined, it created loss upon loss that I needed to grieve. I kept believing as long as I was being honest and open that I could handle all of those traumas at once. Don't make the mistake I did. I should have resisted tackling one or two of those Little t Traumas until I was stronger because I was fragile from my Big T Trauma.

Grief is exhausting. Don't expect yourself to go on with your normal life as if nothing had happened. Look at your calendar and consider what you can cut out during this time, especially anything that already tends to be draining.

Coaching Question: Is there something that you should consider resisting until you are less fragile?

Reliance

Reliance is dependance upon or trust in someone or something. In times of transition, you will recover faster if you let yourself rely on others for support.

I am embarrassed to admit that I hate relying on others. *There, I said it*. I am a Three on the Enneagram. We are "get it done" kinds of people. I prefer to be capable enough to handle any transition through competence, confidence, and Jesus. But guess what? I need people, just like you do.

When I relaunched my coaching business, relying on possible leads, introductions, and connections opened more doors than I could have imagined. The season of transition when my dad died meant more responsibility for my mom. This required me to lean more into my husband, who continually rises to the occasion to help with driving, errands, and doctors' appointments.

Ultimately, we know our reliance falls squarely on relying on God Himself. There is nothing we need that He cannot and will not provide for us. Any reliance we have in our seasons of transitions starts with relying on Him.

But it doesn't end there. God has made us for community, and He wants us to bear one another's burdens (Galatians 6:2). Reach out to family and friends for both emotional and practical support during your transition. It might be picking up groceries or bringing your family a meal. Maybe they could refer you to a good counselor for professional support. Or maybe it's just them sitting with you and reminding you of all the good they see in you.

It requires both humility and courage to ask for help, but it's so worth it. It's a gift to yourself and a gift to those you rely on to have the opportunity to serve you in your time of need.

Coaching Questions:

- Admit in prayer your dependence and reliance on God and ask Him to show you people and resources you can rely on during this transition.

- Name a list of people you can start or continue a conversation with about helping you in and through your transition.

Resilience

Resilience is the ability to spring back into shape. I always think about an elastic waistband or rubber band when I think of being resilient. It stretches out and then snaps back to its natural shape.

If you've been on this planet for more than a few years, chances are good that you've already been through some hard transitions and have recovered. Depending on the loss, it may have taken weeks or months or even years, but you found your way through and started feeling like yourself again.

There is a rhythm to resiliency. We've already looked at Ecclesiastes 3:1-8, which teaches us that there is a time for everything and a season for every activity under the heavens. Look at the contrasts I've pulled to show the elastic nature of our life's seasons. A time to:

Born/Die   Plant/Uproot   Kill/Heal   Tear Down/Build   Keep/Throw Away

In your transition, allowing something to end creates space for something new ahead that God will fill in His time and according to His purpose. Remembering your need for resilience in this season will help you bend, but not break.

CHAPTER 7: HOW DO I LET GO WHEN THINGS END?

Coaching Questions:

- What is a time in your life when you were resilient? Have you raised children? You were resilient when you went from just you and your spouse to a family of three, four, or more.

- Have you lost a person who was close to you? A pet? Have you moved away from a home?

All of those things require resilience. Think about how hard that time was and the fact that you recovered, and draw strength from your former resilience.

Release

Now it's time to make room for what is coming next. In order to receive what is coming soon, we have to release our expectations of what we thought our life would look like.

Take a moment and grip your fists tightly. Pretend you are gripping the thing you lost or that ended. Do you see how you cannot receive anything new while your hands are gripped so tightly?

Now, open your hands softly. Lift your palms to the ceiling. Let your expectations go and remain open to receive what God is turning into new and good things for your future.

Release your expectations of the unknown, yet *don't release your hope*. If you hold too tightly to what you expect the season ahead to be and how you think God will answer prayers, then you set yourself up to be disappointed and potentially miss the open doors God is preparing ahead. You have heard the saying that "Expectations are premeditated resentments." The more you script these times in advance, the more disappointment or resentment you will face in your already fragile, new season.

Instead, try to release your old expectations for your life. You may need to spend some time grieving those things too. Sometimes there's the primary loss and then the secondary loss of all the other things that will be different because of that primary loss. For example, maybe you lost your corporate job with the great benefits and prestige, but that also means you won't get to go to visit the London office next summer like you had planned. There can be all kinds of expectations and plans you have to let go of in times of transition.

But endings are also beginnings. What might replace those plans you've had to release?

We can pray Psalm 5:3 that says, "to lay [our] requests before you and wait expectantly." We can be reminded that God is doing exceedingly, abundantly more than we could ask or imagine, as He says in Ephesians 3:20. If you have already thought of or imagined it, remind yourself that God wants to do abundantly more, but you cannot be the definer of what abundantly more looks like from God's perspective. This is where you rely on Him, release to Him, and receive from Him.

Coaching Questions:

- Take time to write down some of the plans and expectations you're having to release as a result of this transition. Allow yourself to grieve those losses.
- Then consider, what does this loss or ending make possible?

Regroup

Once you accept your season, you need to begin to regroup. Plans need to change when your direction changes.

When my dad died, I had to regroup in order to create space in my days, weeks, weekends, and year to care differently for my mom. I have a friend who lost their son in his early twenties in a tragic accident. This accident happened locally, and some days, they were strong enough to pass the scene of the accident, but sometimes, they needed to regroup and learn a new way home. Maybe for you, there is a part of your schedule that needs to be changed due to your transition or loss.

Transitions can often make new things possible that your previous season wouldn't allow, so it's a great time to revisit your values and determine what you want to prioritize in this new season. When I transitioned from a full-time Executive Director to an independent entrepreneur, I wanted to value a pace that ensured I was helping my mom and not working on weekends or evenings. I wanted to reclaim using my voice professionally in a strong and confident way. By naming those values, I was able to enter into that new season prioritizing those things and building them into my new habits.

It's also good to consider the good things about what you're letting go of that you want to bring with you into this new season. Ponder the legacy of a lost loved one that continues on in you. If you are facing a divorce, celebrate that your union brought you the children you have. If you've moved, what connections do you want to keep with those in your old city? What was good about your old job or position that you want to keep doing in some form?

Regrouping means considering how you want to inhabit this next season—who you want to be in this next role.

Coaching Questions:

- What are you willing to leave behind that is no longer serving you in the midst of your transition? What are four or five things about *this loss* that you want to carry forward into this new season?
- What do you want to value in this transition?
- Is there anything you want to reclaim? Maybe it's a past hobby or an attribute that you've put aside during your old season.

Reinvent

Anne Roiphe writes, "Grief is in two parts. The first is loss. The second is the remaking of life."

All transitions are an open door and provide an opportunity to grow and reinvent yourself. I want to be sensitive again here. If you've lost someone special, you won't be excited about reinventing yourself, but you will need to reinvent some things about yourself in order to grieve well and move forward.

I have a friend who lost both her parents when she was in her thirties. It was so hard and unexpected. However, after their passing, it created space for her career that catapulted her into amazing professional opportunities because she was not needed to care for aging parents in her fifties. Would she rather have her mom and dad here? Of course, but she recognized this loss made it possible for her to devote extensive time into her career.

What is it for you? Let God give you His imagination for how He sees you. In Genesis 18:10, God promises Sarah that "this time next year" she will be a mom. . . even though she was way past childbearing years. A future as a mom is what God saw for Sarah. Let God give you the faith to believe that this transition will open a pathway to reinvent part of your life, your career, yourself, your awareness, etc. With God, the possibilities are endless.

Coaching Questions:

- What do you know to be true about God through this? What Scripture is carrying you right now?

- Is there something you can start that you've never done before? Maybe something you've always dreamed of trying?

- Spend some time praying and journaling about what new possibilities are before you now and what areas of your life might be ready for reinvention because of this transition.

The Story Continues

We all go through transitions in life, some are fairly easy, while some are extremely difficult. Transitions are just a part of life. We can't avoid them. All we can do is learn to navigate them well and make the most of the new opportunities they offer.

When you're going through a transition, remember that there will be some degree of loss. Be kind to yourself as you grieve. Find a place to grieve regularly.

When endings feel unfair, remember that there is a difference between thick skin and a hard heart. Grieving well helps us keep our heart soft, even as we thicken our skin to withstand the blows of difficult circumstances. If you're tempted to harden your heart, move forward, and numb or distract yourself to keep from feeling the pain, remember that those feelings will eventually come out in an unhealthy and dysfunctional way if you don't address them now.

> **GRIEVING WELL HELPS US KEEP OUR HEART SOFT, EVEN AS WE THICKEN OUR SKIN TO WITHSTAND THE BLOWS OF DIFFICULT CIRCUMSTANCES.**

If your life was a book being written, this transition might be the end of a chapter, but it's not the end of the book. When you are ready, turn the page and watch as God writes the next chapter with new ink. Leave behind what no longer serves you, hang onto what you need, and keep your hands and your mind open to the possibilities that are opening up in your new season.

Reflect & Respond

1. Is there something you need to let go of that you've been holding onto? It could be a change you need to make, or it could be something you've already lost that you're holding onto emotionally. Ask God to show you what you need to let go of in order to pursue your calling more freely.

2. Where are you within the four personality styles of transition outlined above? What can you learn about your instinctual response to transition from looking at your SHOE personality and your grief plan?

3. Which of the seven R's feels the hardest to you? Why? How can you encourage yourself to lean into that step toward healing?

Chapter 8

How Do I Get There?

> *"We can make our plans, but the Lord determines our steps."*
>
> Proverbs 16:9 NLT

I'm a planner. I don't know if it's by nature or nurture. It seems both my parents and my siblings are planners, as well. I like to consider all of the ways that my plan could get interrupted, thwarted or ended before it has a chance to begin. That's why I chose Proverbs 16:9 for this chapter.

There are two kinds of approaches I've used in my life when I think through the Bible verse above. One approach is to plan everything I want to see happen during my annual goal-setting process, draw a bullseye around my plans, and ask God to bless the target I'm aiming at.

The second way is to pray and plan my goals, dreams, and priorities and then surrender them to God. I truly sit with these things and ask, "Have I heard you correctly, Father? May I pursue these?" I still have a target in my mind for any given area of my life. I still create action steps that will get me to the target. But I also hold these plans loosely as each passing month brings twists, turns, and obstacles. Some of the obstacles I create by my own self-sabotage. I might procrastinate the action steps that are required. Or I may get ahead of God's best for me. Then there are the obstacles life throws at me. Speeding curveballs come at me in the forms of unexpected illness of myself or a loved one, financial challenges, and life interruptions.

YOUR CONFIDENCE COMPASS

Over the years, I have learned that the key to moving forward with true confidence is to take the second approach, adjusting along the way to God's timing, life, and the consequences of my own setbacks. As much as I have wanted to blame others for why I can't arrive faster, am unable to make progress, or keep hitting walls, I must leave my excuses out of the suitcase I've packed to my destination. I have to create an action mindset by leading myself into the required steps to achieve my goals. This is where I have to trust God, but also do the work I can do.

Have you heard the saying that "God won't move a parked car?" He wants us to participate in the plans He has for our lives by first asking Him about them and paying attention to how the patterns, the words others speak to us, our experience, our spiritual gifts, and our wiring aligns with the plans ahead. It's also common for us to just start and, before you know it, we are so fixated on the target goal that we are not moving in God's timing and are operating without His blessing.

NO COMPASS CAN HELP YOU IF YOU DON'T KNOW WHERE YOU ARE NOW AND WHERE YOU'RE GOING.

The title of this book is *Your Confidence Compass*. A compass is a directional tool that helps keep you from getting off course. But no compass can help you if you don't know where you are now and where you're going. Even once we identify our destination, we have to put the car in drive and put miles behind us to reach it. This portion of the book will require you to employ self-leadership to create pathways of behavior for the life you've designed in the previous pages. You've figured out where you want to go. Now it's time to map out the path you'll take to get there.

Planning Your T.R.I.P.S.

In order to make a long trip successfully, you have to think through all the steps along the path to get there. You can't just decide you're going to drive from California to New York City and then hop in the car and drive East, hoping you'll get there. You have to consider the various routes you could take, make sure your car is in good shape, prepare financially to cover your expenses, and decide where you'll stop along the way. You will also do well to anticipate roadblocks and check the weather, maybe planning what you will do if you have to take a detour.

Achieving a big goal is no different. You'll be much more successful if you think through exactly what it will take to get from where you are to where you want to end up.

I like to use the acronym T.R.I.P.S. (Target, Reality, Investigate, Predict, Steps) to help my clients do this. Let's map out your T.R.I.P.S.

T: Target

What target are you aiming for? Where do you want to end up? This is your mountaintop goal that you named in Chapter 6. It could require a lot of side roads to get there. But it all starts with knowing where you want to go and getting really clear about the target you are taking aim at. Remember, if you're aiming at the wrong target (or not aiming at all), you have virtually no chance of hitting it. Write two or three of your dream destination targets below.

R: Reality

Next, consider where you are now in relation to your target. Your target might be to establish a workout routine five days per week. Your reality is that you are not working out at all beyond walking up the stairs to bed each night. Honestly assessing our current reality is crucial. This is where your human behavior needs to actual numbers and tangible representations of where we are so we can't lie to ourselves (like stepping on the scale to measure your weight). Being honest might mean getting a 360-degree assessment at work in order to remove blind spots.

Being honest might reveal limiting mindsets like, "I'm too old; I'm too young; I don't have enough money; I can't quit my day job; I need more education to do this dream, etc." Write down any limiting belief that might be holding you back so you know how to redirect your mindset! (*More about that in Chapter 10.*) While these beliefs may not be accurate, they are part of your current reality, so it's important to acknowledge them.

This is also a great place to bring in some of the things you learned about yourself in Part I of this book. What strengths and weaknesses do you bring that will impact your journey toward this goal? How are you wired to be realistic, pessimistic, or overly positive?

I: Investigate

Investigate options for creating a clearer pathway toward your target. Look at what you wrote down for your reality. There's a good chance you've listed several limiting mindsets that you'll need to clear up before you can move forward. To put it more bluntly, you're probably using many of the things you listed as excuses. You don't want to take excuses with you on your trip.

For example, maybe you wrote, "I'm too old." Who told you that? Unless your dream literally is a job that has an age requirement, you are believing a lie that will keep you from taking your next steps. There are hundreds of people who start a second career when they are over fifty. I have a friend who was a successful bank executive who retired by fifty, went to seminary, and now pastors around the East Coast.

Some of what you wrote might be an accurate statement about your reality, but you don't have to let it hold you back. Now is the time to investigate possible ways you might change that reality. For example, maybe you wrote, "I don't have enough money." Rather than use money as an excuse, let's use this time to brainstorm ways to make money. It could be selling some pieces you own, getting a loan, cutting your expenses by selling your car and using public transportation, meal planning instead of eating out, only wearing what you have in your closet for a year, or becoming an Uber driver for a season to supplement your income.

Similarly, maybe you wrote something like, "I can't quit my day job," which in your mind meant "I don't have enough time to pursue my dream." Again, you don't have to let this reality—needing to keep working at your day job—hold you back. I coach dozens of leaders who are the breadwinners for their families and provide great income and solid benefits that are necessary, yet are still able to allocate several hours a week or month to pursue their ultimate calling. You can stop scrolling social media and use those hours to research, educate, or equip yourself with the skills you need for a new season ahead.

Maybe part of your reality is that you need additional education or qualifications to accomplish your dream. What are the possible ways you might get that? Start today to research the education required to reach your target goal. Is it getting a master's degree? Going to seminary? Attaining some form of professional certification? This research phase will give you tangible action steps for how much this will cost, how long it will take, and how to budget your money and time in order to hit your target.

The goal of Investigate is to explore your options and think outside the box, so you can break free of those limiting mindsets.

P: Predict

Predict the obstacles ahead. Based on your investigation of the options above, predict the obstacles you might face if you chose to pursue one or more of those paths. Again, this is a good time to consider what you've learned about yourself in our previous chapters and how your strengths and weaknesses will help you arrive at your destination or hinder you from getting there.

Everyone encounters obstacles. But you want to do what you can to prepare for predictable ones. It's like when you see that red line on your GPS route and the accident symbol. You can't change the fact that there's an obstacle ahead, but you can adjust so that the impact of it is not as bad.

In real life, you won't be able to anticipate all of the obstacles you'll face, but you probably know yourself well enough to predict a few like, a lack of follow through; starting but not finishing; giving up when it gets hard; not budgeting enough time to take steps forward; or a fear of failure or success. As humans, we are often our own worst enemy, because we consciously or subconsciously sabotage our own success.

Think about what's happened when you've tried to go after big goals in the past. Where did you get stuck or give up? Which parts felt particularly hard?

Once you've identified a few obstacles you're likely to face, think about how you might plan now to minimize their impact. This might involve letting go of other commitments in order to make room for this new pursuit.

One good way to maneuver around the obstacles you identify is through accountability. Who is someone in your life that wants you to hit your target? No, not your competitive neighbor or negative family member, but who is the cheerleader in your life who will be thrilled to hear you making plans to hit your target? Reach out to them and share about the work you are doing in this book. Ask them to hold you accountable to keep moving forward, especially as you begin your "trip" and hit bumps in the road. This could also be a good time to hire a coach. Most of the clients I coach are high-functioning professionals who use our monthly coaching meetings as accountability sessions so they can keep pursuing their plans.

S: Steps

What are the steps you need to take to move forward toward your goal? I coach my clients to reverse engineer the path to their mountaintop goals. It starts with having the end goal in mind (your fulfilled dream) and stepping backwards mentally in order to create action goals that will get you there.

When I decided to write this book, I had to reverse engineer my goals. Here is what they were:

- Confirm subject matter and gather all related content.
- Investigate whether to traditionally publish or self-publish.

CHAPTER 8: HOW DO I GET THERE?

- Determine who to meet about traditional publishing and set a meeting.
- Determine who to meet about self-publishing and set a meeting.
- Create goals for the book that supports investing time and money into it.
- Develop a budget for time and money required to produce a book.
- Write the first draft of the manuscript.
- Make the edits.
- Investigate focus group options.
- Interview local and national PR/Marketing options.
- Identify networking group ideas to help promote the book.
- Plan a launch party.
- Celebrate a major dream coming true.

Each one of the goals above also had dates associated with them to make sure I could keep all the moving parts on schedule up through the publish date.

It's time to turn all your dreaming into action. Take all of the information you've collected above and create detailed action steps. Reverse engineer the dates on your calendar from your target.

Let's look at an example of becoming a therapist, putting our T.R.I.P.S. together.

Target: Become a therapist.

Reality: I work as an accountant in corporate America. I love people and am a natural listener. But I don't have a counseling degree and don't know if I can really succeed in school at my age.

Investigate: How much of my schooling transfers to getting a degree in counseling? How long will it take me to get my degree while working full-time? Do I need internship hours to graduate? How much can I make annually as a full-time therapist? (Create a budget based on this answer.) Who do I need to get support from in this process (babysitters, grandparents, cooperative spouse, etc.)?

Note: *You will get answers to the questions above as part of your Investigate step.*

Predict: I know I love the idea of being a therapist, but in the past, I have lacked follow-through when I have studied in other areas. I will need a solid time management plan or I could waste the time and money required to get me over the finish line. I need to lay down coaching my kids soccer team and being the treasurer of the PTA during this season to create time. I typically like to sleep in Saturday mornings, so I will need to slate that time to get up and study at a coffee shop and coordinate that with my spouse or partner.

Steps:

- Research where to attain my degree.
- Use money from my savings account or 401K to fund my education.
- Register for continuing education (due by May 1).
- Study five hours a week.
- Plan four weekends a year for longer study times.
- Let my sister-in-law and my BFF hold me accountable by reaching out to me each week to check on my progress.
- Graduate in 2026.
- Begin taking clients within three months of graduation

After you have mapped out your T.R.I.P.S., you should restart the process for your next goal.

Now it's your turn to put this into practice.

Trip

My Mountaintop Goals:

1. _____
2. _____
3. _____

Reality

Where I Am Now in Relation to My Goals:

1. _____
2. _____
3. _____

Investigate

What I Discovered About the Path to Each of My Goals:

1. _____
2. _____
3. _____

Predict

Obstacles I Might Face with Each Goal and How I'll Handle Them:

1. _____
2. _____
3. _____

Steps

1. _____
2. _____
3. _____

Setting Up Basecamps

When I was a little girl, we would leave Kittaning, Pennsylvania, to drive to Bradenton, Florida, to visit my grandparents. One of the highlights for me was stopping at Busch Gardens in Virginia. Not only did this break up the long drive, but it also created a mini-celebration on the way to those warm beaches. The same is true as we begin to work toward our destination in various areas of our lives.

Remember my client who climbed Mt. Kilimijaro? They couldn't climb all the way to the top in one long hike. They needed basecamps along the way. We need those too as we travel toward our mountaintop goals. These are places where we can rest, celebrate our progress, and regroup for the next leg of the journey.

Let's use the example of setting goals in January for the year ahead. Your first basecamp might be in March of the same year:

- Mountaintop Goal: Master's Degree.
    - March Basecamp: Complete 1 class in my continued education
- Mountaintop Goal: Lose 50 pounds.
    - March Basecamp: Lose 10 pounds
- Mountaintop Goal: Connect to 50 potential clients.
    - March Basecamp: Complete 20 client networking meetings
- Mountaintop Goal: Save $10,000
    - March Basecamp: Save $2,000

Basecamps serve two purposes:

1. They're a chance to celebrate what you've achieved so far and help you stay motivated toward a long-term goal.
2. They're a chance to check in with yourself to make sure you're on track to reaching that big goal.

From time to time, you will need to make sure you are making strides toward your goal. Are your actions bringing you closer to your desired destination or farther away? Creating basecamps along the path to your mountaintop goal with their own due dates helps you check in and assess your progress. These milestones will keep you on track even when the mountaintop goal still seems far away.

Remember, self-awareness (knowing yourself and the goals you want to reach) without self-leadership (setting clear, specific intentions and taking action steps) is just a lot of information. Your mountaintop goal stays a dream and never becomes your reality. You are the only person who can set your dreams in motion by creating the behaviors required to drive you there.

> YOU ARE THE ONLY PERSON WHO CAN SET YOUR DREAMS IN MOTION BY CREATING THE BEHAVIORS REQUIRED TO DRIVE YOU THERE.

I want you to pause and remind yourself of your personal "Mt. Kilimijaro" goal that you set in Chapter 6 and plan out some basecamp milestones with due dates. You should also do this for your life area goals.

Mountaintop Goal:

Basecamp Goals:

1.

2.

3.

Next, it's time to look at the behaviors that will help you make progress toward these basecamps—the daily actions that are necessary to move you steadily toward your goals.

Habits—Your Well-Worn Pathway to Success

My favorite beach destination is Hilton Head, South Carolina. There are pathways from homes and condos over the large dunes to the gorgeous sea line as far as the eye can see. In 2016, Hurricane Matthew hit the small island of Hilton Head. Upon our first visit after the hurricane clean-up was done, the dunes were higher than we had ever experienced them on Palmetto Dunes, our favorite destination. The walk down the pathway prior to Hurricane Matthew was easy, even when we were loaded down with chairs, coolers, beach bags, and umbrellas. However, after Hurricane Matthew, the dunes were so high that we could barely get to the top. The reason? Prior to Hurricane Matthew, there was a well-worn pathway to the beach. The hurricane had destroyed that pathway and, until frequent beach travelers wore down another pathway to the beach, we would have to struggle over the dunes. In fact, *we* were the travelers beginning to wear down a new pathway to the beach.

The same is true for our habits. Every new habit feels like walking up a pathway that has not yet been built. It is our disciplined efforts that make walking out this habit easier over time. But, initially, we are pioneers building a well-worn pathway.

> **PATHWAYS ARE NOT BUILT AS MUCH AS THEY ARE WORN BY FREQUENT TRAVEL.**

This was punctuated for me when I ran across this quote: "Pathways are not built as much as they are worn by frequent travel." We need to build pathways of habit that will help us travel to our final destination. Habits are what turn intentions into realities.

We all have great intentions. As I write this, we are one month into a new year. Most New Year's resolutions and intentions have fallen away. When they were set thirty days ago, our intentions were solid. We want to save more money, cut out excess sugar, workout more often, catch up on our doctors' appointments, get up an hour earlier, start reading the Bible, finish reading the Bible, prioritize friendships more than work, etc. But the fact remains that until our behavior matches our intention, we stay stuck.

Our human nature resists doing the very things we want and need. Romans 7:18-19 says ,"For I have the desire to do what is good, but I cannot carry it out. For I do not do the good I want to do, but the evil I do not want to do—this I keep on doing." The truth is that our intentions alone will not carry us to our desired destination.

I lived out the truth of creating a pathway in 2016 when I decided to reassess my health and include more consistent workouts. For years before that, I had exercised at a local YMCA near my work at the time. It was a well-worn pathway for my workout habit. But, in 2014, I had taken a new position in a totally different part of the city. The thirty-minute drive to work in a new direction meant I drove less often to the Y and, when I did, it was so crowded, I couldn't find parking or locker space. And so, my workouts dwindled.

It was in 2016 I received a random Facebook ad for a Pilates studio that was on my way home from work. Knowing myself and my habits, this was one step in the right direction for me to workout. Since it was such a small studio, parking was plentiful and locker space was provided for everyone. Fast forward almost nine years later and I have completed over 2,000 classes and even trained for two years to become a certified Pilates instructor. I started working out six days a week for an hour a day. I loved being in control of my health and became stronger than I'd ever been.

The secret to this habit all began because it was on my well-worn pathway to work, so it was easy to incorporate it into my existing behavior.

This demonstrates the power of what James Clear, author of *Atomic Habits*, calls "habit stacking." It's where you add a new habit onto one that's already well-established. Since every new behavior feels hard to remember and hard to do at first, it helps if you can attach it to something you already do regularly. Clear also recommends making the habit as easy to do as possible when you're starting out. An example he shares is putting your running clothes next to your bed before you go to sleep so you can put them on to run first thing in the morning.

The great thing about habits is that, once you get them established, they become much easier and you almost accomplish them automatically. Think about something you do every day that you've done for years, like brushing your teeth or washing your hands after using the bathroom. Or even something like drying your hair. Developing habits is a little like riding a bike. It's hard to do at first, and you'll probably fall a lot as you're learning, but once you've got it, you don't even have to think about it. That's the power of habits.

What habits do you need to develop in order to make consistent progress toward your goals? Here are a few examples using the life areas:

Finances – The habit of eating out less means you're building a well-worn pathway to consistent menu planning, grocery shopping, meal preparation, and cooking time.

Career – Perhaps reaching the next level in your career requires continued education or certification. This means creating a pathway to research educational opportunities, setting a budget that will pay for this additional education, scheduling conversations with your supervisor to confirm this is supported by your firm, or even considering a job change after this additional education.

Physical – Do you want to change the way you eat and strengthen your body through workouts? That means cleaning out cupboards of food that isn't your best fuel (or having a plan for those in your home who will continue to eat differently than you), finding a meal service or recipes that incorporate your new plan, grocery shopping and meal prepping, signing up for a gym membership or workout classes, and planning to work out a certain number of times each week. Maybe it also includes scheduling annual appointments you've let slide.

Spiritual – Do you want to deepen your morning meditation and study in the Bible? This will require a routine of setting an earlier alarm, jumping right out of bed, arming yourself with coffee, finding a great location in your home, and using the study tools you need.

Relationships – Perhaps most of your relationships involve something work-related and you desire to deepen your friendships. Who are the friends you want to meet more often? Make a list of these friends and figure out times when you are both available to get together. If it's your spouse or partner, this might mean planning a weekly date night or beginning a hobby together.

Lifestyle – Do you need a morning routine? Make sure the pathway you create is keeping what you need at your fingertips (including an alarm set across the room to force you out of bed). Perhaps your cluttered home is causing a lack of productivity. Identify one easy space to declutter per day, like one drawer or one shelf in your pantry. Then, you'll need to maintain this decluttered area with the habit of always putting things away as soon as you're done with them. Do you work too much over the weekends? Removing your email from your phone creates a pathway to a habit to keep you from over-working.

Your habits will be unique to you and to your goals. Take a moment now to think about a few habits you want to develop that will help you reach the targets you outlined in the previous section.

Target:

Habit:

Target:

Habit:

Target:

Habit:

Your Habit Toolbox

Here are a few of the best tools to keep in your toolbox as you create a successful habit:

Accountability—This could be your best friend, spouse or partner, supervisor, sister, or even a coach. For Pilates, accountable so I don't sleep in and cancel a class is being charged $20 for a late cancel. This has made me workout more times than I can tell you (including this morning).

Know Yourself—Think about your wiring and what motivates you. Does it help you if a new habit is fun? Easy? Competitive? How have you succeeded in the past? What obstacles can you predict that could trip you up? What are ways you've self-sabotaged in the past?

Know Your Why—Remind yourself of why you want to develop this habit in the first place. What is the goal helping you achieve, and why is that goal important to you? Envisioning what will be different once you've mastered this habit is important. Instead of saying "I want to work out," say, "I want to work out because I want to be strong and flexible to play with my grandson."

Create a Trigger—Once you know your habit and envision your preferred future, why not turn it into your screen saver on your phone? You can also create a vision board and keep it somewhere you see it daily. Writing it down and saying it out loud can also reinforce your purpose. This is also where habit stacking can come into play. What existing habit can you connect this new habit to? Maybe you can connect prayer time to drinking your coffee, or start making your lunch for the next day after you clean up from dinner. Whatever it is, create a trigger for action.

Focus on One Habit at a Time – Having too many habits you're trying to work on at once sets you up for failure. We can only handle two or three, at best. If possible, focus on one solid habit for six to eight weeks and once that pathway has been well-worn, add on another habit.

Be Specific -- Being too vague about your habit makes it hard to accomplish. Instead, be clear and specific so you know what success looks like. The habit "I want to get healthy" is vague. "I want to incorporate weight training two times a week and eliminate sugar for 90 days" is clear.

Perseverance – A lack of quick results is the main reason New Year's resolutions fizzle out by January 21st. The motivation wanes when the initial excitement wears off and the results are slow. Perseverance is key along with your accountability when you want to give up. Keep in mind that it takes about six weeks for a new habit to form and for that pathway to get worn down enough for it to become easy. Keep going!

Make it Easy – Think about simple ways to make it easy for yourself to complete your new habit. For example, if you want to eat out less, don't pick recipes filled with ingredients that are hard to find or too complicated to cook at the end of a workday. Instead, pick simple recipes with easy-to-find ingredients. Better yet, use a meal kit service to get you started. You can always get more complicated or change it up later once you're used to cooking more regularly.

Beat Procrastination – Procrastination is actually the result of fear, but it can feel like inertia. It's that "I can't get off the couch" feeling. Rather than putting on our workout clothes and driving to the gym, we scroll Instagram for "just another minute or two." Often, the hardest part is getting started. One way to overcome this is by using Mel Robbins' "5 Second Rule." It goes like this: whatever you are trying to do count down from five and then hop up and do it. It can also help to tell yourself you're just going to do the hard thing for five minutes, and then you can stop if you want to. "I'll de-clutter my closet just for five minutes." "I'll jog for just five minutes." Telling yourself it will be over soon helps you get started, and many times, once you're in motion, it will feel easy to keep going a little longer. All you have to do is start. Are you willing to take the first step to create your well-worn pathway?

> ALL YOU HAVE TO DO IS START. ARE YOU WILLING TO TAKE THE FIRST STEP TO CREATE YOUR WELL-WORN PATHWAY?

Remember, pathways are not built as much as they are worn down by frequent travel. The more you do your new habit, the easier it will become. Soon, you'll be moving toward your goal without even breaking a sweat.

Our next step is to take a hard look at your calendar and carve out time for your new habits and goals.

The Myth of Time Management

Oh, how complicated our relationship is with time management. Why do we continually wrestle to manage our time? Time is not manageable. It is fixed and no one has any more than another. Our lives hold twenty-four hours each day and 168 hours each week. These are the limits to our time. Pause for a moment to consider that the President of the United States, Taylor Swift, your boss, and Tom Brady all have the exact same limits on their time as we do. No one has one minute more than another human being each day. The difference is how they choose to use our time. And so, it goes back to that choice of what gets onto our schedule.

We will talk more about our time capacity in another chapter, but for now, we must make sure that we are able to focus on our dream destination in the spaces of our days, weeks, months, quarters, and years ahead. The Investigation and Steps from our T.R.I.P.S. work above need to be written down on our calendar.

A good place to start is one quarter into the future. Look at the next three months and add the priorities you've identified that are necessary to keep moving each week or month. Then, when someone tries to schedule something the exact same time, you can simply and honestly reply, "I already have a commitment at that time."

We must dedicated time for what we want the most, like better relationships, more time with friends, career development, and time with God (and no, that doesn't mean you get to cheat yourself on your rest hours to just cram more into your day).

There are many people and forces in your life who are planning your days for you: social media influencers, late night shows, your supervisor, your friends, your Bible study leader, your pastor, the PTA, and the soccer team. The list goes on and on. But only you can let your "yes" be yes and your "no" be no in order to create room for the priorities you've identified in this book. God's direction and your voice need to be clear on what goes into your schedule and what does not, at least not for now.

> ONLY YOU CAN LET YOUR "YES" BE YES AND YOUR "NO" BE NO IN ORDER TO CREATE ROOM FOR THE PRIORITIES YOU'VE IDENTIFIED IN THIS BOOK.

Another important yet overlooked aspect of time is not only what we do, but *when* do we do our best work. Time is also about understanding what gives us energy and what drains our energy. Then we can strategically plan to do assigned tasks during the best part of the day for us. Are you a morning person? Your hardest projects, conversations, and thinking should be scheduled in the mornings. More routine tasks that require attention but not a lot of thinking should be done when you have the least energy during the day.

Here are some Coaching Questions to help you make the most of your time:

1. What times of the day are you at your best and most productive? Begin to time block those times for your most important and demanding tasks.

2. What times of the day are you at your least productive? Plan to do mindless or easier tasks (like responding to easy emails or folding laundry) at those times.

3. Do you have a rhythm of reflection and planning at the end or beginning of each month? If not, consider starting one. Consider the most recent month and evaluate what drained you and what energized you. What do you want to keep doing and what do you want to do less of? Then, put the most important things on your calendar and block out that time.

Proact vs. React

I walked into the board room for the monthly meeting that my coworker attended. It was just the two of us and about ten minutes before the meeting began, being my jovial self, I made some crack about the weekend and immediately was taken aback by their response . . . or lack thereof. *Did they not hear me?* Being a Stiletto with a strong need to be liked and entertaining, I continued to try to woo my coworker over through clever quips and conversation. Wow. Their eyes burned a hole through me and their curt answers helped me understand that I had interrupted the concentration time they needed prior to the meeting. I assumed since we were in a public space that banter would be appreciated and returned. I was so wrong.

Thinking about it later, I realized I had been operating on autopilot. I hadn't considered how many times in the past this coworker was what I would call rude and unengaging. Instead of reviewing past interactions with them and responding intentionally, I reacted by trying to win them over causing greater distance. After that, I started to think about my meetings in advance and consider who would be in the room and what I should expect. It was a great way for me to get ahead of reactions. I no longer expected cordial conversations prior to meetings with this coworker. I also did not let it deter me from being myself with other meeting guests. I learned to be proactive rather than reactive. I also learned to read the room better when people might be mid-task not a good time to interrupt.

One of the greatest ways to become more emotionally intelligent is thinking through the timing, personalities, and other factors at play before we enter a situation, so that we can bring the most appropriate and helpful parts of ourselves to the table. Our ability to communicate in important conversations, family settings, team meetings, and even Bible studies can be vastly improved if we proact (know ourselves and others) before we react (respond instinctively, which may be an appropriate response in some situations, but a horrible choice in others).

As I coach clients on proacting versus reacting, we start by creating self-awareness about what current personal and professional situations have brought out the worst in them. I encourage clients to become observers of themselves. What is happening around them when this basement part of their personality is drawn out?

Are they H.A.L.T. (Hungry, Angry, Lonely, or Tired)? Proactively considering how I am feeling as I enter into family settings, conversations, and meetings is using self-awareness and emotional intelligence to impact the way I behave. If I'm super tired, I will remind myself that my emotions will come more quickly and to not react without a chance to think things through.

Hungry? Grab that Snickers bar (or almonds). Angry? Well, this self-awareness requires you knowing that you could be a loose cannon, so you need to ask for time to process and realize that being angry is like walking on thin ice in any relationship. Lonely? This is a larger situation that cannot be solved in business meetings, but you can pray through it and even use this book to help you solve this as you learn to coach yourself. However, you can still remind yourself not to expect your business associates to talk to you like a friend in the meeting and to stay professional. Tired? Try doing a few jumping jacks to get your blood pumping or grab some coffee to curb your weariness.

Next, I ask my clients to consider if there is a pattern to when the worst of themselves comes out. For example, it might be that monthly Tuesday business meeting. When I use that as an example with my clients, most of them immediately know of a meeting or gathering that they dread and react rather than proact. Then I ask them to become curious about themselves. What is happening in that monthly meeting that brings out their basement (the worst of their personality)? Are they consistently overlooked?

> I ASK THEM TO BECOME CURIOUS ABOUT THEMSELVES.

Are they working out of a lesser skillset (like me in budget meetings, for example)? Does the meeting go too quickly or too slowly? Lastly, we consider if there are ways to improve that meeting or ultimately accept it for what it is.

Finally, I ask if a certain personality or actual person seems to bring out the worst in them. Sometimes a Workboot personality and a Flip Flop might generally rub each other the wrong way because they are more opposite. The same is true of the Stiletto and Mary Jane (which was the exact case with me and the above-mentioned coworker). Also, if it is a specific person who brings out a reaction from you, why is that? Think about the coworker example I mentioned above. Their response to me was taking me into a basement and causing me to feel like I wanted to prove myself. When I stood back and realized that I could not change their behavior, but I could keep myself from taking the bait and having it ruin my day, I arrived at true freedom. Who is that person for you? Just thinking it through is the proactive approach you need to engage your self-leadership prior to the next interaction. Perhaps every Thanksgiving there is mother-in-law drama over your cooking or décor. You cannot change or control your mother-in-law's choices, but you can create a healthy detachment by not reacting to her behavior.

Proacting versus reacting also applies to:

- Our Health: Ignoring doctors' appointments and dental cleanings (instead of proacting by doing them) can lead to health crises and gum disease which will require you to react.

- Our Finances: Consistently paying for DoorDash more and more frequently (react), instead of meal planning and eating in (proact) will impact our waistlines and lead to wasted cash that could be saved.

In fact, proacting versus reacting can be applied to each area of our seven life areas of Physical/Mental Health, Career, Relationships, Spiritual Life, Hobbies, and Life Balance/Pace.

> IF THERE'S AN AREA OF YOUR LIFE OR A MONTHLY EVENT OR EVEN A TIME OF DAY THAT CONSISTENTLY GIVES YOU TROUBLE, TAKE SOME TIME TO SELF-REFLECT AND LOOK FOR PATTERNS

If there's an area of your life or a monthly event or even a time of day that consistently gives you trouble, take some time to self-reflect and look for patterns. Then, using what you know about yourself and about any other people involved, how could you be more proactive by adjusting your expectations and preparing yourself before that moment arrives?

Forming the habit of proaction instead of reaction will help you make progress on the path to your goals—and have a lot more fun doing it.

Planning Ahead for Travel Interruptions

Having been raised in Pittsburgh, Pennsylvania, we often had weeks of bitter cold temperatures and inches of snow. (This was before global warming caused more mild winters.) It was widely known that you always kept some emergency supplies in the back of your car, such as a blanket, bottled water, and chains for your tires. (Yes, I'm that old.) You never knew when you ventured out in the winter months if you would get stranded either due to the icy roads or unexpected snow squalls. These emergency items could keep you safe in the event of unexpected winter weather.

The same is true with my life and my coaching clients' lives as we seek to prepare for what we know is coming, and also for what we could never predict but will need to respond to. In our day-to-day, this preparation might look like making sure to add margin to your calendar for the unexpected, being aware of how you have interrupted your own goals in the past, or planning around any obstacle you can predict will ensure smoother travels ahead.

> IT DOES YOU NO GOOD TO *SAY* YOU WANT TO BE DIFFERENT. YOU HAVE TO ACTUALLY *DO* SOMETHING DIFFERENT.

Keep this quote that's attributed to Aristotle in mind: "You are what you repeatedly do." It does you no good to *say* you want to be different. You have to actually *do* something different. That's what this chapter is all about.

I have no doubt that your Investigation and Prediction phases of the T.R.I.P.S. pointed out that you need a new or stronger habit, managing yourself and your energy around time to create space for your goals is important, and being proactive rather than reactive can make all the difference in your success (or failure) as you pursue your goals.

This is all part of self-leadership, learning to manage yourself—your strengths and your weaknesses—like a good coach manages a sports team and makes a specific plan of action. You've named your big goals, you've outlined the steps to get there, and you've named the habits that will help you make progress. You cannot step onto the playing field and expect to win without these steps.

Now it's time to start doing it!

Part III will help you stay the course when you're tempted to quit and guard your capacity so you don't get distracted or burned out. Remember, this is the trip of a lifetime. It's more like a marathon than a sprint as you become the person God is calling you to be.

Reflect & Respond

1. Revisit the habits you identified in this chapter and see if you can use some of the tips in the Habit Toolbox to set yourself up for success. What will you start doing this week to begin creating this new pathway toward your goals?

2. What areas in your life could benefit from you thinking more proactively than reactively? Take some time to reflect on what has happened before, look for patterns, and plan how you could be more proactive in the future.

IF THERE'S AN AREA OF YOUR LIFE OR A MONTHLY EVENT OR EVEN A TIME OF DAY THAT CONSISTENTLY GIVES YOU TROUBLE, TAKE SOME TIME TO SELF-REFLECT AND LOOK FOR PATTERNS.

PART 3

Self-Acceptance Through Self-Control

"But the fruit of the Spirit is love, joy, peace, forbearance, kindness, goodness, faithfulness, gentleness and self-control."

Galatians 5:22-23

You've made incredible progress in the previous chapters. You've learned so much about who you are, where you are in your life right now, where you want to go, and, most importantly, why you want to go there. You've charted your own course for your life and created a map to keep you on track, including stop-over points to refuel. You've also named the habits you'll need to keep you moving down the path.

Now it's time to plan for the obstacles you're likely to encounter and prepare to keep yourself on track when the going gets tough. It's also time to make sure you know how to read your gauges so you can add more oil or take a break before your engine grinds to a halt.

As you will learn in this section, a large part of leading yourself well will include accepting the realities of your limitations, seasons of life, skillset, and expectations. In a phrase, you will begin to learn to accept yourself.

One of the things you've learned about me as I've written this book is how much I invest in Pilates as my primary workout. As I've done Pilates through the years, I've become so much stronger and confident in the strength of my body. However, I do not expect to be able to work out like a thirty-year-old. I intend to work out the best my sixty-plus-year-old self can. There is a lovely Pilates exercise called the arabesque that requires me to be inverted on the Reformer. For a few seconds, my entire body is off the ground, supported by my upper body and one foot. It is a challenging exercise. But you know what makes it more challenging at my age? One of my feet has chronic arthritis in the ball of the foot. In order to my do the arabesque on my left side, I need to use a support for my right foot. This is a minor example of self-acceptance, but I could be frustrated trying to pretend that I can push through and heal that foot (which the doctor says I cannot). Instead, I accept that when I do that exercise on my left side at my age, I have to adjust.

LEADING YOURSELF WELL WILL INCLUDE ACCEPTING THE REALITIES OF YOUR LIMITATIONS, SEASONS OF LIFE, SKILLSET, AND EXPECTATIONS.

It will be the same for you in various areas of your life. Single mothers do not have the luxury of extra hands to help with school projects. My friend who was a pilot knows that their travel schedule puts limitations on family time. Perhaps your self-acceptance needs to be focused on more fully understanding your financial state. We all have varying physical health experiences. Some of them can be changed and some need to be accepted.

Many of the women I coach are forty years or older, and many of them are going through perimenopause, menopause, or post-menopause, all of which are challenging to control, at best. Our bodies feel like they are betraying us as our hormones (or lack thereof) manifest themselves in surprising ways, impacting our sleep, focus, waistline, and beyond. There are some things we can do, but self-acceptance is one of the most importance choices we can make to keep us moving forward on our trip of a lifetime.

One of my regular Coaching Questions in any given situation is "What about this can you change?" After a thorough conversation about that question (making sure the client isn't tempted to use an excuse not to change), we land on accepting the things they can't change. Once we clarify what they can and cannot change about their situation, the next question is meant to expand their view as they ask themselves, "What does this make possible?" Life gives us limitations, yet, as any entrepreneur knows, limitations can be the doorway to a breakthrough. This could be the first time in your life you've surrendered control and truly accepted the season of life you are traveling through.

As we drive down the highway to the life God is opening up before us, I want you to picture yourself behind the wheel of your car. When your car begins to veer slightly off the road, you are jolted back into your lane when you hear the grinding of your tires over the rumble strip. The rumble strip helps to keep you safe and arrive safely at your destination. Think of this section of the book as the rumble strips you insert into your life to help you course correct if you veer off the road.

This all requires self-control. It's about getting yourself into action and providing prompt feedback for yourself if you start going off track. As parents, we are good at keeping our kids' lives on course. In our jobs, we focus on leading our teams across the finish line of the project. Even in our Bible studies, we keep our groups on track through the homework and discussions. But do you use the same level of leadership with your own progress toward your dream destination?

One of the fruits of the Spirit is self-control. Self-control in this verse comes from the Greek word *egkrateia*, which means "self-mastery" or "self-restraint." But we also know from this verse that the fruits of the Spirit come from God, flowing from our deep relationship with Him. Remember that as we walk with God, we have access to the supernatural power of self-control.

You are on the path, but we all get distracted from time to time. The exercises in this chapter will help you not get bogged down when you hit a rumble strip, but instead go right back on the road, determined to stay the course.

"WHAT DOES THIS MAKE POSSIBLE?"

Let's create systems for your trip of a lifetime that will ensure you stay on the path and enjoy the ride.

Chapter 9
How Can I Guard My Capacity?

"Be honest in your evaluation of yourselves, measuring yourselves by the faith God has given us."

Romans 12:3 NLT

It was our weekly grocery store run. I was carrying the bags into the kitchen from the garage. Instead of the typical brown paper bags, our groceries had been loaded into plastic ones. Like Superwoman, I started stacking the bags into the crook of my right arm and then on my left arm, the skin above each elbow bulging from the weight of two armfuls of bags. As I made my way into the kitchen, I swiveled around in such a way to launch the bags on the counter. It was then that one of the handles broke, leaving a supersized glass jar of red spaghetti sauce dangling precariously over my ceramic tile floor. All because I wouldn't make two trips, there was something very fragile in danger of breaking because I was over my capacity.

ADJUST BEFORE YOU COMBUST.

Just like my overloaded arms and that glass jar of spaghetti sauce, when we live beyond our capacity, we find fragile things like relationships, marriages, children, finances, and mental health in danger of breaking. This chapter will help you adjust before you combust.

Burning Bright or Burning Out?

Have you noticed the panic that sets in when you are watching your phone battery decline and you forgot your charger? Perhaps you're on an airplane, on a phone call in traffic, or using it for your navigation. Our phones have become a required tool to stay connected to our families, work, GPS, and entertainment. Even the most forgetful among us will make sure that they can keep their phone charged and ready. Yet we don't pay nearly so much attention to our own internal batteries. We allow them to drain until they are almost empty before we admit we need to slow down.

When your phone is dangerously low on battery, it might go into "low-power mode." Certain functions are suspended, and it doesn't work as fast as it normally does. This is similar to what happens to us when we over-extend ourselves and hit burnout.

Statistics show burnout is on the rise in all generations. A recent Gallup survey has discovered that 76% of employees experience workplace burnout at some point. That's a big number—three out of four employees. Even those who are solopreneurs or non-paid workers are experiencing more stress.

We live in a Western society that values overworking. We would never allow someone to sit next to us and repeatedly drink themselves into oblivion, yet we reward overwork more often than not. We wear busy as a badge of honor. And in church and ministry, it is often worse. Ministry leaders take on more because there is no finish line. We need to learn to lay down work each day, knowing that there will always be more ministry to be done.

Richard Swenson says, "What is clear to us in the context of physical limits is less clear regarding other limits." We would never try to bench press 300 pounds if we have only ever lifted fifty, but somehow, we are willing to try to put 300 pounds into our calendars, emotional banks, and mental loads. And then we wonder why we feel numb and joyless and can't bounce back even after a week's vacation. The truth is, we have become a society that is managing adrenaline rather than living a life.

Burnout is most often experienced by adding minor commitments to our schedule and not removing other commitments along the way. We burn out bit by bit, rather than in big chunks. The more we add into our lives, the more stress that is associated with each responsibility. Even wonderful things in our lives still add responsibility and stress.

> WE BURN OUT BIT BY BIT, RATHER THAN IN BIG CHUNKS.

Some of the symptoms that we experience as we approach a state of burnout include being numb, fatigued, exhilarated yet exhausted, restless, distracted, and unsettled. Often, we feel a combination of all of these symptoms at the same time.

Burnout is more than feeling stressed. WebMD states that "Workers with burnout are more likely to take sick days or wind up in the emergency room. These feelings of stress and despair can result in long-term impacts on your physical and mental health." Other symptoms of burnout include sleep interruption, headaches, stomach problems, ulcers, lack of focus, irritability, and a lowered immune system.

Just like we display our trophies on our living room mantle, we often celebrate working ourselves to exhaustion on the figurative mantles of our lives. It's time to walk to the mantle of our lives and remove the trophy of exhaustion.

The world needs your kind of "shine." So much of what we've talked about thus far in this book is about how you shine to the world through your confidence, creative wiring, and calling. But even if you know all those things and are burned out, your light will dim. Burnout causes even the most playful person to become serious and the most organized to become chaotic. You want your light to burn bright rather than burn out, and guarding your capacity will help us do that.

Guarding Your Capacity

A sure-fire way to avoid or heal from burnout is to guard our capacity.

What is capacity? Capacity is the space between what you have committed to do and what you've been designed to do sustainably.

Guarding our capacity means being proactive in our lives, assessing our seasons and responsibilities, saying no to new opportunities that don't' fit our goals, and removing commitments that no longer serve our calling, goals, or season of life.

In 1 Corinthians 9:27 (NLT), Paul says, "I discipline my body like an athlete, training it to do what it should." The word discipline in that verse is the Greek word *egkrateuomai*. This word means "to be self-controlled," which we know is a fruit of the Spirit.

Guarding your capacity is dependent upon your self-control. No one else can guard your capacity other than you. But how?

Let's use a visual for the remainder of this chapter. Picture a large rubber band. If you have one, go grab it. Now stretch it out as far as it can possibly go and hold it there. What will happen to that rubber band if it stays stretched? It will break and so will you—if you stay stretched to your limit. Envision that all of your time, energy, responsibilities, and commitments you've made are inside the rubber band. Is there still elasticity (margin) in the band? Are you stretched for just a season or have you gotten so used to being stretched to the fullest that it feels normal to you? You may have no idea how close to breaking you might be.

As a ministry leader, I am constantly reminded of the importance of being able to delegate tasks. However, self-control cannot be delegated. You are responsible to keep your rubber band in check. Yes, to allow it to expand in various seasons, but also to make sure it has time to contract and not stay stretched out. This is how we avoid burnout. Our lives will have seasons of being stretched. It is staying stretched that is the problem.

A wise woman, Carole, once told me, "Lisa, you can do it all . . . Just not all at once." What a lovely reminder that some things will need to remain outside of our rubber band because, in any given season, they are simply not the greatest priority.

Greg McKeown teaches that the word "priority" was introduced into the English language in the 1400s as a singular word. It wasn't until the Industrial Revolution in the 1900s that it became a plural word, "priorit*ies*." The truth is that you can only prioritize one thing at a time. When we carry multiple ongoing priorities day to day, week to week, and month to month, we begin to stretch beyond our mental capacity and risk burnout.

One of the sure signs that I am approaching burnout, I am ashamed to say, is I consistently look for someone to blame. I often say, "I must do it all. Why does no one honor the time we committed to? I guess if it's going to get done, I have to do it myself."

This desire to blame others goes right back to Genesis 3 when Eve blamed the serpent for an action that she had taken. Do you relate to this blame game? Sometimes we feel overwhelmed, restless, weary, and anxious and we know we are frustrated, so we seek to blame others rather than recognize we got ourselves here and, more importantly, we are the only person who can get us unstretched.

In my burnout seasons of life, my heart is restless. My soul is weary. I find myself searching for someone—anyone—to blame for this feeling. It was in the midst of this rumination years ago that I heard the voice of God whisper, "Lisa, you stretched yourself." I felt gently reminded that the only blame that could be assigned was to myself for allowing my life's rubber band to become overstretched. I am the reason I got too stretched and I needed to be the reason my rubber band would contract to have some margin.

> SELF-LEADERSHIP MEANS TAKING RESPONSIBILITY FOR THE CONSEQUENCES OF OUR DECISIONS AND EXERCISING SELF-CONTROL TO AVOID STRETCHING OURSELVES TOO THIN.

Self-leadership means taking responsibility for the consequences of our decisions and exercising self-control to avoid stretching ourselves too thin.

Reading Your Gauges

Imagine you are driving down the road and your car is operating just fine. Or, so you think. The engine light comes on. You don't see anything overtly wrong with your car. What do you do?

A. Pull over immediately.

B. When you arrive home, check your owner's manual to see what the light is telling you.

C. Ignore it.

If you choose A, you will also do B, most likely. Sadly, however, many of us choose C. We ignore it and act like an ostrich with its head in the sand, hoping it is some quirky glitch that means nothing and will eventually go away.

That's what I almost did about four months into the lockdown during the 2020 pandemic. One morning, I had rehearsed in my head how well I felt I had handled the transition with resilience. My husband and I were figuring out how to be together all day, every day working from home. Both of my grown kids had transitioned themselves into a healthy living and working space. My parents were tucked into a lovely assisted living space where meals were delivered to their front door and all necessary precautions were in place. And my team of twenty-two staff had responded well to Zoom meetings, digital icebreakers, and meeting our customers' needs, all while exceeding many of our goals.

It was that particular morning I decided to head out to do a few socially-distanced errands. I was on my way home when I found myself at a red light next to a car. I had clearly offended the driver somehow. I have no idea what I did, but they were ticked at me, which was confirmed by a particular hand gesture. Out of nowhere (or so I thought), when the light turned green, I found myself downshifting and chasing that car. Yep, an Executive Director of a national ministry decided to enter a car chase with the anonymous driver I had offended. Thankfully, I had made it about a half mile when the Holy Spirit nudged me in a non-audible way, saying, "Lisa, what exactly are you going to do if you catch them?" I immediately took my foot off

CHAPTER 9: HOW CAN I GUARD MY CAPACITY?

the gas and drove home. I sheepishly confessed this whole scenario to my husband, who promptly reminded me of everything that could have happened. I went on about my day.

But the next morning during my time with God, I realized that the car chase had been my check engine light. My gauges were telling me, even though everything was "in place" during a challenging season of the pandemic, that I needed to pull back and put some vitamin-D-outside-daydreaming-time on my schedule. I needed to adjust to have margin before I suddenly combusted.

Our lives offer warning lights over and over again, but sadly, we too often ignore them, hoping they are nothing. If we are going to grow in our ability to self-lead, then reading our gauges from time to time is crucial for our confidence and self-awareness. Just like in a car, the windshield washer fluid warning isn't as life-threatening as check brakes warning. As we grow in our self-control, we will know when our gauges indicate that we need a restful weekend, a Sabbath, an earlier bedtime, or a boundary. The gauges could be more serious like heart palpitations, bleeding gums, or too many emotional reactions. All these are signals for us to slow down and focus on our physical, dental, and mental health, because, if left unchecked, these symptoms could lead to losing our health (or *life*), losing our teeth, or losing our job.

When I take my car in for service, there are regular diagnostics that are run to ensure my car can function for the next few months without my dashboard lighting up. Here is an overview of some gauges you will want to check and evaluate honestly as you assess your capacity and looks for signs of burnout:

Physical Symptoms

These include starting to grind your teeth, carrying stress in your shoulders or stomach, or nervous habits like shaking your leg or picking your cuticles. Sometimes, the physical symptoms are more serious like high blood pressure, heart palpitations, and beyond. If you are experiencing these serious symptoms, it is important to see your doctor to assess the it, determine its root cause, and take the cure for it. A doctor visit is a good start to for even mild burnout symptoms.

How long has it been since you've had a physical? Start with your primary care doctor. Talk to them about any physical symptoms you are experiencing.

Over (or Under) Reactions

When we're working past our capacity, our emotional reactions tend to get out of proportion to the situation. For some, these can be overreactions. This is particularly true for Workboots and Stilettos. For Flip Flops and Mary Janes, they can sometimes underreact by withdrawing from stressful situations—only to explode later. Both underreactions and overreactions are a sign that you need to check your engine.

Become curious about your reactions. Are you H.A.L.T. (*Hungry, Angry, Lonely, or Tired*)? Are your reactions based on a specific relationship that could benefit from boundaries? Do you need to bring in a third-party to observe and guide this interaction? Is it your hormones? Don't underestimate the impact of hormones on your reactions. Is it unresolved grief coming out in an unhealthy way?

Avoidance Behaviors

Numbly scrolling or doom-scrolling through social media, online shopping that leads to overspending, and over-drinking and over-eating all can be signs that you're beyond your ability to cope in healthy ways.

What exactly are you avoiding? A good place to start is with a feelings wheel. Get granular in naming what you are feeling. Next, determine if you are avoiding a work project, a family meeting, a neighbor, or having a hard conversation. An initial way to deal with avoidance can be searching for Scripture that applies to the feelings you are experiencing and turning those Scriptures into prayers. Talk with a friend and share that you have been using scrolling, binging Netflix, or spending to deal with your feelings of overwhelm. Ask them to help you plan to replace those negative avoidance behaviors.

Exhaustion or Sleep Problems

Chronic stress can cause insomnia, so you may experience a combination of being extremely tired and also not being able to sleep well.

Establishing a bedtime routine including no screen-time for sixty minutes before you sleep and charging your phone across the room, so you don't have it at your fingertips is ideal. Avoid sleeping in on the weekend and establish a consistent bedtime and wake up time for every day of the week. Eliminate late day caffeine. Getting some exercise during the day can also help your body rest well.

Loss of Interest in Things That Used to Give you Passion and Joy

If you're no longer interested in doing something you usually love, that's a strong indication that your engine needs attention.

This could be due to grief, depression, or burnout. Burnout does not happen in a week, nor is it cured in a week. Using this book to assess your rubber band capacity, setting required boundaries and resuming self-leadership can reverse burnout.

Neglecting Self-Care (Nutrition, Exercise, or Other Basic Needs)

If you find yourself skipping meals (and eating out of a vending machine), suddenly not exercising anymore, going days without bathing, or neglecting other areas of basic self-care, it's time to stop and assess what's really going on.

The best way to start caring for your body is to create a menu plan, remove tempting foods from your pantry, meal prep once a week, and enlist a friend or family member to help you. The best way to begin a workout is simply to begin. Select a day and time. Will you do it online or at a gym? Can you include a friend to workout with you? If not, ask a friend to hold you accountable as you establish this routine.

If you answered "yes" to any of these gauge-reader clues above, please write down which categories apply to you here:

_____

_____

_____

_____

_____

Remember that in addition to addressing the symptoms you identify by reading your gauges, those "check engine lights" can also be signs that you're over-extending yourself more generally. Has your rubber band been stretched too far for too long? Don't just try to fix the symptom, such as by exercising or taking sleeping aids. Take those flashing red lights as signs to look at your life more holistically and evaluate how you're using your time and energy.

Just like taking your car into a mechanic is better than trying to fix the problem yourself, another set of eyes will help you assess how to address what your gauge is telling you. Do you need to talk with your BFF, pastor, or Bible study leader about what you've learned?

I also want to remind you that it might be time to put down this coaching book and contact your pastor or counselor. Coaching and counseling hold hands and, while this book is helping you self-coach, nothing replaces the need for face-to-face professional counseling. Several of the symptoms listed above can be signs of depression or anxiety, so please seek professional help if these symptoms are more pronounced or continue for several weeks or more.

Staying Stretched

Over my last twenty years of life, I have entered the fray of burnout a couple different times. The problem isn't *being* stretched. The problem is *staying* stretched. Again, let's think about your life as a rubber band. Stretch it out as far as you can and hold there. It's no problem for a short time, but if the rubber band stays stretched, it will break . . . and so will you.

Ecclesiastes 3 shows us that God has woven elasticity into the ebb and flow of our lives. There will be times our lives are stretched too wide for a short time. You won't find me here to beat you up about that. But we need to recognize that when our priorities shift and our rubber band goes back to normal, we need to give ourselves some space to recover before our next stretched season.

> **THE PROBLEM ISN'T *BEING* STRETCHED. THE PROBLEM IS *STAYING* STRETCHED.**

Most of us put off important things until some future time when we think we'll have more time. Somehow like a genie in the bottle, our lives will magically open up room within our rubber band.

Does this sound familiar?

- When the board meeting is finished, I can focus more on my physical health.
- When the kids go back to school, I'll start digging into my Bible reading and grow my faith.
- When the kids get out of school, I'll have more time to spend with my friends since I won't be on an intense school schedule.
- Once I am an empty-nester, I'll get my master's degree.
- As soon as I finish my master's degree, I will be fully present in the evenings.
- After this busy season, I won't work weekends.

What is the myth you are believing in your life? What are you waiting for in order to finally start doing the things you want to do and know are good for you?

This is an important time to introduce the concept of the six-to-twelve-week myth. We all fall for it. "In six weeks, I'll be able to . . ."—*fill in the blank*. We believe after the holidays or during the summer or once the big project is completed that we will have time to put the priority back into our rubber band. But here is the truth: in six weeks, there will be something waiting for you to crowd out the thing you are putting off.

The real problem comes when the thing we are putting outside of our rubber band is important and fragile . . . Our marriage. Our parenting. Our education. Our physical health. Our finances. Today is the day to adjust before you combust—or before you drop one of those precious, but fragile balls and it shatters.

I am constantly reminded that there is freedom that comes from knowing our limits. Let me explain. There was a popular research study that observed two swing sets on playgrounds. Swing Set A had no fence around it. Swing Set B was fenced. The children playing near Swing Set A all huddled close to the swing set even though there was plenty of green grass surrounding it. Swing Set B (the swing set with the fence) showed the children playing all the way to the fence beyond the swing set. The limits of the fence gave the children comfort about how far they could go and remain safe. God has woven limits into each of our lives.

THERE IS FREEDOM THAT COMES FROM KNOWING OUR LIMITS.

If you live alone, you have a different set of limits than if you have a roommate or children. Having a predictable nine-to-five job means you have different limits than someone who travels frequently throughout the week. Having responsibilities for children or aging parents sets limits that are different from someone without kids or without the responsibility of their parents. The ability to identify these limits and work within them will help you guard your capacity.

Take a few minutes to work through the following Self-Coaching Questions:

- ⊚ What are a few limits that your current season of life has placed upon you? Limits can be joyous, wonderful things like rocking babies to sleep, studying for midterms, or caring for aging parents. But they are responsibilities that limit other areas in your rubber band.

- ⊚ What is currently in your rubber band that needs to be placed outside of it? And what is sitting outside of your rubber band than needs to be given priority and placed inside of it?

Fueled or Fatigued?

I love public speaking. It fuels me and gives me energy. Bible teaching, however, requires an attention to detail that is hard for me.

I recall a peer of mine who led a large ministry that did events several times a year. We occasionally met to compare notes, gain insights, and learn from each other. She stewarded a large platform and I had been blessed to be in the audience for this event more than once. In one of our discussions, she mentioned that she felt like I would be a good speaker for a possible future event. Having attended this event many times, I knew I was not her girl. This isn't false humility or insecurity about accepting this assignment. They needed a Bible teacher and I am much more of a practical coaching speaker who is Biblically-based. I told her that I was honored to be considered, but I was not the right fit for the event.

She was stunned. I remember every part of her reaction because it was so unexpected to her. She relayed that there were dozens of women each year who wanted to be included on that event stage and my willingness to say "no" to an opportunity like that was an example of self-awareness she wanted to learn more about.

Don't get me wrong, I was totally tempted to accept and make it work, but in my gut, I knew it was a "no." I wasn't the right fit for her event, and the event wasn't the right fit for me. It would have been a stretch for me to try to do it, and it would have taken a lot of energy—energy I could better spend on something I was more suited for.

If you are an extrovert (like a Stiletto), you are fueled by being with people. It gives you energy when you work as a family, collaborate with your teams at work, and serve on committees at church. However, if you are more reserved by nature (like a Mary Jane), then brainstorming with teams, too much family time without alone time, or a weekend full of church meetings will fatigue you because your energy comes from spending time alone.

If you are fueled by relationships (like Stilettos and Flip Flops), then work projects based on analytics and strategy will fatigue you quickly. If you are more task-oriented (like a Workboot or Mary Jane), you will be fueled by brainstorming strategy, analysis, and problem-solving.

An important concept to consider is the reality that some people, projects, and predicaments *fuel* our lives and others *fatigue* our lives. For me, one-on-one in person meetings and networking tend to give me energy. These engagements fuel me. Working on budgets and planning business strategies fatigues me quickly. Therefore, I try to schedule a balance of those things. I don't spend three straight days focusing on budgets and business. I space them out.

I worked with a client in the accounting field whose career advancement required much more networking for prospective clients. The field they started in created a quieter, more independent work-life that fueled them. Conferences, networking, and business dinners fatigued them. So, we started to implement a monthly at-a-glance review of their upcoming fatiguing days and weeks. Then, we made sure to bookend those types of events with quiet, independent work to help them refuel.

HOW MUCH OF YOUR DAY OR WEEK INCLUDES FUELING ACTIVITIES? HOW MUCH REQUIRES FATIGUING ACTIVITIES?

The first key to managing this fuel and fatigue is awareness. How much of your day or week includes fueling activities? How much requires fatiguing activities? If your job description requires an abundance of fatiguing activities, you need to fill your life outside of work with fueling activities in order to avoid burnout.

Ephesians 4:16 emphasizes that everyone is different in the Body of Christ, and each does its own work. The word work in this verse is the Greek word *energian* from which we get our English word "energy." Our lives need the fuel of God-directed, God-assigned work and self-directed control to live a sustainable life.

Ephesians 5:15-16 (ESV) says, "Look carefully then how you walk, not as unwise, but as wise, making the best use of the time." How are you making the best use of your time? You cannot look at your time without considering your energy. You need a combination of work, rest, recreation, daydreaming, enjoyment, exercise, hobbies, and relationships. Some of the assignments you have within each of these areas will fuel you and give you energy, while other assignments will fatigue us. Walking through a season of caring sick loved one or aging parent may feel weighty and will need to be counterbalanced with less weighty commitments.

Saying "no" to certain opportunities because they demand more time or energy than you can currently give without sacrificing your priorities is an essential part of guarding your capacity.

It's hard to tell people "no," because we don't want to disappoint them, or we think, "Well, I *could* do that." But when you know who you are (and who you aren't), decisions like the Bible teacher event I turned down are clear. Saying "no" when we're the wrong woman for the event also creates room for the right woman. I like to remember that when I say "no," it makes room for someone else to say "yes." It's a win-win.

Navigate Your Time

As we examine our rubber bands, we begin to evaluate and redeem our time. Remember that this part of the book is about our self-leadership. Not only do our life responsibilities set limits on our time, but we have to also set limits on our time.

Our choices are a major contributor to our stress level, burnout, and capacity. Small choices, good or bad, over time can affect the person we become. Similarly, small changes pay off over time.

YOU ARE A LIMITED RESOURCE.

You are a limited resource. As we previously discussed, we all have only twenty-four hours in a day and 168 hours in a week. If those hours were dollars, where do you need to invest your time and energy so that you get the maximum return on the investment of *you*? What is the best ROI on you?

Navigating your time well is the difference between burning out versus burning bright. Just like our car navigation system gives alternative routes, you have options about how to spend your time, how to use your voice, how to steward your energy for maximum productivity, and how to guard your relationships and priorities.

Each one of us has a unique set of demands and priorities on our time based on our season of life, marital status, career season, health, and more. Therefore, it is not helpful to look at our coworker or neighbor and expect them to be able to navigate our time in the same way someone else does. Although we all have the same twenty-four hours in each day, the way we invest them looks very different.

We cannot get more time or make more time. Thus, we need to get good at limiting the things that creep into our schedules.

Below are a few tips to help you maintain your priorities while you're navigating your time:

Spend Time with God

Part of guarding our hearts requires us to have consistent time with God.

Are you able to seek God daily, read His Word and pray? If you have this time, is it fresh or stale? Are you taking a weekly Sabbath? I used to feel pretty proud of my weekly Sabbath time until God showed me that I was not having a Sabbath, I was simply exhausted which required me to do nothing one day each week. There is a different between engaging in the spiritual discipline of the

CHAPTER 9: HOW CAN I GUARD MY CAPACITY?

Sabbath in pursuit of a deeper relationship with God and just being so exhausted that you look forward to one day all to yourself to do nothing. There is a difference between the discipline of silence and being silent simply because you've used all your words in a week.

Guard Your Calendar

We cannot navigate our time without focusing on our calendar. If you're like most people, we live and die by the schedules written into our calendars. We swap calendars with our spouses and our work teams and have shared family calendars.

As you look at your calendar each week, where are you seeing white space? White space on your calendar is the much-needed margin that will allow you to have the resiliency you need in your life. Things to consider when you look at your calendars is:

- How many nights a week do you want to have a commitment?
- How early will you rise and when is your consistent bedtime?
- How many kid's activities can you handle each week?
- How often can you travel for work or pleasure any given month?
- What needs to find space on your calendar?
- How are your relationships prioritized on your calendar?
- What are your power hours? (*See Chapter 8*.) Are they blocked off for your most important and demanding work?

You will also need to keep margin in your band to allow for interruptions like traffic, a sick child, a new work project, etc. This will allow margin to be available when you need it without stretching your rubber band to the max over and over every week.

Leviticus 19:9 says, "When you reap the harvest of your land, do not reap to the very edges of your field or gather the gleanings of your harvest." This verse is written to leave "gleanings" of the crop for the poor to gather. But it also highlights the concept of leaving gleanings of our time (margin) in our calendars for the unexpected that arises. If you are fortunate enough in any given week to not have an interruption, then you get bonus time to read, rest, daydream, or tackle an extra item on your to-do list.

Set Limits

It may seem counterintuitive, but a limit can be freeing. Just like the swing set illustration above, when you know exactly how much time you have or don't have, when you have prioritized what is inside and outside your rubber band, and when you have the elasticity of margin, you experience true freedom. Limits show us a realistic picture of where we are and what is possible with our time, energy, and resources.

There is freedom in understanding the truth. The opposite of this understanding is denial. Denial in any given area of your life can lead to damage than cannot be undone.

Think about these areas that, if left without limit, will lead to stress, exhaustion, depression, and ruin:

- Screen Time (Emails, Text Messages, Social Media)—We could literally stay on our phones all day, every day. We'll never run out of content to explore. The average cell phone user touches their phone 2,617 times per day. Each user is on their phone for two and a half hours over seventy-six sessions. Clearly, we need to set limits in this area.

- Finances (Bankruptcy, Foreclosure, Credit)—If we don't set limits in our finances, then we have to ask our banker, mortgage officer, or creditors for permission to live rather than them asking us.

- Physical Heath (Cholesterol, Weight Gain, Depression, Diabetes, Heart Disease)— Our overall health can suffer the consequences of a lifestyle without limits.

- Career—If we want to advance in our careers, then we need to spend time developing ourselves professionally. This may

CHAPTER 9: HOW CAN I GUARD MY CAPACITY?

mean reading books on leadership or taking a class online. We need to limit how we spend our free time to make room for what we need to do in order to advance our careers. Conversely, we may need to limit how many hours we work a week in order to make time for ministry or family.

These limits lead to freedom, though they *all* come at a cost.

What in your life could benefit from the freedom that comes from imposing a limit? It's good to return to our Life Wheel in Chapter 6 as you consider this.

Don't Fear the Disappointment

Whether you consider yourself a people pleaser or not, you could likely have something inside your rubber band that is not your priority, but someone else's. What is in your rubber band because you know taking it out will disappoint someone?

Working in ministry is complicated because I genuinely want to help people. Yet, I have learned that you can't make everyone happy. They won't like the boundaries you have on your time or they won't like the structure of your small groups. People will want parts of your budget to fund their passion projects, which can be really good things, but not something that aligns with the larger goals you've committed to.

After a season of feeling like I was disappointing people more than meeting their needs, I reached out to my mentor, Mary Ann, who was in long-term ministry. As I processed each area during our long and much-needed conversation, she said, "The longer I'm in ministry, it seems the more people I disappoint." She then dug deeper and asked me if the things I had to say "no" to were things I had prayed about. After I told her that I had, she said that my saying "no" was a matter of obedience. This led me to come up with the phrase, "I am willing to disappoint you in order to obey God."

Don't get me wrong. I never say this to anyone, but I do rehearse it to myself. I cannot allow the priorities God has given me to be crowded out by other people's expectations. If you make a decision based on God's direction, then it's a matter of pleasing (or obeying) God, rather than people. *I'm willing to disappoint you in order to obey God* is not a bumper sticker, but it is a guiding mindset that will free you from being overstretched.

Fan the Flame

As you consider your capacity, a question I always like to ask is "What are the things that only I can do?" Make sure the answers to that question are aligned with the priorities you are identifying within your rubber band. What are several things that only you can do? You cannot delegate these things. There are some things you can hire others for or swap time for. But some assignments can only be done by you.

Pay attention to time-stamped seasons of life and consider some no-regret decisions. What is something outside of your rubber band that needs to be inside of it? Focusing on your marriage? Continuing your education to advance your career? Parenting during a special season, like the last year before kindergarten or senior year? These need to go into your rubber band first.

We see an example of this with the disciples in Acts 6:2-4: "It would not be right for us to neglect the ministry of the word of God in order to wait on tables. Brothers and sisters, choose seven men from among you who are known to be full of the Spirit and wisdom. We will turn this responsibility over to them and will give our attention to prayer and the ministry of the word."

The apostles modeled prioritizing what only they could do (focus on prayer and the ministry of the Word) and delegating what others could do (waiting on tables). This was not them saying they were too good to wait tables. They were assessing what needed to be inside and outside their rubber bands and adjusted according to the priorities God had given them.

CHAPTER 9: HOW CAN I GUARD MY CAPACITY?

2 Timothy 1:6-8 says, "For this reason I remind you to fan into flame the gift of God, which is in you through the laying on of my hands. For the Spirit God gave us does not make us timid, but gives us power, love and self-discipline."

The phrase "fan into flame" above in the Greek means to "kindle anew or kindle afresh." What a perfect illustration for how we combat our burnout. *We need to adjust before we combust.* We need to kindle anew our lives.

When I was little, we lived in a parsonage in Sharon, Pennsylvania, that had a wood-burning fireplace. Often on the weekends in the winter, my parents would have fires in that fireplace. On the mornings after the fire, my mom would scrape the old ashes onto a brown paper bag to dispose of the ashes. Sometimes, while scraping those ashes, we would find one hot ember still remaining from the previous night's fire. Even when it looked like everything had been burned up, there was still one burning ember. If you are burning out, you can believe that God has left one burning ember inside of you that needs to be cared for, so that it can burn brightly again.

Do the work to identify burnout and adjust your life so you can heal from this burnout and be able to burn brightly again. You may need to enlist the help of a pastor, counselor, or coach in order to process how to adjust your rubber band.

I also recall from our wood burning fireplace that if you took that one burning ember buried in the soot and added it to fresh wood and new kindling and blew onto the burning ember, the fire would be blaze again. This chapter is an exercise in guarding the burning ember that remains, placing new wood in your life, and letting the Holy Spirit blow upon your life, so you can burn passionately like a blazing fire once again.

As you finish this chapter, I want to encourage you with this quote: "Set yourself on fire with passion and people will come from miles to watch you burn. "

Reflect & Respond

1. Go to the Appendix to access the Capacity Assessment. Talk to a trusted friend about your reality and your concerns about your capacity. Give yourself permission to pause a few commitments as you heal and reflect.

2. Which tasks or activities fuel you and which fatigue you? Write a list of the most energizing and the most draining tasks you have to do on a regular basis.

3. Look back at the life wheel again and how you rated each area. Which areas would benefit most from some limits?

Chapter 10

How Can I Maintain My Mindset?

"For as a man thinks in his heart, so is he."

Proverbs 23:7 NKJV

In 2022 after taking over 1,000 classes in five years of Pilates, I embarked on becoming a certified Pilates instructor. Of all the things that I've done well through the years, such as parenting, leading people, real estate management, coaching, and ministry, they were all things that came more naturally to me. Although these things required me to learn, grow, and put in hard work, I was able to engage in them easily.

However, working out has not always been a strong suit for me. I'm not naturally athletic, I don't love to sweat, and my favorite part of the gym is always leaving. I like knowing I've gotten a great workout in, but I am glad it's over. So, learning muscle groups, understanding the philosophy of Pilates, and guiding others in their daily workouts, was quite a stretch for me.

I grabbed my practice client who happened to be my daughter, took several hours of training with my host studio in NYC, and then began the practicum hours that were required to lead up to a 60-minute exam to lead a 60 minute class without notes cueing proper form, noting required adjustments and maintaining pace in the exact order required. *Whew!* It was hard, but I did it. I gained so much confidence in what I am capable of when I put my mind to grow in an area I've not been in before. I built upon past experiences of doing hard things, doing things afraid, and learning something new.

I remember coming across the quote "Everything is hard before it's easy," and it helped me keep moving forward when it felt too hard. It was like riding a bike without training wheels. It's hard until it's easy.

For you it may not be getting a Pilates certification, but it may be starting a new career later in life, walking forward after a hard divorce or the death of a spouse, emphasizing healthy eating and working out instead of taking medications for cholesterol, or something else entirely. What is it that you need to have the confidence to pursue? It's ok that it's out of your wheelhouse, experience, or understanding. You can achieve more than you know, especially if you have the right mindset.

Facing the Unknown

Confidence is moving forward in uncertainty and into what you have never experienced before.

> CONFIDENCE IS MOVING FORWARD IN UNCERTAINTY AND INTO WHAT YOU HAVE NEVER EXPERIENCED BEFORE.

The truth is that, if you've already experienced a circumstance in your life (had a baby, survived an illness, learned how to set and reach goals, etc.), you probably already have some confidence that you will be able to do that again.

However, true confidence, I've found, exists when you move forward into the unknown. This is where the importance of our mindset comes in. We often fail to move forward because of our limited mindset.

Science has proven that the more we think a certain thought, it creates pathway in your brain. The more you think this thought, the more your brain uses this pathway and your behavior reflects this thought. However, the same science says that if you can create a new pathway, you can also produce an open, abundant mindset.

CHAPTER 10: HOW CAN I MAINTAIN MY MINDSET?

This is known as a growth mindset. Having a growth mindset doesn't guarantee the outcome will be what you would call "success," but the greatest success is that you took action and tried.

I once coached for a large organization that required me to use technology that I had never used before. I am not what you would call intuitive with anything tech-related. On top of that, I use a Mac and this organization used Windows, which created even greater technological challenges. Then, at the last minute, I was told I needed a second screen to manage the interactions of fifty people on a telecast. I wanted to throw in the towel and declare myself unqualified. But I coached myself in that moment. I spoke the truth that I had done things for the first time before and I had committed to this training. So, I would move forward as prepared as I could be and learn from the process. And guess what? The attendees had no idea how I was sweating and the training went great. I did need a good nap afterward! *LOL!*

You can self-coach yourself into the right mindset to keep you moving forward on your pathway. How do we build, maintain, and rebuild the appropriate mindset?

A Gallup Strengths conference incorporated this phrase that helps with our mindsets: "First, we think it. Then we say it. Then we do it."

For over five years, I have had in my "goals" for the year ahead to write the book you're reading. Admittedly, the timing was not right for a couple of those years. However, the next couple of years, I kept having the following thoughts in my head: *"I'm a good coach, speaker, and communicator, when it came to being a writer? An author? Not in my wheelhouse."*

That mindset kept me from rolling up my sleeves to write. One day, I just started translating so many of my messages and coaching exercises into potential chapters until the book you're holding came into being. As I am continuing to prepare for the release of this book, I am actively pursuing a mindset narrative that will carry my heart, hands, and head through the uncertainty of a first-time book release. I have decided to write out a narrative in advance that is positive and supportive of the goals God has given me for this book.

> **MINDSET WILL ALLOW US TO MANEUVER INTERRUPTIONS AND CHALLENGES RATHER THAN TURN THEM INTO DOOM AND GLOOM.**

Now, mindset is not "name it and claim it." But mindset will allow us to maneuver interruptions and challenges rather than turn them into doom and gloom.

For the book you are holding, I had to *think it* . . . I prayed and pondered about it for years. I had to *say it* . . . I interviewed agents and publishers and asked my friends and family to pray for me. I had to *do it* . . . I invested time, energy, and resources to bring this dream into a reality.

In order to shift or create a mindset, you have to recognize what your current mindset is. Is it serving you? Would you talk to your children the way your mindset is talking to you? Would God talk to you the way you are talking to yourself? If you are a follower of Christ, you have the benefit of having the mind of Christ and seeing yourself through His lens. Your identity is solid and complete in Jesus. You wear His righteousness. You claim Him as your Father. His royal blood was passed to you. You are who He says you are. I would recommend reviewing Psalm 139 and Ephesians 2:10 to remind yourself of how He sees you and wants you to see yourself.

Let's discuss some practical ways to build or maintain a confident mindset as you pursue your calling.

Write Affirmations

If you grew up in a certain generation, you probably remember watching a Saturday Night Live skit about Daily Affirmations with Stuart Smalley. His mantra was "I'm good enough. I'm smart enough, and, doggone it, people like you." My affirmations change from job to job and from season to season. I have shared my affirmations in the Appendix, but I am including a few examples based on my own to get you started.

Rehearse Why I Am Qualified: I am qualified as a coach because I spent hours of time studying for and attaining my certification. I was observed and graded with practicum clients. I have coached for hundreds of hours. I have invested in ongoing professional coaching development to grow my skillset.

This Is My Wiring: I can lead my team because I have the spiritual gift of leadership and my wiring as a Workboot means I am a natural leader.

My Calling Statement: My Calling Statement is to encourage, inspire, empower and equip women to be the unique individuals God created them to be and leave His mark on their world through their lives. I am reminded that I am certified and trained in four areas, including DISC, Gallup Strengths, the Enneagram, and Values, which help me affirm how each client is unique.

Other things to include in your affirmations is a Scripture verse, a quote or phrase that inspires or challenges you, your unique education, skillset or life experiences, and the values you identified in Chapter 4. You can include some or all of these elements in your affirmations.

Writing and then repeating your affirmations out loud is a strong way to orient your mindset in the right direction. There are many other resources on mindset by Margaret Feinberg and Craig Groeschel that can be used for further application.

Name Limiting Beliefs

There is a movie from 2002 called *A Beautiful Mind*.

Spoiler alert: *In the first half of a movie, we meet John Nash as a college student who then becomes a government spy. It isn't until midway through the movie that we learn that his college roommate, little girl, and the boss of his spy ring are all hallucinations. John Nash then goes through a myriad of treatments so that he can resume a normal life. In the end of the movie, he receives the Nobel Peace Prize with his faithful wife in attendance. At the end of the movie, you can see him looking off to the side and noticing those same three companions. None of them were real. He still saw them, but he no longer chose to give them power.*

This is a powerful illustration of how you can choose not to give power to limiting beliefs. You can pick up these limiting beliefs from various places. It can be the demanding mother-in-law who is always disappointed in your efforts, or the demeaning boss who pushes you, yet never appreciates your contributions. Perhaps the echoes of your teacher's voice calling you stupid or incompetent. All of these situations can cause us to believe "Things will never change. I will never be good enough." However, just like John Nash couldn't change seeing those three imaginary companions but chose to move past them without giving them power, you can go into Christmas with your mother-in-law, knowing she may not ever change, but you don't have to let her attitude toward you ruin your day.

> **WE ALL HAVE LIMITING BELIEFS, AND THEY KEEP US FROM OUR BEST LIFE.**

We all have limiting beliefs, and they keep us from our best life. They mock us and tell us that we will fail, be laughed at, aren't educated enough, don't have enough money, are too old, are too young, or some other lie.

Start by writing down the internal dialogue of your limiting beliefs—write down anything that makes you feel small. Ask yourself if it is true. Enlist a trusted friend to safely share your limiting beliefs. What would the opposite of that belief be? If you feel like you are too old, then how can you shift this limiting belief to a Kingdom mindset where you say, "God knows my age and has called me into this project. I will trust He will provide all I need to accomplish what He's asked."

Memorize 2 Corinthians 10:5 to combat those limiting beliefs: "and we take captive every thought to make it obedient to Christ."

Consider incorporating a correction to your limiting beliefs into your affirmations.

Make a Brag Sheet

One of the exercises that you can do is list out how you've overcome obstacles and learned new things in the past. Have you gotten a degree or certification? Have you learned a completely new skill or changed careers? Have you learned to parent? Even hard things like surviving a divorce or being widowed can give you confidence in how you've adapted, reinvented yourself, and learned new things.

If you struggle with this, ask someone close to you what growth they've seen in you. You might be surprised!

Write down all the obstacles you've overcome so you can refer to them when you need a boost.

Reframe Hard Circumstances

During a bedroom update in our home, I found myself replacing some very old picture frames with chic, newly designed ones. The new frame totally updated the photos, but the photos remained exactly the same. I use this same technique with clients called "reframing." Coaches define reframing as "changing the way people see things and trying to find alternative ways of viewing ideas, events or situations."

Sometimes there are things that God allows in our lives that He allows to remain unchanged, no matter how much we've prayed and asked Him to intervene. Perhaps it is a difficult marriage, a season of illness, a wayward child, or a difficult work situation. What is it in your life that you need reframed with a fresh perspective?

Once you identify the object, circumstance, or season of life you need reframed, spend some time with God asking, "What does this make possible in my life?" If you are like me when a circumstance arrives that you cannot change no matter how you have worked, prayed, and tried, you have probably already considered everything that is *not* possible. But I want to encourage you to reframe the situation and consider what it *does* make possible. As unbearable as it was to watch my sweet mom lose our precious dad, what I saw that it made possible was for her to become a powerful prayer intercessor and pick up the mantle of prayer my dad used.

With a little practice, you can learn to reframe any hard circumstance:

- Being stuck in a job makes it possible to receive training for another position, learn new skills, or take a class to sharpen your professional skillset.
- Being single and wanting a husband makes it possible for you to travel or invest deeply in friendships.
- Struggling with a wayward child makes it possible to deepen your trust and faith in God and to experience Him in ways you never have before.
- Struggling with an ongoing illness makes it possible for you to lean into other people and let them help and serve you as you learn to receive.
- Consider how to assess things if you are being overly optimistic or decidedly pessimistic and try to shift into being more realistic.

Now hear my heart here . . . I am not making light of any of the above situations. As our hearts yearn for situations to change, our ability to reframe them helps deepen our faith and perspective.

Develop a Growth Mindset

I am not a camping kind of gal. I enjoy creature comforts more than most. So, in 2010 when faced with the invitation to travel across the world to Burundi, Africa, to work with ministry teams and pastors, I knew it was way out of my comfort zone. I felt led to say "yes" and was grateful to receive cross-cultural training and learn from seasoned travelers who had gone before me. It was one hot night as I lay trying to go to sleep covered by a mosquito net that I sensed God equip me with inner fortitude by reminding me, "Lisa, you are stronger than you think you are."

A growth mindset frames every challenge and mistake as a learning opportunity. It comes from a deep faith in ourselves and a conviction

CHAPTER 10: HOW CAN I MAINTAIN MY MINDSET?

that God equips us for the tasks He sets before us. It comes from believing that we are immensely capable of learning and growing.

Dan Sullivan and Benjamin Hardy's quote captures how we should shift our mindset: "The way to measure your progress is backward against where you started, not against your ideal." The concept is to focus on what you have gained, which is birthed from a growth mindset, instead of emphasizing the gap you have which comes from a fixed mindset.

YOU ARE STRONGER THAN YOU THINK YOU ARE.

Changing your mindset from a limited mindset to a growth mindset allows you to see obstacles and turn them into opportunities. It is positive and realistic, rather than negative and doom and gloom. When things feel particularly hard, remind yourself of what you are learning and look for the part of the situation you *can* control. This is especially important when we make mistakes or feel like we've failed.

Changing your mindset will take some intentional practice. Below are examples of how a fixed mindset and a growth mindset each view a situation:

> **Fixed:** "Nothing is ever going to change. This is too hard"
>
> **Growth:** "I will try. I've done hard things before."
>
> **Fixed:** "I am overwhelmed with technology."
>
> **Growth:** "I can learn this. I can find someone to mentor me on this."
>
> **Fixed:** "I feel like giving up."
>
> **Growth:** "There are things out of my control, but what can I control in this situation?"

Learn from Failure

A phrase I love is "Failure isn't fatal." Missing an outcome, goal, or deadline truly doesn't kill us. We can use past failures by learning from them, changing what we can, and accepting the experience so we don't make the same mistake again.

Begin by defining what you saw as failure and why. Then, begin the autopsy. Was your original goal realistic? What are the variables you could not control (the weather, illness, the economy, someone else's response, etc.)? Were there variables you could control? If so, what could you do differently next time?

Even if you can't identify anything you could have done differently, you can see failure as an opportunity to grow in humility and maybe practice the art of apologizing. You might be surprised at the beauty that can come out of a sincere apology.

Grieve Well

Sometimes we have an unhealthy mindset because we have not taken the time to acknowledge a loss. If we don't allow ourselves to move through sadness, it can come out as anger, bitterness, or denial. As I mentioned in Chapter 7, the larger the loss, the longer and more intense the grief. To move forward, we need to name what we have lost. These can be the ending of a familial season, the loss of a good friendship, the betrayal of a family member, the loss of beloved pet, or the death of someone dear. What do you need to name, process, surrender to, and accept?

Increase Self-Awareness

Sometimes we learn something about ourselves when we're younger and then grow past it without realizing we have. We are like the elephant that cannot break free from the chain around its leg. What happens is that an elephant is tied to a stump with a chain when it is young and eventually learns that it can't break free from the chain. As the elephant grows, it never tries to break

CHAPTER 10: HOW CAN I MAINTAIN MY MINDSET?

free again because it remembers that it failed in the past. When it is an adult, the elephant could easily rip the entire stump from the ground, but it never tries because it does realize how much it's grown.

I used story this in a coaching group recently to identify how business owners were allowing their mindset to "shackle" them into procrastination or even failure. One of the women took it to heart and said, "I am not an elephant!" This was a declaration that she is not allowing herself to be held captive to her past limiting beliefs.

The key is to look at yourself objectively and evaluate your current strengths, rather than resigning yourself to something that was true a long time ago.

It's also helpful to consider what I call the five D's of coaching insight. These can lead to deepened self-awareness if you're feeling stuck or lack confidence.

- **Development:** Do I need further development to keep moving forward? This could mean getting a mentor, taking a class, pursuing a graduate degree, viewing a webinar, reading a book, listening to podcasts on a certain subject, or getting a new certification.

- **Design:** What about my unique design, personality, and wiring is helping me in this situation and what about my design is hindering me? How can I use my God-given design to leverage success in my desired future?

- **Discipline:** Does my future success require a new discipline, such as getting up earlier, eating healthier, driving home a different way from work to make it to the gym, being accountable to implement my spiritual practice, or having the self-control to eat in to save for retirement?

- **Dream:** Do I need more clarity about a dream I am pursuing? Is it a side hustle I want to create or a calling I'm sensing from God? Is it a career move or a way to minister to others? Am I in a transition season and want to shake things up to create a more purposeful life?

- **Decision:** Am I struggling to make a decision about moving forward? Should I seek counsel by hiring a coach, meeting with my personal board of advisors, or referencing what God's Word says about what I am facing?

Ask Questions

As a coach I have continually seen how one question can change the trajectory of a life, goal, project, or mindset. While working with a client, I once asked, "How are you making this too hard?" and it was life-changing for her as she reflected on her work ethic and perfectionism. It's amazing what curiosity can do to change our mindset. If you are stuck in a fixed mindset, read through the questions below and see if they can shift you from being stuck to moving full-steam ahead.

- What is the best next step?
- How are you making this too hard?
- What is at risk if you don't change, decide, grow, etc.?
- What can you say "yes" to? What will this require of you?
- When was the last time you moved past this kind of discomfort?
- What do you want to say about this at the end of this year?
- Are there specific resources you need to keep moving?
- What would happen if you did nothing?
- How would you advise a friend about this?
- What are all your options? (Write them all down.) Which option do you feel ready to act upon?
- Where are you now in relation to your goal?
- Why do you think you haven't done this before? What do you think is stopping you now?

Making Up Your Mind

Human behavior tends to settle into a groove, which is good unless the groove becomes a rut. As you coach your mindset, what does it look like to stretch outside your comfort zone? Often, our greatest accomplishments lie just outside of our comfort zone.

We also need to stretch the way we are viewing a situation. Having a mindset of abundance will help you see the possibilities ahead of you.

If you're like most of us, our parents had a way of correcting the way we spoke that went something like, "watch your mouth." This was often followed with the threat of soap in our mouths if we didn't correct how we talked. It was a good warning that the way we spoke needed to be corrected and to use our words in an appropriate way.

> **HUMAN BEHAVIOR TENDS TO SETTLE INTO A GROOVE, WHICH IS GOOD UNLESS THE GROOVE BECOMES A RUT.**

The same is true if you say, "watch your mind." How you think ultimately directs where you go and who you become. How you think becomes your reality. You cannot change what life deals you, but you can change your mind set in any situation.

Henry Ford once said, "Whether you think you can or think you can't, you're right." Your mindset is that powerful.

This is where self-control really comes into play. We can't control our circumstances, and we can't even always control what actions we are able to take, since they often depend on circumstances. But we can always control our mindset.

Reflect & Respond

1. What are two or three healthy mindsets you currently possess? Did you always have that mindset or did you learn it?

2. Which of the mindset strategies above would you like to work on improving or starting to use for the first time?

3. What is a limiting belief that has journeyed with you throughout your life? What is the affirmation you will speak over it?

4. Name a friend, group, or teammate who you can be vulnerable with and share that you are trying to redirect your mindset.

Conclusion

Self-Acceptance That Grows Our Confidence

> *"Don't copy the behavior and customs of this world, but let God transform you into a new person by changing the way you think. Then you will learn to know God's will for you, which is good and pleasing and perfect."*
>
> — Romans 12:2 NLT

Over thirty-five years ago, I found myself sitting in a circle of chairs in a twelve-step meeting for families with loved ones fighting for sobriety. I'm grateful that within that same year and for every one of the thirty-five years since, my husband has remained sober. But I will never forget the desperation and disappointment expressed in those tiny circles.

One family in particular had three children, yet their oldest, who was not yet eighteen had relapsed again. They had been in and out of rehab facilities but sobriety continued to be elusive. The parents made the brave decision to allow their oldest to experience the consequences of the addiction and to focus on rebuilding their relationships with their other children. Addiction had taken its toll and the family was going to rebuild while keeping a door open for their oldest son to return.

I was young, naïve, scared—and more than a little shocked that a parent would need to make such a hard decision. It was in this spirit that the Serenity Prayer was applied over and over.

"God, grant me the serenity to accept the things I cannot change.
The courage to change the things I can.
And the wisdom to know the difference."

One of life's greatest challenges, especially for high-achieving women, is discerning what *can* be changed and accepting what *cannot*. Many of my clients have conquered the business world, found victory in ministry leadership, written books, climbed literal mountains, raised families, thrived after a divorce, and so much more. We are used to achieving, producing, and conquering. As we mature (a.k.a. age), it can be difficult to accept an aging body, feel invisible in an "under-forty" world, and realize that some dreams can simply not be achieved.

> ACCEPTING OUR LIMITATIONS IS AN ESSENTIAL PART OF TRUE CONFIDENCE.

Yet, accepting our limitations is an essential part of true confidence. We have to own everything about us, releasing the things we cannot change so we can focus our energy on the things we can change.

Let's consider some of the common challenges that may need to be accepted rather than overcome. For each one I provide a statement that you could use as a mantra.

Accepting the Scars of Your Past

THE CONFIDENT WOMAN LETS HER SCARS CHANGE HER FOR THE BETTER.

I had a C-section with our daughter. The first month after the operation, I was understandably protective of the developing scar. Sneezing, laughing, and nursing all were accompanied by a pillow over my abdomen to protect the healing incision. Over time, a scar formed and I never thought about it again. It is a reminder that scars form as callouses that actually protect us. Our bodies instinctively take over and begin rebuilding.

CONCLUSION: SELF-ACCEPTANCE THAT GROWS OUR CONFIDENCE

The Latin root of the word callous means "hard skin." Our modern vocabulary thinks of the word "callous" as something negative. If you are a callous person, you are insensitive or lacking compassion. However, a callous after surgery thickens the skin to allow healing.

Sometimes, we feel ashamed of our scars, even when they have fully healed. Deep wounds will leave permanent scars that become part of us. We have to learn to accept these marks as signs that we have survived something hard and come out stronger on the other side.

What is a scar from your past you find yourself wanting to hide? This might be a painful loss of a friendship or a divorce, or it might be much deeper like the traumatic experience of abuse or violation. How could you shift to seeing this scar as a badge of honor, as a part of what makes you uniquely suited to the calling God has given you?

As I have mentioned throughout this book, if you need help processing the healing of a scar, please reach out to a counselor or pastor.

Letting Go of Unrealized Dreams

THE CONFIDENT WOMAN ACCEPTS WHAT SHE CANNOT CHANGE.

No matter how much we've prayed, planned, and put ourselves in a position to create a life that fulfills our dreams, some will remain unrealized. We have taken webinars, attended conferences, and made vision boards. Yet, the preferred life we imagined remains out of our reach.

It's the woman who realizes that her forced early retirement will require her to accept roles that pay her bills, but no longer allow her to be the leader of the pack in her industry. Those who have dreamed of marriage or remarriage, now need to learn to live passionately as strong single women. It's the women who have always wanted to have children, yet their age, bodies, or season made that dream fade away.

These are all circumstances in life that we wish we had not been dealt. But just like the parents at the AA meeting in the last chapter, the decision to keep living while accepting the limitations that have been placed upon us is crucial. We keep moving forward. We accept the things we cannot change. We learn to not only survive, but to thrive while rejecting the notion that our life, while different than we expected, is somehow diminished.

> SOME THINGS COME OUR WAY AND THEY SIMPLY CANNOT BE SOLVED. THIS IS WHERE THE GIFT OF THINKING STRATEGICALLY BECOMES AN IDOL OF OVERTHINKING.

Some people I work with, especially leaders, often try to strategize their way out of these situations. When life sends us disappointments, it is natural and wise to begin to think through alternatives to help us cope, survive, and then thrive. However, some things come our way and they simply cannot be solved. This is where the gift of thinking strategically becomes an idol of overthinking. Overthinking steals our joy, our mindset, and our energy. If you have prayed about it and asked God to solve it and the answer isn't what you expected, like the Psalmist in Psalm 46, it is time to stop striving and know He is God. This season may be one of accepting some uncertainty, moving forward without all the answers, and walking in the tension of transitioning from what you expected to the reality of where you are.

As we explored in Chapter 7, part of this process is grieving what we have to let go of. Only then can we open our hands to receive what God is sending us next.

What dreams are you needing to let go of in order to move with more acceptance into this next season of your life? Is it possible that those things are making room for the larger calling you have identified in this book?

CONCLUSION: SELF-ACCEPTANCE THAT GROWS OUR CONFIDENCE

Accepting Your Appearance

THE CONFIDENT WOMAN IS COMFORTABLE IN HER OWN SKIN.

We've talked a lot about being comfortable in who we are from the inside out with our personalities, values, skills, and beyond. We also have to be comfortable with who we are from the outside in.

It was around age fifty-five that this became hard for me. Like most women my age, I had conquered workouts, engaged in healthy meal prep, and ate well, only to find nothing was working any longer. My body felt like it was betraying me in this area. I was healthy and strong, thank God . . . but, pounds piled on me that simply would not budge. I spoke with my two long-term doctors who confirmed I was strong and healthy. They told me I was within quite a normal weight for my age group and to keep up the good work. It was then my confidence took a dive. I had never battled weight gain that a few strategic meals and workouts couldn't conquer. I was staring down the truth that it wasn't so much that I didn't like the woman in the mirror that I am. I was simply missing the woman I had been. Acknowledging and grieving these little losses will help us move forward confidently.

This process of aging led me to reevaluate my mindset in order to surrender to my healthy reality about my appearance. I applied the tools we learned in the mindset chapter that allowed me to stop nit-picking myself and overanalyzing posted photos, so that I could move toward healthy self-acceptance. I reframed my view to that of a strong woman, (working out five to six days a week), being healthy (able to lift my growing grandson over and over from a deadlift), and having a body that allows me to do things that I take for granted every day.

As women, we are bombarded with airbrushed and filtered models, influencers, and actresses who distort the view of the skin we are in. Turning thirty, forty, fifty, sixty, seventy, and beyond stretches the view of our skin as we watch it literally bump, sag, and bulge in ways we hadn't imagined. Somehow, we thought we would be different.

To accept the skin you're in requires perspective. The plumbline we measure ourselves against has to shift as we age. When I work out, I need to expect to build the body of a sixty-year-old woman—and the sixty-year-old woman that has my body shape, chemistry, and metabolism. Not the body of a thirty-year-old and not the body of the sixty-year-old who was simply blessed with great genes. If I'm trying to compete with a forty-year-old, I will lose every time and it will cause me to dislike the skin I'm in. But, when I use a sixty-year-old plumbline, I'm strong.

This kind of self-acceptance also means we like the skin we're in, even without the props we prefer to use. We all have props or tools we use to "improve" our appearance according to our standards and preferences: highlighting our hair, working out, dressing in the latest fashion that complements our body, great shoes, Botox, fill-in-the-blank. It's ok to use tools like these to boost our confidence in certain situations. But we have to let the props serve us, not us serve our props. If we have something that adds a little pep to our step, then we should let that prop serve us. I have said for years that a cute blazer and great pair of shoes just make me feel more confident when I speak. But don't be tempted to think props are necessary to be the confident woman you are.

Go ahead and dye those roots, my friend. Just remember, like we learned during the pandemic when we couldn't get our roots touched up, we are loved and worthy, even with grey roots. You do you, boo. But, don't let these things define you.

I have decided I like the woman who looks back at me in the mirror. She has laugh lines that reflect my favorite part of my personality—my sense of humor. She has a unique fashion sense and style that she isn't afraid to display. She has that Lisa Rinna style haircut that has become her signature. She is not forty anymore, but she has taken on sixty with style and confidence.

My new slogan is "Confidence is the new beauty cream." Let this be a reminder that the most attractive feature any woman can have is the quiet confidence that comes with knowing who she is and what she's been put on this earth to do.

CONCLUSION: SELF-ACCEPTANCE THAT GROWS OUR CONFIDENCE

Being Willing to Be a Beginner . . . Again

THE CONFIDENT WOMAN IS WILLING TO TRY AND KEEPS MOVING FORWARD.

When I relaunched my coaching and speaking business a few years ago, I had to strengthen my entrepreneurial skills. I was used to a staff, a team, and tons of support. I didn't need to network. I only needed to open my office door and attend the meetings on my calendar. I became willing to grow as an entrepreneur by attending webinars, having coffee with lots of other entrepreneurs, joining a networking group, and even learning Canva. I had to start with the basics and learn a new skillset in some areas, even though I had been doing other parts of it for decades. At times, that meant I had to swallow my pride and let myself be a beginner.

Sometimes, when we start pursuing new goals later in life, we have to face the fact that we're going to be beginners in certain areas for a while. This might mean doing something even though we are scared, trying something unknown, or persevering when you want to give up before you even try.

As mentioned earlier, confidence is simply the willingness to try. It requires believing you are capable of learning new skills and growing and the humility to be a student rather than an expert.

CONFIDENCE IS SIMPLY THE WILLINGNESS TO TRY.

If we are too proud to admit we need to start with the basics and learn as a beginner when we're trying something new, we'll never be able to reach our big goals.

When we're truly confident in who we are and our God-given purpose, we aren't shaken by admitting we don't know how to do something. It's just another opportunity for growth, leading to another milestone on our adventure of a lifetime.

Your Confidence Compass

I read a story recently about a woman who was settling in on a Friday night to watch a movie with her family. At the beginning of the movie, she saw her father's name come up as an incoming call. She had seen the beginning of this movie before, but told her family, "I'll call him back tomorrow." She was wrecked by regret that her father died later that night and tomorrow never came.

This is not a statement about boundaries on family movie night. Rather, it's a warning not to wait for tomorrow (or next week or next year) to get started.

You've done great work making it to the end of this book. Please accept this as an invitation to not let the call go to voicemail. Today is your day to take action and follow God on the trip of a lifetime.

We don't *stumble* into our best life. We get there through careful choices followed by deliberate actions. This book is filled with exercises and tools that will act as your compass as you move from self-doubt to self-leadership. With God as our True North, we can chart our course to fulfill our calling and become the confident women He's created us to be.

WE ARE ALL GOD'S MASTERPIECES, BUT WE ARE STILL BEING MOLDED AND SHAPED BY HIS HOLY HANDS.

Confidence is a cycle that requires curiosity and humility. It's a continuous process where you go back to self-discovery when something changes. We gain victory over self-doubts and insecurity once and for all in some areas of our lives. You may conquer pleasing your mother-in-law by not taking the bait, not engaging in futile discussions, and adjusting your expectations. Other areas, like speaking in front of groups, for example, can sneak up on us, requiring a cycle of self-awareness, self-reflection, and the self-leadership needed to reflect again.

CONCLUSION: SELF-ACCEPTANCE THAT GROWS OUR CONFIDENCE

```
         SELF-DISCOVERY
        ↗              ↘
SELF-ACCEPTANCE      SELF-AWARENESS
     ↑                      ↓
SELF-CONTROL          SELF-REFLECTION
        ↖              ↙
         SELF-LEADERSHIP
```

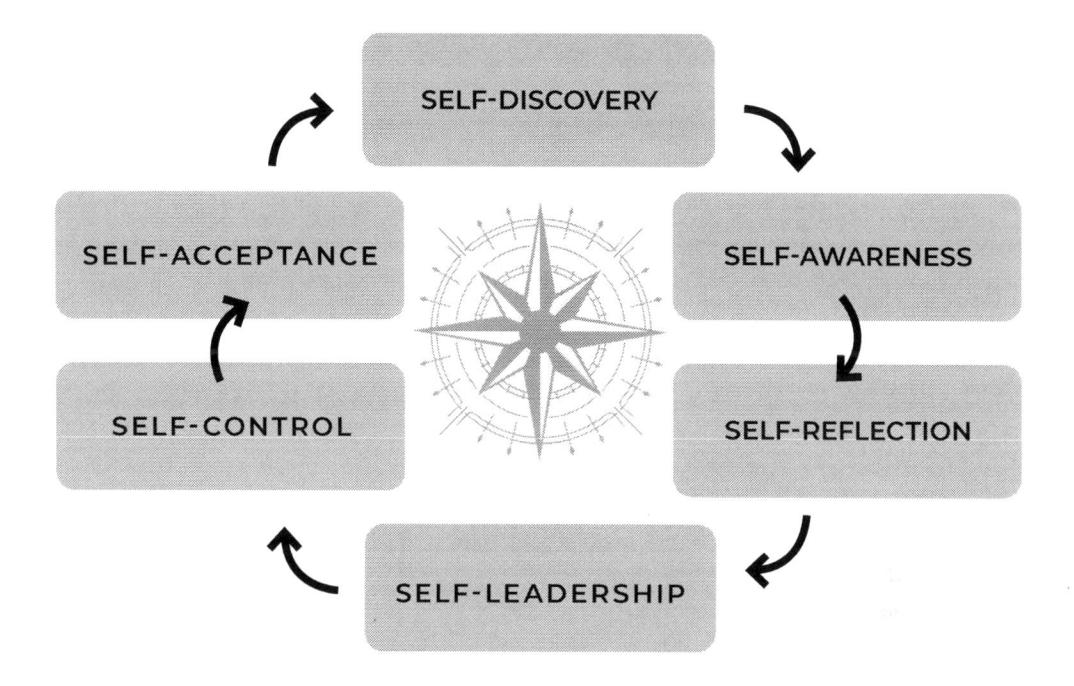

If your hard-won confidence begins to lag in one area, don't lose heart. This is a normal part of the cycle and simply means it's time to return to the steps in this book to remind yourself of who you are, where you're trying to go, and what strengths you can bring to the situation you're facing. I want to encourage you with the words of Hebrews 10:35-36, which says, "So do not throw away your confidence; it will be richly rewarded."

If you feel tempted to give up, whether on a big goal or a small habit, remind yourself that self-control is a fruit of the Spirit given supernaturally to those who seek God. He will give you the self-control and the courage to start the confidence cycle again.

The confident woman knows she's a work in progress. We are all God's masterpieces, but we are still being molded and shaped by His holy hands.

Self-acceptance means recognizing that we're never too old or too "finished" to need the tools in this book. I use them myself all the time. Confidence doesn't mean we have it all figured out or that we've "arrived" and no longer have anything to learn or work toward.

True confidence means trusting that, with God's help, we can face any challenge that comes our way with resilience, perseverance, and faith. Just like Michaelangelo saw the Statue of David masterpiece in the block of marble, God sees every part of your life as a way to polish your best and chip away at anything that doesn't serve you. We can trust Him in every season of our lives to strength and empower us to face the unknown roads that life is opening up ahead of us.

Let's close with the entire Serenity Prayer. I invite you to pray this with me over your life and to repeat it as often as you need as you step out confidently into the unknown.

> *"God, grant me the serenity to accept the things I cannot change.*
>
> *The courage to change the things I can.*
>
> *And the wisdom to know the difference.*
>
> *Living one day at a time, enjoying one moment at a time*
>
> *Accepting hardship as a pathway to peace.*
>
> *Taking, as He did, this sinful world as it is. Not as I would have it.*
>
> *Trusting he will make all things right if I surrender to His will.*
>
> *So I can be reasonably happy in this world and supremely in the next."*

Acknowledgments

Any project of this magnitude can only be accomplished through the empowerment of the Holy Spirit and the support of friends and family.

To my husband, Bill, who looked me in the eye and said, "*Go do it, Lisa,*" thank you for believing in me and giving me the courage to write this book. You have always been a huge support for my calling to minister to women for which I am so grateful.

Kelsey, Justin, Connor, and McKenzie, thanks for being excited for me and being Guinea pigs for all the personality coaching I've learned and tried through the years. I pray the content in this book will inspire and guide you long after I leave this earth for Heaven.

To my sweet Mom (and Dad in Heaven), you allowed me to be myself and remained proud of me at my best and at my worst. This foundation of unconditional love gave me my earliest confidence. You reflected Jesus to me every day of my life and I'm grateful. I view this book as an extension of the ministry you both did in the local church for 42 years.

To Janet, Wendy, and Amy, you truly are best friends and sisters to me. You have prayed for my calling, my assignments, open/closed door—and have prayed this book into existence. Thank you for your love and support.

To Mary Ann Ruff, Marilynne Chadwick, Forest Hill Church, and Proverbs 31 Ministries, you have sharpened the tip of my arrow spiritually and professionally for which I am grateful.

To Mandy Roberson, Mara, Raejen and the MRM Team, you have exceeded my expectations as my publisher. Thank you for being professional and creative in bringing this book into the world.

About the Author

Lisa Allen is a passionate advocate for women, blending her love for Jesus, coffee, and leopard print into a dynamic and relatable presence. With over two decades of experience in faith-based non-profit leadership, including past roles as Executive Director at Proverbs 31 Ministries and Women's & Life Group Director at a large church, Lisa possesses a deep understanding of the challenges and triumphs of both women of faith and women pursuing faith.

Lisa is a board-certified life coach and speaker with extensive experience that has made her a highly sought-after keynote speaker, conference presenter, and workshop facilitator. She guides her audiences to view their lives through the lens of God's word, delivering messages that resonate deeply and leave them inspired with renewed passion, a strong sense of calling, and unwavering confidence.

In addition to her speaking engagements, Lisa enjoys coaching large groups, bible studies or one-on-one on topics she's been certified to facilitate including Gallup Clifton Strengths, DISC Personality Profile, Uniquely You Spiritual Gifts, and the Enneagram. Her clients find their calling, cultivate their confidence and create much needed capacity to live a purposeful and sustainable life.

Lisa lives in Charlotte, NC, with her husband, Bill. She is the momma of two grown, married children and a darling Yorkie named PJ. However, Lisa's favorite title is "LiLi" (Grandmother) as the family welcomes baby Noah as the first grandchild.

For Speaking Inquiries: ljallencoaching.com/contact

For Coaching Inquiries: ljallencoaching.com/individual-coaching-intake-form

Appendix

As a reader, you get special access to the assessments and templates on my website. My prayer is that these resources help you on your journey to become the self-confident woman God intends for you to be!

SHOE Assessment

This is a fun assessment consisting of four separate columns of statements. As you read through each statement, place an X next to each statement that is true to you. After you have completed all four columns, add up the total number of X's in each column. The two highest totals are the two SHOE combination personalities you most relate to. Most people are a blend of two or more SHOEs.

Please note: *The SHOE Assessment is based on the DISC theory, just in a more shortened and relatable format. This SHOE Assessment is not scientific. If you want a more detailed DISC assessment, please go to:* https://uniquelyyou.org/catalog/online-profiles/disc-profiles.

Values Assessment

Instructions:

1. Start with all of the values listed below and eliminate any that you immediately do *not* identify as your core values. (They should represent about half of the total values.)

2. Next, go through the remaining values you were drawn to and eliminate about half of them again.

3. Keep doing this until you have narrowed your values down to your five top values. You may have more than five, but typically, it's the top five or so that are "squeezed out of you" during times of stress.

Sometimes you don't know what your core values are until they've been violated, so it can be helpful to think about what gets you fired up.

Here are some questions to consider as you identify your more important values:

- What are you willing to stand up for or against? What causes do you actively support, and why?

- What upsets you? I recall being at a three-day retreat where someone criticized that "they only prayed during the first session opening of each day—no other corporate prayer was offered (beyond a prayer room)." I was then reminded that this woman had the gift of intercession and an extremely high value of prayer. Thus, though many attendees appreciated the opening prayers and didn't think a thing about them, my friend was disappointed there wasn't a greater emphasis on prayer.

- What is so important that you hold on to it even if no one else knows or sees? If you have a value of responsibility or perfection, you will put a shopping cart back into the stall even if no one knows.

- What values do you have that are so important that you might quit your job if they were violated (even if nothing illegal or immoral was happening like I repositioned my role at church)?

Things to keep in mind to help you get accurate and insightful results:

- Pay close attention to similar values that you are wrestling with. See if you can ask yourself *why* you are debating between them. It may be good to journal a bit about the values you are wrestling with. It's also good to make note of *why* you ultimately chose the five you did.

- There are no "right" or "wrong" choices if you are being honest. For instance, if you value material possessions or prestige/power and feel there is selfishness or pride associated with them, please still claim them as a value (they still drive your behavior). Don't fall prey to "I *should* have this value" and adopt it because you *want* or *wish* you had it. Only select those values that drive and motivate you.

- ⊚ We have included a couple blank boxes so that you can write your own value as you go through this assessment if you feel the need. Should you choose to, please also write your definition of this value.

- ⊚ If you are struggling with having too many values and are unable to narrow them down significantly, we suggest leaving them on your desk overnight or even for a week and ponder them as you go through your day.

Capacity Assessment

Sometimes, it's hard to have the proper understanding of just how much we can hold as we pursue the lives God calls us to live. I've created the Capacity Assessment, so that you can know what your limits are and how you should orient your life as you chase the life the Lord created you to live.

Spiritual Gifts Assessment

As Christians, we have all been endowed by the Holy Spirit with spiritual gifts. If you would like to determine what your spiritual gifts are, you can take the quiz by accessing the QR code.

Writing Your Affirmations

Writing down your affirmations is not an exercise to make you feel good about yourself. It's a practice that helps ground you in your divine calling, reminds you of your God-given identity, and strengthens you against attacks from the Enemy, as you rehearse the various experiences and education that affirm and qualify you for your calling. Sometimes, it can be hard to get started when writing your affirmations. That's why I'm sharing my original affirmations when I first began women's ministry.

YOUR CONFIDENCE COMPASS

I am delighted to continue this coaching journey with you! All of the resources and assessments mentioned in the Appendix can be accessed using the QR code below.

Endnotes

Introduction

1. Philippians 1:6 (NIV).
2. "Coach (n.)." Etymology. Accessed February 26, 2025. https://www.etymonline.com/word/coach.
3. 2 Corinthians 12:9 (NIV).
4. James 1:22 (AMP).
5. Romans 7:15 (NIV).
6. Galatians 5:22-23 (NIV).
7. Warren, Rick. *The Purpose Driven Life*. Michigan: Zondervan, 2002.
8. Proverbs 3:5-6 (NIV).

Part I

1. Psalm 139:23-24 (NIV).

Chapter 1

1. Ephesians 2:10 (NLT).
2. Philippians 2:3 (AMP).
3. 1 Samuel 17:38-40 (NIV).
4. Peculiar | Definition in the Cambridge English Dictionary. Accessed February 27, 2025. https://dictionary.cambridge.org/us/dictionary/english/peculiar.
5. Hebrews 10:10 (NIV).
6. Devil's advocate | English Meaning - Cambridge Dictionary. Accessed February 27, 2025. https://dictionary.cambridge.org/dictionary/english/devil-s-advocate.
7. Trent, John. "4 Animals Personality Test." Focus on the Family, February 19, 2025. https://www.focusonthefamily.com/marriage/4-animals-personality-test/.
8. "Ποίημα (Poiēma) - Ephesians 2:10." Greek concordance: ποίημα (poiēma) -- 1 occurrence. Accessed February 26, 2025. https://biblehub.com/greek/poie_ma_4161.htm.

9. "Poem (n.)." Etymology. Accessed February 26, 2025. https://www.etymonline.com/word/poem.
10. Romans 12:4-5 (The Message).
11. 2 Corinthians 12:9 (NIV).
12. "Quote Origin: You Just Chip Away Everything That Doesn't Look Like David." Quote Investigator, January 22, 2025. https://quoteinvestigator.com/2014/06/22/chip-away/.
13. Ecclesiastes 7:18 (NIV).

Chapter 2

1. Romans 12:18 (NIV).
2. Trent, John. "4 Animals Personality Test." Focus on the Family, February 19, 2025. https://www.focusonthefamily.com/marriage/4-animals-personality-test/.
3. Conflict language is loosely applied from the Christian Coach Institute DISC Training.
4. Perry, Elizabeth. "7-38-55 Rule of Communication: How to Use for Negotiation." BetterUp, January 21, 2025. https://www.betterup.com/blog/7-38-55-rule.

Chapter 3

1. Ecclesiastes 4:9-12 (NIV).
2. Jim Rohn quoted in Canfield, Jack, and Janet Switzer. *The Success Principles: How to Get from Where You Are to Where You Want to Be*. New York: Collins, 2005.
3. "10 African Proverbs, Their Origin, and Meaning." Refinedng.com. Accessed February 26, 2025. https://refinedng.com/10-african-proverbs-their-origin-and-meaning/.
4. "New APA Poll: One in Three Americans Feels Lonely Every Week." Psychiatry.org - New APA Poll: One in Three Americans Feels Lonely Every Week, January 30, 2024. https://www.psychiatry.org/news-room/news-releases/new-apa-poll-one-in-three-americans-feels-lonely-e#:~:text=The%20latest%20Healthy%20Minds%20Monthly,they%20are%20lonely%20every%20day.
5. Gallup, Inc. "Gallup's Q12 Employee Engagement Survey." Gallup.com, February 21, 2025. https://www.gallup.com/q12/.
6. Chapman, Gary D. *The 5 Love Languages: The Secret to Love That Lasts*. Chicago: Northfield Publishing, 2024.
7. Seitz, Amanda. "Loneliness Poses Risks as Deadly as Smoking: Surgeon General." AP News, May 3, 2023. https://apnews.com/article/surgeon-general-loneliness-334450f7bb5a77e88d8085b178340e19.
8. Proverbs 20:5 (NIV).
9. Romans 12:4 (NIV).

ENDNOTES

Chapter 4

1. Luke 10:42 (NIV).
2. Nelson, Sara. "Widow Auctions off Husband's Burial Plot above Marilyn Monroe." Daily Mail Online, August 18, 2009. https://www.dailymail.co.uk/news/article-1207357/Widow-auctions-husbands-burial-plot-Marilyn-Monroe.html.
3. Luke 10:38-42 (NIV).

Part II

1. 1 Timothy 4:16 (AMP).

Chapter 5

1. 1 Corinthians 4:12 (NIV).
2. Marshall, John. "Off-Target at Olympics, Matt Emmons No Stranger to Adversity." AP News, September 15, 2024. https://apnews.com/off-target-at-olympics-matt-emmons-no-stranger-to-adversity-28d642af37d540b69e0ae54cadda0222.
3. Sinek, Simon. *Start With Why*. Portfolio, 2009.
4. "Intention (n.)." The Free Dictionary. Accessed February 27, 2025. https://www.thefreedictionary.com/intention.
5. Proverbs 29:18 (NKJV).
6. "Provision (n.)." Etymology. Accessed February 26, 2025. https://www.etymonline.com/word/provision.
7. Ephesians 2:10 (AMP).
8. "Voice (n.)." Etymology. Accessed February 26, 2025. https://www.etymonline.com/word/voice.
9. Guinness, Os. *The Call: Finding and Fulfilling the Central Purpose of Your Life*. Nashville, Tenn: Thomas Nelson, 2003.
10. Ephesians 4:1 (NIV).
11. "Κλήσεως (Klēseōs) - Ephesians 4:1." Ephesians 4:1 lexicon: Therefore I, the prisoner of the lord, implore you to walk in a manner worthy of the calling with which you have been called,. Accessed February 26, 2025. https://biblehub.com/lexicon/ephesians/4-1.htm.
12. "Κλήσεως (Klēseōs)." Strong's Greek: 2821. κλῆσις (KLÉSIS) -- calling, invitation. Accessed February 26, 2025. https://biblehub.com/greek/2821.htm.
13. Luke 5:16 (NIV).
14. Psalm 42:1-2 (NIV).

15. Ephesians 3:1-8, 3:11 (NIV).
16. Ephesians 4:16 (NIV).
17. "'Ενέργειαν (Energeian) - Ephesians 4:16." Greek concordance: ἐνέργειαν (energeian) -- 7 occurrences. Accessed February 26, 2025. https://biblehub.com/greek/energeian_1753.htm.
18. 1 Corinthians 12:7-11 (NIV).
19. "Passion (n.)." Etymology. Accessed February 26, 2025. https://www.etymonline.com/word/passion.
20. Esther 4:16 (NIV).
21. Exodus 4:10-12 (NIV).

Chapter 6

1. 1 Corinthians 9:26 (NIV).
2. Turner, Ph.D. Randall. "The Difference 1 Degree of Change Makes." LinkedIn, March 2, 2018. https://www.linkedin.com/pulse/difference-1-degree-change-makes-randell-turner-ph-d-/.
3. "Decision (n.)." Etymology. Accessed February 26, 2025. https://www.etymonline.com/word/decision.
4. "Freewill Lyrics." Rush.com. Accessed February 26, 2025. https://www.rush.com/songs/freewill/.
5. Joshua 4:20 (NIV).
6. Nehemiah 6:3 (NIV).
7. Cloud, Henry. *Necessary Endings*. United States: Harper Business, 2011.
8. Galatians 5:22-23 (NIV).
9. Romans 5:3-5 (NLT).
10. Warren, Rick. "Your Commitments Shape Your Life." Pastor Rick's Daily Hope, October 8, 2021. https://pastorrick.com/your-commitments-shape-your-life-2/.
11. Clear, James. *Atomic Habits*. Avery, 2028.

Chapter 7

1. Isaiah 43:18-19 (NIV).
2. Craig. "Beginnings - An End Is Only a Beginning in Disguise." Craig Lounsbrough, March 31, 2024. https://craiglpc.com/beginnings-an-end-is-only-a-beginning-in-disguise-2/.
3. Ecclesiastes 3:1-8 (BSV).
4. Cloud, Henry. *Necessary Endings*. United States: Harper Business, 2011.

ENDNOTES

5. Transition, noun - | Oxford Advanced American Dictionary. Accessed February 27, 2025. https://www.oxfordlearnersdictionaries.com/definition/american_english/transition.
6. Galatians 6:2 (NIV).
7. Psalm 5:3 (NIV).
8. Ephesians 3:20 (NIV).
9. Roiphe, Anne Richardson. *Epilogue: A Memoir*. Harper Collins, 2009.
10. Genesis 18:10 (NIV).

Chapter 8

1. Proverbs 16:9 (NLT).
2. Romans 7:18-19 (NIV).
3. Clear, James. "How to Build New Habits by Taking Advantage of Old Ones." James Clear, February 4, 2020. https://jamesclear.com/habit-stacking.
4. Batchelor, Marlena. "Mel Robbins' '5 Second Rule' for Success." The CEO Magazine. Accessed February 26, 2025. https://www.theceomagazine.com/business/management-leadership/the-5-second-rule/.
5. Soschner, Chris. "Did Aristotle Say, 'We Are What We Repeatedly Do'?" Medium, May 13, 2023. https://medium.com/illumination/did-aristotle-say-we-are-what-we-repeatedly-do-3dbda3f2dceb.

Part III

1. Galatians 5:22-23 (NIV).
2. "'Ἐγκράτεια (Egkrateia) - Galatians 5:23." Strong's Greek: 1466. ἐγκράτεια (egkrateia) -- self-control, temperance. Accessed February 26, 2025. https://biblehub.com/greek/1466.htm.

Chapter 9

1. Romans 12:3 (NLT).
2. Wigert, Ben. "Employee Burnout: The Biggest Myth." Gallup.com, July 21, 2023. https://www.gallup.com/workplace/288539/employee-burnout-biggest-myth.aspx.
3. Swenson, Richard A. *Margin: Restoring Emotional, Physical, Financial, and Time Reserves to Overloaded Lives*. Colorado Springs, Colo: NavPress, 2004.
4. "Burnout: Symptoms, Risk Factors, Prevention, Treatment." WebMD. Accessed February 26, 2025. https://www.webmd.com/mental-health/burnout-symptoms-signs.

5. 1 Corinthians 9:27 (NLT).
6. "Egkrateuomai Meaning - Greek Lexicon: New Testament (NAS)." Bible Study Tools. Accessed March 6, 2025. https://www.biblestudytools.com/lexicons/greek/nas/egkrateuomai.html#:~:text=Egkrateuomai%20Definition,government%2C%20conduct%2C%20one's%20self%20temperately.
7. Graham, Jennifer. "This 'Essentialist' Explains Why the Word 'Priority' Shouldn't Be a Priority." Deseret News, December 20, 2023. https://www.deseret.com/indepth/2021/3/16/22333870/words-of-wisdom-from-greg-mckeown-essentialism-podcast-effortless-time-management/.
8. Fence Study – source needed?
9. "Lexicon - Ephesians 4:16." Ephesians 4:16 lexicon: From whom the whole body, being fitted and held together by what every joint supplies, according to the proper working of each individual part, causes the growth of the body for the building up of itself in love. Accessed February 26, 2025. https://biblehub.com/lexicon/ephesians/4-16.htm.
10. Ephesians 5:15-16 (ESV).
11. Leviticus 19:9 (NIV).
12. Comer, John Mark. *The Ruthless Elimination of Hurry: How to Stay Emotionally Healthy and Spiritually Alive in the Chaos of the Modern World*. WaterBrook Press, 2019.
13. Acts 6:2-4 (NIV).
14. 2 Timothy 1:6-7 (NIV).
15. "Ἀναζωπυρεῖν (Anazōpyrein) - 2 Timothy 1:6." Greek concordance: ἀναζωπυρεῖν (anazōpyrein) -- 1 occurrence. Accessed February 26, 2025. https://biblehub.com/greek/anazo_purein_329.htm.
16. John Wesley – attributed, not sure about citing here

Chapter 10

1. Proverbs 23:7 (NKJV).
2. "Gallup 2024 Certified Strengths Coaching Conference," 2024.
3. "Stuart Smalley - Daily Affirmations." YouTube. Accessed February 26, 2025. https://www.youtube.com/watch?v=6ldAQ6Rh5ZI.
4. "A Beautiful Mind - The Story of John Forbes Nash Jr." A Beautiful Mind - The story of John Forbes Nash Jr, November 15, 2018. https://www.abeautifulmind.com/.
5. 2 Corinthians 10:5 (NIV).

6. Sullivan, Dan, and Benjamin Hardy. *The Gap and the Gain: The High Achievers Guide to Happiness, Confidence, and Success.* Hay House Business, 2021.
7. Andersen, Erika. "21 Quotes from Henry Ford on Business, Leadership and Life." Forbes, February 20, 2024. https://www.forbes.com/sites/erikaandersen/2013/05/31/21-quotes-from-henry-ford-on-business-leadership-and-life/.

Conclusion: Self-Appreciation That Grows Our Self-Confidence

1. Romans 12:2 (NLT).
2. "Serenity Prayer." Beliefnet. Accessed February 26, 2025. https://www.beliefnet.com/prayers/protestant/addiction/serenity-prayer.aspx.
3. "Callous (Adj.)." Etymology. Accessed February 26, 2025. https://www.etymonline.com/word/callous.
4. Psalm 46:10 (NIV).
5. Hebrews 10:35 (NIV).

Made in the USA
Middletown, DE
18 April 2025